W9-CBY-050

SAMUEL WILLARD, 1640-1707:
Preacher of Orthodoxy
in an Era of Change

SAMUEL WILLARD, 1640-1707:
Preacher of Orthodoxy in an Era of Change

by

SEYMOUR VAN DYKEN

WILLIAM B. EERDMANS PUBLISHING COMPANY
Grand Rapids, Michigan

To my wife

Barbara Mae

Abbreviations

A.A.S. Proc.	*Proceedings of the American Antiquarian Society*
A.A.S. Trans. and Colls.	*Transactions and Collections of the American Antiquarian Society*
Pubs. C.S.M.	*Publications of the Colonial Society of Massachusetts*
C.S.P.	*Calendar of State Papers, Colonial Series, America and West Indies*
D.A.B.	*Dictionary of American Biography*
M.H.S. Colls.	*Collections of the Massachusetts Historical Society*
M.H.S. Procs.	*Proceedings of the Massachusetts Historical Society*
N.E.Q.	*New England Quarterly*
Mass. Records	*Records of the Governor and Company of the Massachusetts Bay in New England*

Preface

Although Samuel Willard has been acknowledged by both his contemporaries and by historians as one of the most important preachers among the second generation of New England Puritans, one who summarized the theological thought of seventeenth-century American Puritanism, no extended study has been published on either his life or his thought. As one of the chief propagators and defenders of this inherited orthodoxy in an era of social, economic, political and religious change, in a distinct sense he epitomized the New England mind, and kept alive the orthodoxy which with modifications was to become more efflorescent in the next generation.

Willard's voluminous sermons and treatises constitute the heart of this study. Since he left no diary or autobiographical materials, extensive use has been made of the diaries of contemporaries. The official records of Massachusetts and Third (South) Church, Boston, furnish valuable information on the life of the time. Willard's thought is viewed in the light of the inherited orthodoxy of Puritanism and the generic Reformed tradition by the use of representative New England, English, and Continental sources as well as the contemporary writings which challenged orthodoxy.

The prosecution of the necessary research was aided by the unfailing helpfulness of the staffs of the libraries of Princeton Theological Seminary and Princeton University, as well as those of the Boston Atheneum, Brown University, American Antiquarian Society, Boston Public Library, Congregational Library (Boston), Harvard University, Library of Congress, Massachusetts Historical Society, New York Public Library, Purdue University, Union Theological Seminary (New York), University of Chicago, and Yale University.

This work is the result of a pilgrimage of study which received its inspiration in the seminars of Professor Lefferts A. Loetscher at Princeton Theological Seminary, and I am indebted to him for his scholarship,

7

unstinted suggestions, criticisms and encouragements, as well as to Professor Edward A. Dowey, Jr., for his incisive theological insights. My secretary, Jean Stuk, has given excellent assistance in the preparation of the manuscript. I owe most to my wife, Barbara, for her unfailing encouragement and patience.

—Seymour Van Dyken

Grand Rapids, Michigan

Contents

CHAPTER ONE

THE FORMATIVE YEARS

Deep in the woods of the Massachusetts frontier, at the newly organized town of Concord—if one could call it a town—a son was born on January 31, 1640, to Simon and Mary Willard, the town's leading citizens. With a Puritan predilection for Biblical names they named him Samuel, not knowing that, like his Old Testament namesake, he was destined to become a leading prophet in their new Israel. That one day, at the center of New England life, he would fight to preserve the very orthodoxy they had so recently hazarded the sea to enjoy, was beyond their thought. That in his lifetime he would not only battle heresy, but cross swords with royal governors, rebuke witch hunters, and eventually head Harvard College, was beyond imagining, wrapped in the womb of the future. Not until a new century had dawned would men pay tribute to the many contributions of his checkered career.

Not least among the formative influences in his life was his family. One generation is linked to another, and a bequest of spirit is often patent. While it is not invariably true that children reflect their parents, in Samuel Willard's case it was quite apparent that his temperament and character, his attitudes and convictions, owed much to his religious and venturesome father.

"His Descent was Honourable"

The Willards had arrived in the Bay Colony only a few years before from the southeastern tip of England. There the name was ancient in the counties of Sussex and Kent, with records going back to Walter Willard in 1208 and William Willard, provost of the city of Canterbury in 1218. The family tree, with all the variety of old English spelling—

Wilard, Wyllarde, Wellarde, and Wyllerde—has been traced back to John Willard, who resided at Hailsham in Sussex in the reign of Edward III, and Richard Willard, who was baron of Cinque Ports, probably in the reign of Richard II. Socially, however, the family was mainly middle class, as record notations such as "yeoman," "clothmaker," and "husbandman" indicate.[1]

The county of Kent, jutting out with scenic rolling hills from the border of London into the Dover Straits, was advantageously situated for trade and commerce, and its revenues were the highest in England. Most of the gentlemen farmers, it was said, were also trained in law and "acquainted with good letters," and nowhere were the yeomen more "free and jolly." They were a manly and brave folk, "the forward of all battels belongeth to them," observed a contemporary; ". . . there were never any bondmen or villeins, as the law calleth them, in Kent."[2] Here in 1605, in the rural parish of Horsmonden, forty miles southeast of London, Samuel's father, Simon Willard, was born.

Samuel's grandfather, Richard Willard, thrice married and prosperous, was solidly established in Horsmonden until his death in 1616, and all his children were baptized in the established Anglican Church.[3] One cannot be certain whether he was wholly in accord with episcopacy or a sympathetic Puritan within the bosom of the church, for nonconformity had not yet come out into the open. In naming his son Simon he may have betrayed a Puritan leaning, for it was an unusual name in England at the time.

Simon himself did not come out openly for the Puritan cause until mature young manhood. Orphaned at the age of twelve,[4] he learned self-discipline early. As a youth he witnessed the persecution of the Puritans by Bishop Laud. With the elevation of this arbitrary prelate to the See of Canterbury, and the subsequent intensification of the persecution, a heroic decision was triggered in Simon Willard's mind. He became a thoroughgoing Puritan. As the tumult over establishment and Arminianism increased, adventurous Puritans read the handwriting on the wall, and sensing that there was little hope for their cause in England, they began the great migration to New England. Though it meant sundering ancestral ties, thwarting emigration hurdles thrown up by the authorities, a perilous journey by sea, and settlement in an undeveloped and savage-infested continent, Simon Willard resolved to

1. Joseph Willard, *Willard Memoir: or, Life and Times of Major Simon Willard*, pp. 21-80, 125; Charles Henry Pope, ed., *Willard Genealogy*, p. 1.
2. Willard, *op. cit.*, pp. 115-116, 122, 129.
3. *Ibid.*, pp. 126, 130. Richard Willard's death on February 20, 1616 (old style), corresponds to March 2, 1617.
4. Willard, *op. cit.*, p. 128.

join them, for beckoning him was a truly English asylum where one could practice religious conviction undisturbed. He was twenty-nine, his wife, Mary Sharpe, twenty-one, as together with their first child they set sail on the flood tide of Puritan migration for New England in April, 1634.[5] The passengers were "entertained in the ship with Mr. Willard ... and others of good account,"[6] one of them noted, and after a comparatively short voyage they arrived mid-May at Boston.

The infant colony consisted mainly of scattered small communities spread out in a thin band along the coast. The only incorporated towns were Boston, Salem, Charlestown, Medford, Watertown, Roxbury, Dorchester and Cambridge. There, at Cambridge, Simon Willard acquired a house, on a hundred-acre tract on the banks of the Charles River;[7] but soon he was out looking for larger quarters. He declined to associate himself with a sizable party at Cambridge under the leadership of the powerful Reverend Thomas Hooker, who, hoping to escape the orbit of the dominating Reverend John Cotton of Boston, moved to the Connecticut Valley. Through fur-trading contacts with the Indians Willard had discovered a rich tract off to the northwest, and he interested a number of families in settling there, including the distinguished Reverend Peter Bulkeley. On September 2, 1635, the General Court granted to "Mr. Bulckley and——[Simon Willard], merchant, and about twelve more families, to begin a town at Musketaquid, for which they were allowed six miles upon the river, to be free from publick charges three years."[8] They named it Concord.

Without waiting they set out on their trek "up further into the *woods*," though fall was hardly the most propitious season for establishing a settlement in the wilderness. They purchased the land from the Indians with *wampumpeag*, cutlery, cloths, and other objects, and built their lodgings. That first winter the town had neither an organized

5. Commenting on the exodus of 1634, Sir Symonds D'Ewes wrote: "I could not but wonder withal at God's providence, that this year, especially in the spring-time, put into the hearts of so many godly persons, as well women as men, to hazard themselves, their children and their estates, to go into New England in America – at least three thousand miles from this kingdom – by sea, there to plant, in respect of the doctrinal part, one of the most absolutely holy, orthodox, and well-governed churches in Christendom, or in that other world." "Autobiography of Sir Symonds D'Ewes," *M.H.S. Colls.*, XXXI, 248. Cf. also A. Harold Lancour, "Passenger Lists of Ships Coming to North America, 1607-1825," *Bulletin*, New York Public Library, XLI (May, 1937), 389-410.

6. Willard, *op. cit.*, p. 134; Pope, *op. cit.*, p. 6. The deposition of Elizabeth Bacon is in the files at Hartford, Connecticut.

7. Willard, *op. cit.*, p. 135. On the colony at this stage, see John Gorham Palfrey, *History of New England*, I, 372.

8. John Winthrop, *The History of New England*, I. Thomas Hutchinson, *History of the Colony and Province of Massachusetts-Bay*, I, 40.

congregation nor a church building, but the next summer they duly organized the twelfth "gathered" church in Massachusetts. This significant event was snubbed by some of the invited dignitaries such as Governor Sir Henry Vane, the Reverend John Cotton, and the Reverend John Wheelright, however, for in the brewing Antinomian controversy Peter Bulkeley was deemed a "legal preacher."[9] He was a dominant figure, and as comoderator of the Cambridge Council the next year he denounced Anne Hutchinson as a "Jezabell whom the Devill sent over thither to poison these American Churches with her depths of Satan,"[10] leaving no doubt where he stood in this controversy. Clerical dominance of this sort inevitably had a profound influence on the Willard family.

From the outset the Concord settlers had to grapple with a host of trials. The snow fell early and stayed late. The spring grain was blackened by frosts. The summers were so wet that the English corn rotted in the ground; even the Indian corn refused to ripen. Pigeons and blackbirds pecked out the grain at seedtime, wolves dug up the corn to get at the fish-fertilizer, the rich grass sickened the cattle, and the pigs escaping from the pens were devoured by the lynxes. And death filled the little churchyard cemetery. Many of the graves were those of children, among them those of Elizabeth and Dorothy Willard, the second and fourth of Simon and Mary.[11]

Such was the time and place of Samuel Willard's birth in January, 1640, the Willard's sixth child and second son. According to Puritan tradition he was baptized during public worship at the rude meetinghouse by the Reverend Peter Bulkeley on the first convenient Sunday, though precisely when is unknown, for the early records of Concord were destroyed in the Indian wars and no diary of the immediate family has come to light. Nor is much else known of the personal details of Samuel's early life, other than the fact that he grew up in a busy, growing household, other brothers and sisters following with Puritan regularity, for after Mary's death Simon Willard married Elizabeth Dunster, then Mary Dunster, and in all seventeen children were born in the Willard home.[12]

9. Cotton Mather, *Magnalia Christi Americana*, I (Hartford, 1853), 400.

10. William Cogswell, ed., *The New England Historical and Genealogical Register*, XXXI, 157.

11. Pope, *op. cit.*, p. 8. On Concord, see Townsend Scudder, *Concord: American Town*, pp. 5, 12.

12. Willard, *op. cit.*, p. 128; Pope, *op. cit.*, pp. 8-9. Samuel Willard's brothers chose widely different vocations and professions: Josiah (b. around 1635) kept school for many years at Hartford, Connecticut; Simon (b. November 23, 1649) was deacon of the First Church in Salem, marshal of Essex County in 1689, and commanded a company in the expedition against the Eastern Indians in 1689;

From childhood, however, Samuel was intimately exposed to the political and military life of the colony, his father being a leader in both fields. Justice of the peace and commissioner on several occasions, clerk of writs for Concord nineteen years, and representative at the General Court for fifteen years, Simon Willard was elected to the supreme judiciary of Massachusetts Bay as an Assistant in 1654, a position he maintained by annual election for twenty-two years. Throughout his life he was a military man also, rising from lieutenant-commander of the Concord militia, and sergeant-major of Middlesex County, to commander of the expedition against the Nianticks in 1654.[13] Valuable as these services were to the colony, they were invaluable for the experience of any growing young man with similar potential for leadership.

Samuel's was to be a religious leadership, and this too received early encouragement from paternal example. As superintendent of the colonial fur trade, Simon Willard turned his dealings with the Indians into opportunities for evangelism. His relationships were on such a high plane of integrity that shortly after introducing missionary John Eliot to the Concord sachem, the converted tribe agreed to certain religious and civil laws, and with "unanimous consent . . . intreated Captaine Simond Willard . . . to be their recorder: being very solicitous that what they did agree upon might be faithfully preserved without alteration." Simon Willard established good rapport also with Passaconaway, chief sachem of Merrimack, and accompanied Eliot two successive springs to their favorite fishing place at Pawtucket Falls, with the result that they too were converted. As Eliot recounted it, a good while later the chief indicated "that he would be glad if I would come and live in some place thereabouts to teach them, and that Capt. Willard would live there also."[14]

Such parental involvement in social, political, and religious affairs inevitably left an imprint on the mind of Samuel Willard. Years later the Reverend Ebenezer Pemberton, his colleague and successor at Boston's Third Church, declared: "HIS DESCENT was *Honourable,* from a Sage Patriot in our Israel; whose Wisdom assigned him a Seat at the *Council-Board,* . . . whose Military Skill, and Martial Spirit intituled

Henry (b. June 4, 1655) owned a large estate on the frontier; John (b. February 12, 1657) resided all his life at Concord; Daniel (b. December 29, 1658) was a blacksmith and later a keeper of the Boston jail; Joseph (b. January 4, 1661) was a sea captain and lived at London for a time; Benjamin (b. 1665) was a carpenter and justice of the peace; Jonathan (b. December 14, 1669) was a blacksmith.

13. Willard, *op. cit.,* pp. 147-149, 154, 158, 160, 188, 190, 193; Pope, *op. cit.,* pp. 6, 7.

14. Thomas Shephard, "Cleare Sunshine of the Gospel breaking forth upon the Indians in New England," *M.H.S. Colls.,* XXIV, 38-39, 82-83.

him to a Chief Place in the *Field*."[15] What Samuel Willard made of this birthright, training, and experience was his own responsibility, but of his lineage he could be justifiably proud, or as a New England Puritan more likely would have put it, grateful.

The World of Samuel Willard

In the year Samuel was born Increase Mather, destined to become New England's foremost Puritan, was already six months old at the Dorchester parsonage. Solomon Stoddard, the future "pope" of the Connecticut valley and grandfather of Jonathan Edwards, would not be born for three more years. John Winthrop, New England's influential leading citizen, had but nine years to live. Across the sea in England, Richard Baxter was about to begin his ministry at Kidderminster, and John Owen, refusing to submit to the Laudian discipline, was openly identifying himself as an Independent reformer with the anti-High Church party, while on the Continent in Holland, the theologically influential Hugo Grotius and Simon Episcopius were about to pass off the scene.

The Puritan revolution had broken out in the very year of Willard's birth, and England was in turmoil. Before he was a year old Laud and Strafford were on their way to the Tower in London and eventually to the block, and by the time he was three the Westminster Assembly had been called. The day before his ninth birthday King Charles was beheaded in front of the royal palace at Whitehall. Events so pivotal in their political and religious import were talked of everywhere in Massachusetts, but hopes for the new reformation were soon tempered by strange reports of unprecedented toleration being granted to pulpit and press and sects of all sorts.[16]

In New England itself the early 1640s was a time of great peril to the very existence of the colony, however. The success of the Puritan movement in England had virtually brought migration to a stand-still, the colonists were becoming discouraged by the unproductiveness of the Massachusetts soil, foreign trade had declined, the price of commodities had dropped, and their benefactors in England understandably

15. Ebenezer Pemberton, *A Funeral Sermon on the Death of that Learned & Excellent Divine, The Reverend Mr. Samuel Willard*, p. 63.

16. Valuable for an understanding of the background of the period and the events of the time are Palfrey, *op. cit.*, I, 111ff.; William Haller, *The Rise of Puritanism*, pp. 324ff. See also Haller, *Liberty and Reformation in the Puritan Revolution*, and W. K. Jordan, *The Development of Religious Toleration in England*. From the Convention of the Long Parliament to the Restoration, 1640-1660: The Revolutionary Experiments and Dominant Religious Thought.

were beginning to advise removal to more propitious places—Ireland, the Bahama Islands, or Jamaica.[17] That very year, however, the voluntary incorporation of the New Hampshire towns under the jurisdiction of Massachusetts, and, of still greater moment, the consummation of the long-discussed confederation between Massachusetts, Plymouth, Connecticut, and New Haven in 1643, gave new strength to each settlement as well as to the whole. And the formation of this league of mutual defense and assistance was an act of sovereignty accomplished in the nick of time, for the English parliament was finally turning a critical eye toward the American colonies. By confidently taking affairs into their own hands New Englanders, at least for a time, thwarted interference with local administration.[18]

Ecclesiastical and educational developments of significance for Willard's life were taking shape also. The Cambridge Synod of 1646 adopted tentative conclusions on the power of magistrates and the nature of church synods; two years later it approved the Cambridge Platform (establishing Congregational polity) and the Westminster Confession of Faith.[19] A system of common schools was inaugurated in Massachusetts by the historic law of 1647. After the legislation of 1642, which had put the responsibility for elementary education on the heads of families, had proved ineffective, the General Court, recognizing the scheme of "that old deluder, Satan, to keep men from the knowledge of the Scriptures," forced the towns to provide proper teaching, "that Learning may not be buried in the graves of our fore-fathers in Church and Commonwealth." Every town of fifty families was ordered to appoint a schoolmaster to teach reading and writing, the cost to be underwritten by parents or townsfolk, provided it did not exceed the expense of educating their children in a neighboring town. When a town numbered a hundred families it was to establish a grammar school that young men might be "fitted for the University." The penalty for default was a fine of five pounds, payable each year to the neighboring school.[20] Samuel Willard's town folk at Concord chose to pay the annual fine.

The Education of Samuel Willard

In whatever way Samuel Willard received his elementary education, therefore, at home or by tutoring elsewhere, he followed the pattern

17. Winthrop, *op. cit.,* II, 37.
18. Palfrey, *op. cit.,* II, 592, 623-634.
19. See Williston Walker, *The Creeds and Platforms of Congregationalism,* pp. 157-237, for a discussion of the background of the Cambridge Synod and the full text of the Platform.
20. *Laws and Liberties of Massachusetts* (1929 reprint of the 1648 ed.), p. 47;

established in early Massachusetts: the immemorial English hornbook, speller, primer, and catechism.[21]

Having learned to read and write, at eight years of age Samuel was ready for grammar school. The nearest town fortunate to have such a school was many wilderness miles away, however, and more than likely he learned his Latin at the parsonage of Peter Bulkeley, for ministers in small towns often prepared their youth for college. The world of books must have intrigued him. New Englanders had an insatiable appetite for reading, and new titles came not only from the new colonial press at Cambridge but with every ship from England. Close at hand would be Bulkeley's learned but practical sermons on *The Gospel Covenant*, Ward's vigorously intolerant *The Simple Cobler*, Johnson's gripping *History of New England*, the colony's propagandistic *New England's First Fruits*, and Anne Bradstreet's *The Tenth Muse*,[22] all of them capable of communicating to a prep-school lad something of the spirit of their errand into the wilderness.

On July 17, 1655, at the slightly early age of fifteen, Samuel Willard entered Harvard College,[23] New England's only institution of higher learning. The sight of the college yard, a neat rectangle comprising the first college building, Goffe college, and the president's house, would quicken the pulse of any backwoods youth. Just outside the college yard at the edge of the town stood the new meetinghouse of the First Church of Cambridge, where twice each Sunday he would worship in the reserved east gallery built by the college for the students, and for which each student was assessed a fixed charge of three shillings and four pence.[24] The small college community was a quiet pastoral setting, close enough to Boston to enable one to take in important events, but remote enough from the hub of New England life to enable one to devote himself to study.

Not that the campus was without its own kind of ferment, however.

quoted by Samuel Eliot Morison, *The Intellectual Life of Colonial New England*, pp. 67-68. Scudder, *op. cit.,* p. 15.

21. Morison, *op. cit.,* pp. 76ff. See also G. E. Littlefield, *Early Schools and School-Books of New England* (Boston, 1904), pp. 110-117; Paul Leichester Ford, *The New England Primer* (1897).

22. Peter Bulkeley, *The Gospel Covenant: Or the Covenant of Grace Opened;* a second, much enlarged, edition was published in 1651. Nathaniel Ward, *The Simple Cobler of Aggawam.* Edward Johnson, *A History of New England;* reprinted as *Johnson's Wonder-Working Providence. New England's First Fruits* was published in London, 1643. Anne Bradstreet's *The Tenth Muse Lately sprung up in America, or Several Poems* (London, 1650) was published by her brother-in-law without her knowledge.

23. Harvard College Steward's Account Books, i, 269; cited by John L. Sibley, *Biographical Sketches of Graduates of Harvard University,* II, 13.

24. *Pubs. C.S.M.,* XV, 208; XXXI, 332.

An administrative shake-up the year before had ousted President Henry Dunster for repudiating infant baptism. Harvard's scholarly new president, the Reverend Charles Chauncy, alert to the threat to higher learning fomented by the radical English pamphleteers, emphatically agreed with the new provision that "in the teaching of all Arts such Authors bee read as doe best agree with the Scripture truths." Aware of the growing indifference to learning among certain classes in New England, he also vigorously denounced the colony's "covetous earthwormes" who kicked at supporting education, happy "to live in a wast, howling wilderness, without any ministry, or schools, and means of education for their posterity . . . [whose] children may drudg for them at plough, or hough, or such like servil employments."[25] A Concord youth would understand.

By the time he enrolled at Harvard, Samuel Willard had already mastered an impressive classical learning. The entrance requirements for 1655 specified:

> When any Scholler is able to read and understand Tully Vergill or any such ordinary Classicall Authors, and can readily make and speak or write true Latin in prose and hath Skill in making verse, and is Competently grounded in the Greek Language; so as to be able to Construe and Grammatically to resolve ordinary Greeke, as in the Greeke Testament, Isocrates, and the minor poets, or such like, having withall meet Testimony of his towardlinesse, hee shall be capab[le] of his admission into the Colledge.[26]

Futhermore, colloquial Latin only was to be spoken on campus.

Socially he was well accepted. For years the college had been dominated by the New England gentry, the sons of ministers, magistrates, merchants, physicians, and substantial landed families. Most of the students were New Englanders, with a few from other colonies, and an occasional Englander who came to escape the "lewdness" of English universities. Willard's class included Samuel Megapolensis, son of the Dutch minister at New Amsterdam; Charles Brooke, son of an Oxford graduate who had settled Charles County, Maryland, with a Puritan colony of his own; Nathaniel Utie, son of Captain John Utie of Utimaria, York County, Virginia; and Richard Bennet, son of the Puritan governor of Virginia. Social change was evident, however, in a notable increase in sons of artisans and tradesmen; but social status was still hierarchically controlled—there was to be no "excesse of Apparell," nor curling, crisping, or powdering of the hair, and no jewelry "except

25. Charles Chauncy, *Gods Mercy*, pp. 14f.
26. *Pubs. C.S.M.*, XXXI, 329.

to whom upon just ground the president shall permit the same." No
one was to leave his room, however, without coat or gown.[27]

Harvard was not going to take any chances on holding an empty bag,
whatever the changes. Putting an end to easygoing payments, it required of each student before admission that "his Parents or Friends
shall both lay downe one quarter expenses, and also give the Colledge
Steward security for the Future." Samuel Willard's "Tuition, study,
rente and beedmaking [bedmaking]," the account books show, were
thirteen shillings and seven pence a quarter. He met the cost of college,
like many others during the depression of the 1650's, by payment in
kind in addition to a certain amount of hard cash. His bills were paid in
wheat, calf, veal, lamb, mutton, pork, hens, eggs, boards, malt, silver,
meal, and the like, often delivered to Cambridge by friends and ac-
quaintances traveling that way. His quarter bills over the four years
contain three charges for glass repair, two for "fetchinge fower bush of
wheate" from Concord, as well as an occasional charge for tobacco and
other small items.[28]

His day began at six o'clock with morning prayers, followed by
breakfast, lectures, dinner at eleven, afternoon disputations, evening
prayers at five o'clock, and supper at seven-thirty. All meals, opened
and closed with prayer, were served according to academic seniority,
with beer as the beverage. Evenings were for study, with lights out at
eleven o'clock.[29]

Harvard was not solely a theological seminary, however; it was a
school of higher learning for all, the curriculum reflecting Cambridge in
providing young theologues the same liberal education afforded any
other scholar. Willard accordingly took the prescribed course in six of
the traditional seven arts (grammar, logic, rhetoric, arithmetic, geometry, astronomy), the three philosophies (metaphysics, ethics, and
natural science), Greek, Hebrew, ancient history, and finally divinity.[30]

Here, then, was the making of a Puritan divine. Grammar taught him
the correct use of language; rhetoric and oratory, studied each Friday
for three years with such manuals as Omer Talon's *Institutiones Ora-
toriae* or his *Rhetorica*, taught him the Puritan "plain style." "His

27. *Ibid.,* 330; Morison, "Virginians and Marylanders at Harvard College,"
William and Mary Quarterly, XII (1933), 1-9; *Harvard College in the Seventeenth
Century,* I, 73-75.

28. Steward Account Books, I, 270; quoted by Sibley, *op. cit.,* II, 13-14.

29. *Pubs. C.S.M.,* XXXI, 332; Morison, *Harvard College,* I, 89-91, 94-98, 100,
109.

30. Morison, *The Founding of Harvard College,* pp. 248-250; *Harvard College,*
I, 165, 169; *Intellectual Life,* p. 42. For another viewpoint on the founding of the
college, see Winthrop S. Hudson, "The Morison Myth Concerning the Founding of
Harvard College," *Church History,* VIII (1939), 148-159.

Phansy was Copious, tho' not luxuriant, but most Correct," observed Pemberton, "being Obsequious to the Dictates, and kept under the strict Guard of a well-poised Judgment," with none of the "lawless Luxuriances and Extravagances" of ungoverned minds. Logic, that supremely useful gift of God, especially the system of Petrus Ramus who reformed Aristotelean dialectic with the Platonic principle of "dichotomy," enabled him to see that ideas were best understood in pairs or contraries. "His *Apprehension,*" Pemberton continued, "was quick, his *Reason* bright, and his *Judgment* exact and solid. . . . His mind [was] inrich'd with a vast number of noble Ideas, and knew well their several Connexions, Relations and Dependencies, how to separate, and how to unite them in deep searches after Truth."[31]

Willard's exposure to the last three of the arts, however, was comparatively meager, due largely to the maternal example of Cambridge. Arithmetic and geometry, plane and spherical, he was permitted to study in English, so practical they were. The astronomy course was revolutionary; for Harvard, in advance of some of the European universities, discarded the Ptolemaic system, recognizing in the new astronomy of Copernicus a divinely given insight into the created universe.[32]

Philosophy, metaphysics foremost, and roughly equivalent to ontology, Willard studied as a senior, with Aristotle as the unquestioned authority, the main guides being the manuals of Reformed scholars such as Herreboords's revision of Burgersdiscius' *Institutiones Metaphysicae* and Caspar Bartholin's *Enchiridion Metaphysicum.* Natural philosophy (including botany and chemistry), still scholastic and pre-scientific, were given small place in the curriculum. But ethics, or moral philosophy, was important, Keckermann's Aristotelean *Systema Ethicae* being rated highly, while in practical ethics Ames' *de Conscientia et eius casibus* was popular. Mastery of these principles made Willard "an Excellent Casuist," in the eyes of contemporaries. "When any Cases of Conscience came under his thought . . . He deliberated maturely on all Circumstances, and laid the Whole by the unerring Rule, and with great Judgment determined agreably."[33]

Greek and Hebrew were stiff courses. Chauncy, fond of Hebrew and one of the best Hellenists of his day at Cambridge, kept the standards

---

31. Pemberton, *op. cit.,* pp. 63-64. On the teaching of rhetoric, oratory, and logic, see Morison, *Harvard College,* I, 172-174, 177, 179, 191-192. On rhetoric and the plain style, see also Perry Miller, *The New England Mind. The Seventeenth Century,* chapters xi and xii.

32. Morison, *Harvard College,* I, 208-209, 214-217; also his "The Harvard School of Astronomy in the Seventeenth Century," *N.E.Q.,* VII (1934), 3-24.

33. Pemberton, *op. cit.,* p. 67. For the teaching of philosophy see Morison, *Harvard College,* I, 252-254, 258, 260-261, 263. Ames' *de Conscientia* was translated into English as *Cases of Conscience* in 1639.

high at Harvard, even seizing devotions as an opportunity for sharpening one's skills. As a freshman Willard took his morning turn at translating a passage from the English Old Testament into Greek; as an upperclassman he read the Old Testament from Hebrew into Greek. At evening prayer he in turn translated a passage of the New Testament from English into Greek.[34]

Undergraduate theology for Willard was both catechetical (memorization of a treatise in dogmatic theology, such as Ames' *Medulla SS. Theologiae* or Johannes Wollebius's *Christianae Theologiae Compendium*) and biblical (logical analysis of the Hebrew and Greek Scriptures read at morning and evening prayers).[35] With this completed, plus a bit of history,[36] Willard graduated from Harvard in 1659.[37]

Only after he had taken his first degree did he, according to custom, engage in the professional study of theology. Graduate students in this M.A. program, largely reading, were on their own to pursue the course wherever they pleased. Those who remained on campus had the benefit of the Harvard library, a respectable collection of several hundred, perhaps over a thousand, volumes.[38] Most of the works were theological, but there were also the ordinary possessions of a gentleman's library, donated in the main by John Harvard. A few odd volumes had been presented by Sir Kenelm Digby, and about 1650 the library had acquired as its proudest possession the great Antwerp Polyglot Bible. Nearly three-quarters of John Harvard's collection was theological, of which about one half consisted of Biblical commentaries, mainly in Latin, about equally divided between the Old and New Testaments. There was a surprisingly large number of works by scholars of the generic Reformed tradition, and the works of a few Roman Catholic writers. Thus the works of Thomas Aquinas and Johannes Duns Scotus took their places beside the numerous volumes of William Ames, Johan H. Alsted, Robert Bolton, Hugh Broughton, John Calvin, Cornelius A. Lapide, David Chytraeus, Arthur Hildersham, John Preston, Petrus Ramus, Abraham Scultetus. The works of Calvin, strikingly, were more numerous than those of any other. The actions of the renowned Dutch

34. Morison, *Founding of Harvard,* pp. 89-91; *Harvard College,* I, 198-200, 203, 194-195.

35. Morison, *Harvard College,* I, 267-8. Ames' *Medulla* (Amsterdam, 1623) was later translated as *The Marrow of Sacred Divinity* (London, 1642). Wollebius's *Compendium* (Basel, 1626) was translated by Alexander Ross as *The Abridgement of Christian Divinity* (London, 1642).

36. Morison, *Harvard College,* I, 265.

37. Sibley, *op. cit.,* II, 14.

38. The main source of information about Harvard's library at this time is Alfred C. Potter, "Catalogue of John Harvard's Library," *Pubs. C.S.M.,* XXI (1920), 190-230.

Synod of Dordt (1618-19), codifying the five points of Calvinism, were evaluated in a number of volumes. There were sermons, but comparatively little on religious controversy. The classics were represented, often in English translations, as Chapman's *Homer*, Holland's *Pliny*, and North's *Plutarch*. Besides a number of Greek, Hebrew, and English grammars and dictionaries, there were a half-dozen books of extracts or phrases, such as Ockland's *Anglorum Praelia*, La Primaudaye's *French Academy*, and Peacham's *Garden of Eloquence*. English literature and history had a scanty place in the library: Bacon's *Essays* and poems of Quarles and Wither represented the former, and Camden's *Remaines* and a tract on the Plague and another on the Gunpowder Plot covered the latter field. A few volumes on science, scholastic philosophy, medicine, logic, and law completed the collection. Over one fourth of the books were printed in or after 1630. Here, besides these basic materials for a liberal arts education, was an introduction to generic Reformed thought.[39]

In addition to reading widely in theology Willard was required to compose a number of synopses, engage in disputations, present syllogistic expositions of philosophical problems, and deliver a sermon in the college hall. This accomplished, he would be ready for his M.A.[40] But in 1662, when the three-year course could have been completed, the salutatorian complained: "*Mater Academia* has miscarried in the birth of Masters, she has brought none this year."[41] Necessity forced many students to discontinue after their first degree and "enter into the ministry raw and unfinished,"[42] Jonathan Mitchell lamented. Samuel Willard's circumstances seem to have been quite different, but this period in his life is shrouded with mystery. Eventually he did obtain his M.A., precisely when is unknown, the only member of his class to do so.[43]

That scholarly interval was a time of political excitement. The Cromwell regime in England collapsed, and in 1660 the king was restored. "By a strange turn of Providence," John Hull noted in his diary, Charles II was "with all joy accepted," and history seemed to be making a complete circle as New Englanders "heard of bishops; and

39. Perry Miller's generalization that "they studied the reformers less than they did a score of more later formulators of Protestant opinion" (*op. cit.*, p. 93) tends to overlook the fact that the works of Calvin, for example, were not only the most numerous in the Harvard library but were also numerous in other early New England libraries. Cf. Charles F. and Robin Robinson, "Three Early Massachusetts Libraries," *Pubs. C.S.M.*, XXVIII, 107-175.
40. Morison, *Harvard College*, I, 148.
41. *Pubs. C.S.M.*, XXVIII, 23; quoted in Morison, *Harvard College*, I, 275.
42. *Pubs. C.S.M.*, XXXI, 317; quoted in Morison, *Harvard College*, I, 274.
43. Sibley, *op. cit.*, II, 13.

with them the old formalities of surplice, &c. were begun to be practiced again in our native land,—which had been now twenty years expunged,—and many good ministers put out of place." Not until fourteen months later, on August 7, 1661, in Boston, did Massachusetts Bay declare: "Forasmuch as Charles the Second is undoubted King . . . we therefore do, as in duty we are bound, own and acknowledge him to be our sovereign Lord and King." At the end of the reading, the troops at attention, the magistrates on horseback, the ministers, and a great crowd of citizens shouted "God save the King!" The guns of the castle, the fort, the town, and the ships boomed away, and that night "all the chief officers feasted . . . at the charge of the country." [44] Samuel's father, both Major and Magistrate, doubtlessly figured in the event, and we may surmise that young Willard was there. The event so politically portentous for the Bay Colony was, more than he realized at the moment, deeply significant for the young theologue about to enter upon his life's work.

The churches of New England were grappling with another disturbing problem also. As parents of the second and third generation found it increasingly difficult to qualify for full communicant membership by a confession of personal regeneration, baptism for their children became a burning issue. A ministerial assembly in 1657 advised a half-way measure, but strong differences of conviction kept the controversy alive, Chauncy of Harvard strenuously opposing the idea, and Mitchell of the Cambridge Church vigorously espousing the more liberal practice. The Synod of 1662, summoned by the General Court, voted overwhelmingly for what was to become known as the half-way covenant.[45] It was a compromise: members who had been admitted in their minority, who publicly professed the faith, who were not scandalous in life, and who solemnly owned the covenant before the church, might have their children baptized. It was an earnest attempt to arrest the drift of children from the church, but in regularizing the broader practice the synod set the stage for some of the next generation's problems. Here was the ecclesiastical framework within which Willard was to conduct his ministry.

Thus, as the winds of change began to blow, Samuel Willard, a second-generation New Englander, stood ready for the ministry. To this

44. *The Diaries of John Hull, A.A.S. Trans. and Colls.,* III, 195, 203-204. *Mass. Records,* ed. Nathaniel B. Shurtleff, IV (Part II), 30-31, gives the proclamation.

45. For a survey and discussion of the background of the controversy and the adoption of the Half-Way Covenant, see Walker, *op. cit.,* pp. 238-269; and H. Shelton Smith, Robert T. Handy, and Lefferts A. Loetscher, *American Christianity,* I, 202-203.

task he brought a mind and character inherited from a founder of considerable importance and station, conditioned by frontier life and the important events of his time, influenced in boyhood by learned and godly divines, and educated in orthodoxy at Harvard College.

CHAPTER TWO

THE EMERGENCE
OF A CHAMPION

By springtime the next year Samuel Willard, at twenty-three years of age, was preaching at the remote town of Groton, about thirty-five miles northwest of Boston. Located on the Nashua River, the town was on the outermost fringe of civilization, almost as far beyond Concord as Concord was from Boston, and accessible only by river and wilderness trails—a sixty-four-square-mile nature wonderland of wooded hills, ponds, brooks, and meadows.[1]

Groton was indebted for its name to Deane Winthrop, a son of Governor John Winthrop, who as an early settler and petitioner named the town after his birthplace in England when it was incorporated in 1665. At the time, it was calculated that the territory could afford comfortable accommodation for at least sixty families, but four years later a petition reported that the plantation "Continueth Vnpeopled." By 1661 four or five families had been "planted" there, and by 1662 it seems there were enough residents to warrant the calling of the Reverend John Miller, an English nonconformist minister. A year after his settlement in Groton he took sick, however, and Samuel Willard was called in to supply his pulpit.

Groton: "a flock in a more obscure part of this Wilderness"

Willard made such a favorable impression that, when Miller died on June 12, 1663,[2] the church entreated him to stay. On June 21 the

1. Sibley, *Biographical Sketches,* II, 14. Samuel A. Green, *An Historical Sketch of Groton, Massachusetts, 1655-1890,* p. 70; Green, "The Geography of Groton," *Groton Historical Series,* I, No. XV.
2. Allan Forbes, *Towns of New England and Old England, Ireland and*

town voted "that Mr. Willard if he accept of it shall be their minister as long as he lives. w^c Mr. Willard accepts Except a manifest Providence of God appears to take him off." For reasons unknown, five men dissented, and eleven dissented when it was voted that "Mr. Willard shall have their interest in the house &. lands that was devoted by the Towne for the minestry . . . provided they may meete in the house on the lords day &c. upon other occasions of the Towne on meetings." In September Willard's salary was voted at forty pounds for the first year, the shrewdness of the Yankee spirit emerging in the provision that "if God be pleased so to dispose of his & our hearts to continue together after the expiration of the years (w[e] hope) by approving of him & he of us we shall be willing to ad unto his maintinanc as God shall blesse us. expecting allso that he shall render unto our poverty if God shall please to deny a blessing upon our labours." The dissension that clouded these initial experiences was quickly removed as the minority expressed penitence for injuries given, and asked forgiveness of each other and God.[3]

Willard was not ordained, it seems, until the following year, at which time the church was also formally gathered. Ordination was a solemn act, done by each congregation with imposition of hands and prayer, and whenever possible with a representation of other congregations present. There is no mention of this significant event in the town records of Groton, however, and the church records were lost in the war, but the record of the First Church in Roxbury carries the note: "1664. July 13 A Church gathered at Groyton and Mr. Willard ordained."[4]

The next month the bachelor preacher married Abigail Sherman, daughter of the Reverend John and Mary Sherman, of Watertown, a few miles west of Cambridge. The register of vital statistics at Groton contains the simple record:

> Mr. Samuel Willard & Abigail Shearman were maried. August 8th. 1664
>   Received, August. 8, 1664, and here entred
>   by Tho: Danforth, Record^r.

Scotland, p. 145. Green, "The Population of Groton at Different Times," Groton Historical Series, II, Article V, 126; "List of Ministers, with Their Dates of Settlement, and of Death or Dismissal," ibid., Article IV, 193.

3. Town records quoted in Sibley, op. cit., II, 14. In view of the eleven dissenting votes the five initial votes of dissent could hardly have constituted one fourth of the congregation, as Caleb Butler estimates: History of the Town of Groton, p. 156.

4. Quoted in Sibley, op. cit., II, 15.

Samuel was twenty-four at the time, Abigail but sixteen. Socially and religiously Willard had married well. His father-in-law, brought up in England under the ministry of the celebrated John Rogers, was reputed to be "a veritable Chrysostom" as a preacher, a "*first-rate* scholar," a teacher of mathematics at Harvard for a time, and a distinguished leader among New England clergy.[5]

Once settled in the parsonage at Groton, Samuel and Abigail raised a Puritan-size family. In July 1665 they were gladdened with the birth of a daughter, whom they named Abigail; next came a son, whom they named Samuel; then Mary, John, and Elizabeth.[6] The Groton congregation provided them with an increasing maintenance for their growing family. In December of 1665 it was unanimously voted to give Willard and his forever "y^t accomadation formerly stated to the ministry together with the house and all other apurtanances," with but one limitation: if he moved before seven years he should "leauve the half acomadation to the town and be aloued . . . for what improvement he haue mad upon it. But if it shall please God to take by Death, then the house and land to his eayers forever." His salary, voted annually, was fifty pounds for the second year, sixty for the third and several successive years, then sixty-five, and finally eighty pounds: part of it always in country pay, such as wheat, Indian corn, pork, and butter. He identified himself more firmly with the community by the purchase of several sizable tracts of land, totaling in all about three hundred acres, which, in keeping with the practice of the time, produced supplementary sustenance for his family. On May 11, 1670, he became a freeman with the full privileges of citizenship in Massachusetts Bay, a status reserved for Congregational church members.[7]

The Groton parishioners were mainly frontiersmen—trappers, traders, and farmers concerned with hewing cultivatable estates out of the forest. Other members of the Willard family, attracted by the fertile land available, also settled in the area. Samuel's younger brother Henry acquired a large acreage at Groton, and in 1672 his father, after twelve years of residence at Lancaster, moved to his Nonacoicus Farm at Groton, a five-hundred-acre tract granted to him by the General Court

5. *D.A.B.*, XVII, 83; Mather, *Magnalia*, II, 516; William B. Sprague, *Annals of the American Pulpit*, I, 45. Abigail was born February 3, 1647: Pope, *Willard Genealogy*, p. 15.

6. Pope, *op. cit.*, pp. 17-18. Cf. also Green, "A Register of Births, Deaths, and Marriages in Groton, 1664-1693," *Groton Historical Series*, I, No. XIII, 3,5,8.

7. Sibley, *op. cit.*, II, 15, cites the town records on maintenance and citizenship. Green, *The Early Records of Groton, Massachusetts, 1662-1707*, pp. 180-182, gives the details of Willard's holdings.

in 1657 in appreciation for his public services.[8] In addition to making family life at Groton more propinquous, this enabled Willard to keep intimately informed about the latest political and social developments at the heart of New England life through his father's contacts at the General Court.

The spirit of the times and the problems with which frontier folk had to grapple come out in three of Willard's sermons preached on special occasions between 1670 and 1672. The first was delivered on a public fast day observed throughout the colony on Thursday, June 16, 1670. For a number of years the colony had been vexed by a series of calamities, uniformly interpreted by the leaders as "afflicting providences." Waning religious intensity, the vitiating influence of new social and economic conditions, pettiness and an emerging crudeness in Massachusetts Bay are apparent in the sermons, as well as in the Court orders. There were lamentations over the neglect of child training and ministerial support, jealousy and backbiting, drunkenness and immorality.[9]

What did a thirty-year-old preacher have to say to an outpost church in such a situation? Willard's sermon was a typical jeremiad on Jeremiah 7:12—"But go ye now unto my place which was in Shiloh, where I caused my name to dwell at the first, and see what I did to it for the wickedness of my people Israel." After exegeting his text, and drawing out nine doctrines for instruction, he bore down on the need for repentance and reformation. Hypocrisy that covered up iniquity with the "veil of privileges and performances," he warned, would not deceive God—in His own time He would punish. In rare purple oratory he entreated them with a lesson from history.

> When I read the story of *Sodom's overthrow,* me thinks I see the Sun rising in glorious brightness, the *Sodomites* sporting and pleasing themselves in their *opulence and security;* when on a sudden, me thinks I see the heavens covered with those sable clouds, and hear the great Cannon of heaven thundring down tempests upon them, and the streams of fire with horror and dread, till I behold a proud City, on a sudden become a *desolate heap;* when I read *Ierusalems history* me thinks I see the battering Engines placed against the walls, the proud enemy climbing up the battlements, the feble and faint hearted Citizens flying into converns, overtaking by the insulting foe; who without mercy or pity sheaths his sword in their bowels; me thinks I see the fire-balls flying to and fro, and the glorious buildings, the work of

8. Pope, *op. cit.,* pp. 7, 9, 19; Willard, *Willard Memoir,* p. 238; Green, "Simon Willard and the Nonacoicus Farm," *Groton Historical Series,* I, No. XII, 14.

9. *Mass. Records,* IV (Part II), 1661-1674 (Boston, 1854), 653.

> many years, yeelding to that prevailing and mercyless enemy, I
> hear the cries of the ravished virgins and bereaved Orphans, yea, I
> look on till I see all Gods threatnings fulfilled, and the glory of
> the Nation stript of all ornament and become a widow.

It was a standard sermon for days of humiliation, depicting the
mercy and the justice of God, heavy with the note of pleading.

> Look on Shiloh, Look on Ierusalem, look on the number of
> desolate Churches, and take warning by these to fall down before
> God, to receive his reproofs; if you be wise, be wise for your
> selves; turn to him, for why should ye die?[10]

The next year the whole community was thrown into turmoil by the
strange case of Elizabeth Knapp, a sixteen-year-old member of the
church. The girl was seized with what might be called hysteria today,
but to the townsfolk of Groton it was unmistakably witchcraft—a
phenomenon that terrorized New Englanders no less than others. It was
a case that required skillful handling, and Willard made a careful study
of it and sent a notable clinical report to Boston.[11] For a fortnight the
girl had acted strangely, when suddenly on the night of October 31,
1671, sitting at the fireside, she cried out, "Oh! my legs! & clapt her
hand on them, imediately Oh! my breast, & removed her hands thither,
& forthwith, Oh! I am strangled, & put her hands on her throat." In the
days that followed she was obsessed with weeping, laughing, and "many
foolish & apish gestures." She led her family in a futile search of the
cellar for imaginary people, went into periodic fits, and accused a godly
neighbor of coming down the chimney at night and striking her. The
devil often bribed her to sign in blood a book of covenant (promising
money, fine clothes, or seeing the world), and repeatedly tempted her
to murder her parents, the neighbors, the children, even Willard himself.

The physician diagnosed the malady as mainly physical—"the foul-
ness of her stomacke & corruptness of her blood, occasioning fumes in
her braine, & strange fansyes"—and prescribed a "physicke." But when
her spells continued, even after a "soleme day" had been kept for her,
he refused to treat the case further and advised "extraordinary fasting,"
concluding that the distemper was "Diabolicall." This Willard ruled out
when she began to bewail her sins. To his amazement, however, on a
subsequent visit she greeted him with "Oh! you are a great roague. . . .
You tell the people a company of lyes." The voice was hollow, Willard

---

10. *Useful Instructions for a professing People in Times of great Security and
Degeneracy,* pp. 12, 19.

11. "A briefe account of a strange & unusuall Providence of God, befallen to
Elizabeth Knap of Groton, per me Sam^u Willard," *Pubs. C.S.M.,* VIII, Fourth
Series, 555-570.

observed, and came from her throat with no apparent movement of her speech organs, as if someone were speaking through her. "I answered Satan," he reported, "thou art a lyar & a deceiver, & God will vindicate his owne truth one day." But the voice answered, "I am not Satan, I am a pretty blacke boy, this is my pretty girl. I have bin here for a great while."

Willard kept his head in the weeks that followed and continued his investigation. It was an atypical and puzzling case. In spite of her convulsions she gained weight and lost no strength, she spoke even labial letters (B, M, P) without lip motion, and her "revilings" were confined to the moments of seizure. There was something preternatural about the case, Willard conjectured, but deferred final judgment to the more learned and judicious.

> Whither she have covenanted with the Devill or noe, I thinke this is a case unanswerable, her declarations have been soe contradictorye, one to another, that wee know not what to make of them, & her condition is such as administers many doubts; charity would hope the best, love would alsoe feare the worst; but this much is cleare, shee is an object of pitye. . . . She is a monumt of divine severitye, & the Lord grant that all that see or heare, may fear & tremble: Amen.

This was the motivation for the sermon preached to the taut little congregation on that "solemn occasion" sometime during November. Since God unloosed His judgments in the world that the inhabitants might learn righteousness (Isaiah 26:9), the significance of this mysterious phenomenon was clear. "There is a voice in it to the whole Land, but in a more especial manner to poor *Groton*, it is not a Judgment afar off, but it is near us, yea among us. God hath in his wisdome singled out this poor town out of all others in this wilderness, to dispense such an amazing Providence in." To Puritans Satan was intensely real, but Willard, working with the hypothesis that the girl's distemper might be demonic, kept a positive approach, and nothing like hysteria developed. But there was a lesson here for every age group, he warned, and parents especially were to "have a care of letting [their children] have their swinge, and go and come where and when they please, and especially in the night." In words reminiscent of Winthrop he urged the congregation to look upon themselves as "set up as a *Beacon upon a Hill* by this Providence, and let those that hear what hath been done among us, hear also of the good news, and the reformation it hath wrought among us."[12]

12. *Useful Instructions,* pp. 32-33, 35-41.

A third "solemn occasion" came the next summer as Groton suffered another wheat-crop failure. Willard's fast-day sermon on June 13,
1672, points up the farmers' concern to get at the bottom of the
trouble. "We are very inquisitive to know what may be the Natural
Cause of these Blastings which have for many years diminished and
corrupted the best of our Grain," he said, "and hence, many projective
endeavors in vain attempted to prevent it, by seeking to remove that
Cause, which we are to this day baffled in, and as far to seek as ever."
But the spiritual causes which were much more manifest and more
easily discovered, Willard chided, were being overlooked: "no wonder
that the Effect remains."[13] Once more he preached reformation. But
the mildew continued throughout the seventeenth century, and into the
eighteenth, when it was finally attributed not to the hand of God but
to the barberry bush.

The baffled preachers, thrown on the defensive by continually
mounting calamities, had found new notes of lamentation. The ineffec-
tiveness of numerous days of humiliation, the contemning of ministerial
rebukes, even the division of opinion among the ministers themselves,
were an indication that the sinews of society, religion, and the political
order were loosening, Willard warned. Speedy repentance was urgent.

> But if you yet resolve to delay, and put God off, expect swift and
> sudden ruine; you have tasted the Rod, but God hath seven-fold
> more heavy plagues in store, expect to go captive with the first
> that go captive, to be slain with the first that are slain by the
> sword, to be famished with the first that perish with hunger.[14]

Little did he realize how prophetic his words were! On June 24,
1675, after a peace of nearly forty years, the Indians at Swansea, in the
southern part of Plymouth Colony, opened what has become known as
King Philip's War. The population of New England had increased
rapidly during the peaceful decades, and as numerous new towns were
settled the colonists encroached ever farther upon the Indian domain.
Philip, of a different spirit than his father Massasoit, shrewdly perceived
that it would soon be a question as to who would rule the wilderness—
the red man or the white man—and taking the offensive he united the
Narragansetts, Mipmucks, and other tribes in a war of extermination
against the English.

13. *Ibid.*, p. 55. See W. DeLoss Love, Jr., *The Fast and Thanksgiving Days of
New England*, pp. 206n, 473, for the date of the fast. See Robert R. Wolcott,
"Husbandry in Colonial New England," *N.E.Q.*, IX (1936), 235, for the next
century's discovery of the cause of the mildew.
14. *Useful Instructions*, p. 80.

Willard's Groton flock watched with mounting alarm as the war approached ever nearer. Major Simon Willard, in charge of the New England forces, deployed companies from town to town all along the border to one danger point after another. The Indians savagely attacked Deerfield, Hadley, Springfield, and Hatfield, exacting dreadful tolls until winter forced a lull. Early in 1676 the frontiersmen, fearing that a fresh outbreak was imminent, began new preparations for defense. On February 6, Samuel Willard wrote a petition for the town committee of Groton *"To the honored Counsill of the Massachusetts sitting in Boston,"*[15] explaining the precarious safety of the frontier towns and urging immediate changes. Major Willard's scout of forty "troopers & Dragoons" ranging between Groton, Lancaster, and Marlborough was poor defense, they argued. It would be better strategy to put a garrison of soldiers in each town.

The emergency they envisioned came four days later. One of the Christian Indians tipped them off on February 9 that Lancaster was about to be attacked, and the very next day at sunrise the Indians fell upon the town, brutally killing some, wounding others, and leading away among the captives the wife and child of the Reverend Joseph Rowlandson. On March 10, as the churches of the colony met for fasting and prayer, the Indians attacked Groton and Sudbury, killing several. Three days later, while Major Willard was out with his troops, a force of four hundred Indians assaulted Groton as the unsuspecting townsfolk were busy with their chores, and except for a few houses utterly destroyed the town. *"The House of God"* was one of the first destroyed, reported Increase Mather, and having completed this desecration "they scoffed and blasphemed, and came to *Mr. Willard* (the worthy Pastor of the Church there) his house (which being Fortified, they attempted not to destroy it) and tauntingly, said, *What will you do for a house to pray in now we have burnt your Meeting-house?"* [16] After spending the night in the captured garrison house and in the adjacent valley, the savages renewed their atrocities the next morning before marching off.

> They stript the body of him whom they had slain in the first onset, and then cutting off his head, fixed it upon a pole looking towards his own land. The corpse of the man slain the week before, they dug up out of his grave, they cutt off his head and

---

15. The handwriting is Samuel Willard's, though it is signed by James Parker, Thomas Wheeler, Henry Woods. Quoted in Green, *Groton During the Indian Wars*, pp. 22-23.

16. Increase Mather, *A Briefe History of the Warr with the Indians in New-England*, p. 274. For the background see Willard, *Willard Memoir*, p. 264; Palfrey, *History of New England*, III, 183-187; Love, *op. cit.*, p. 475.

leg, and set them up on poles, and stript off his winding sheet. An infant which they found dead in the house first surprised, they cut in pieces, which afterward they cast to the swine.[17]

By the time Major Willard returned four days later the Indians had fled, and Groton lay in desolation. Samuel Willard had lived through the full horror of the destruction. His own family had been spared, but other lives had been lost, and besides other buildings over forty houses had been burned. The three hundred inhabitants resolved to abandon the place, and scattered to temporary quarters in other towns. Samuel and Abigail took their family to Charlestown, it seems, where Samuel's sister was living.[18]

Here Major Willard, overwhelmingly reelected to the General Court by a grateful public, fell victim to a raging epidemic that took the lives of many that spring, and died on April 24 at the age of seventy-two. He was buried with military honors, a force of several hundred soldiers marching in the funeral[19] of this "pious, orthodox man," as John Hull eulogized him.[20]

It was a trying time for Samuel Willard. The loss within a span of a few weeks of home, church, position, and the companionship of an eminent father was a shattering experience.

But Willard stood on the threshold of the most significant period of his life.

Boston: "a more conspicuous Orb"

Within two months Willard was preaching in Boston. He preached the preparatory lecture at Third Church for the Reverend Thomas Thacher, who was ill, and made a good impression. Samuel Sewall, a substantial Harvard alumnus, noted in his diary: "Being distressed with melancholy and troubled concerning my State—I was relieved by Mr. Willard's Sermon."[21] The Artillery Company invited him to be its annual election preacher on June 5, and he delivered a metaphorical mosaic on "The Heart Garrisoned."[22]

Preaching in the new world's foremost city was an auspicious opportunity. Boston was a thriving port city, the social, economic, and cultural link with the old world, the center of colonial affairs, and the

17. William Hubbard, *A Narrative of the Indian Wars in New England 1607-1677*, p. 74; Green, *Groton During the Indian Wars*, p. 32.

18. Pope, *op. cit.*, pp. 9, 16.

19. Willard, *Willard Memoir*, pp. 281, 305, 307.

20. *The Diaries of John Hull, A.A.S. Trans. and Colls.*, III, 241.

21. *Diary of Samuel Sewall, M.H.S. Colls.*, Fifth Series, V, 13, 44, 52.

22. *The Heart Garrisoned.*

seat of New England's chief churches. It was an attractive town of pebble-stone streets and houses of brick and stone. Situated upon an almost square peninsula about four miles around, surrounded by the sea except for a narrow isthmus on the south, the city was fortified by artillery on the hills that commanded a view of the bay and the coast. It was "the Metropolis of this Colony, or rather of the whole Countrey," according to the English voyager John Josselyn, giving him the impression of an English port city, with houses "for the most part raised on the Seabanks and wharfed out with great industry and cost, many of them standing upon piles, close together on each side of the streets as in *London.*" The center of business life in the city was the town house "where the Merchants may confer." The General Court convened each month in the same building on the second floor. There were two "constant Fairs" on the northeast and northwest, and on the south there was a small, pleasant commons where "the Gallants a little before Sunset walk their *Marmalet-*Madams . . . till the nine a clock Bell rings them home to their respective habitations, when presently the Constables walk their rounds to see good orders kept, and to take up loose people."[23]

At the year's end a tiff with the Reverend Increase Mather, the well-established teacher of Second Church, reveals that Willard no longer thought of himself as a refugee or guest minister in the city. Mather's church was lost on November 27 in the great fire that destroyed a large section of the city. His flock scattered, he was given the opportunity of preaching in the other churches of the city, and seemingly he took advantage of this hospitality to satisfy his desire to preach to the largest congregations. Willard, who also knew what it was like to be deprived of a church, reacted vigorously. At a conference with Mather and Joseph Rowlandson on December 18, Sewall sensed that Willard had "some Animosity . . . toward Mr. Mather: for that he said he chose the Afternoon that so he might have a copious auditory: and that when the Town House was offered to him to preach to his Church distinct, said he would not preach in a corner."[24]

This was a time of new joy to the Willard family, but also another crushing loss. On December 6, 1676, Abigail gave birth to a sixth child, whom they named Simon. He was their last child; either at the time, or shortly thereafter, Abigail died.[25]

23. John Josselyn, *An Account of Two Voyages to New-England,* pp. 161-162. Cf. also Bernard Bailyn, *The New England Merchants in the Seventeenth Century,* p. 97; and Walter Muir Whitehill, *Boston,* pp. 13-15.

24. Sewall, *Diary, 5 M.H.S. Colls.,* V, 28-30.

25. Pope, *op. cit.,* pp. 18, 30. When Willard was admitted to membership at Third Church there was no mention of her, and a few years later he married again.

After he had assisted Thacher at Third Church for almost two years, the church resolved in 1678 to call Willard as an associate. On February 12 he was admitted to membership, and on April 10 he was installed as Teacher.[26] In his younger years his Master had committed to his care a flock "in a more obscure part of this Wilderness," declared Ebenezer Pemberton, but "his Lord did not design to bury him in obscurity, but to place him in a more eminent Station, which he was qualified for." The providence that moved him here was a judgment on the whole land, but it was a "mercy" in that "it made way for the Translation of this bright Star to a more Conspicuous Orb, where his Influence was more Extensive, and Beneficial."[27]

Third Church, commonly known as South Church because of its location, was a spacious cedar meetinghouse, with a steeple, galleries, square pews, and a pulpit at the side.[28] It had been organized only nine years before in 1669 as a result of contention in the First Church over the Half-Way Covenant decisions of 1662. South Church not only adopted the accommodation on baptism, a few years later it also made an adjustment on the manner of receiving members. Traditionally candidates for membership, after a searching examination by the elders of the church, gave a public "relation" of their "experience in the wayes of grace," the men orally and the women in a written statement. It was sufficient in exceptional cases, the church decided on February 14, 1678 (and the record is in Willard's handwriting), to present such relations to the elders rather than to the entire church.[29] Such steps towards greater leniency, bitterly attacked by the more conservative leaders, were not startling, but they do indicate that on the more formal aspects of church polity he was willing to accept change.

Six months after Willard began his copastorate at South Church, Thacher, who had been ill off and on for at least two years, again took sick, and died on October 15, 1678.[30] Thus, at thirty-eight years of age, Willard was left to minister alone to the congregation.

Among the two hundred and seventeen members of the growing

Hamilton A. Hill and George F. Bigelow, *An Historical Catalogue of the Old South Church (Third Church) Boston, 1669-1882,* p. 11.

26. Hill and Bigelow, *op. cit.,* pp. 1, 11. Benjamin Wisner, *The History of the Old South Church in Boston,* p. 13. The date March 31 given by Hamilton A. Hill, *History of the Old South Church (Third Church) Boston. 1669-1884,* I, 226, and by Widney Willard, *Memoirs of Youth and Manhood,* I, 5, is according to the old style of dating.

27. *Funeral Sermon,* 70.

28. Hill, *op. cit.,* I, 140; Wisner, *op. cit.,* p. 10.

29. Hill, *op. cit.,* I, 65ff., 229. On the traditional practice see Walker, *Creeds and Platforms,* pp. 106-107.

30. Hill, *op. cit.,* I, 229; Hill and Bigelow, *op. cit.,* p. 227.

church were many of Boston's distinguished and prominent citizens. They included John Hull, the famous silversmith, mintmaster and treasurer of the colony; Samuel Sewall, his son-in-law, also prominent in the business and official life of the colony, and a Harvard graduate who received his M.A. in 1674; and Edward Rawson, Secretary of the colony. Also among them were Thomas Brattle, merchant and one of the wealthiest men of his day; Peter Oliver, an eminent merchant; Joshua Scottaw, a great proprietor; and Hezekiah Usher, bookseller and representative in the colonial government. Thomas Savage, commander-in-chief of the forces in the early part of King Philip's War, was a prominent member, as was Commander William Davis, a man of wealth. The membership also listed representative Peter Brackett; John Alden, the highly respected eldest son of John and Priscilla Alden of Plymouth; Daniel Henchman, a schoolmaster; and the Reverend Peter Thacher, H.C. 1671, son of the Reverend Thomas Thacher.[31] There were others who occupied various lesser positions of responsibility in the political life of the colony among them, and many merchants. The First Church and the Second Church of Boston also had prominent members, but, compared with First Church,[32] the South Church's constituency was proportionately more substantial and influential. The large number of merchants in the membership was a mixed blessing, however, for the economically powerful and politically influential merchants became prime movers in the subtle but fundamental transformation of New England society. The intolerant attitude of the clergy toward religious pluralism, they felt, not only discouraged migration to New England, it was bad for trade.[33] As the merchants in the interest of successful trade promoted a softer and more latitudinarian policy, the religious leaders were faced with the necessity of keeping alive the sense of New England's errand into the wilderness.

For more than a year after taking up the ministry at South Church, Willard had sole responsibility for the care of his family. Samuel had died early, Abigail was now fourteen, Mary almost ten, John six, Elizabeth three, and Simon two. On July 29, 1679, Willard married again, not one of the many commonly sought-out eligible widows, but Eunice Tyng, a twenty-four-year-old member of the First Church.[34] The fact that Eunice was the daughter of Magistrate Edward Tyng, who a decade earlier had done much to impede the establishment of South Church, perhaps explains that for two years after their marriage Eunice

31. Hill and Bigelow, *op. cit.,* pp. 5-11, 213-263.
32. Cf. "First Church of Boston, Records and Baptisms 1630-1687," in the library of the Massachusetts Historical Society.
33. Bailyn, *op. cit.,* pp. 105ff.
34. Pope, *op. cit.,* pp. 15, 17-18; Hill, *op. cit.,* I, 226.

remained unaffiliated with South Church. It seems quite unlikely that Willard would have married one spiritually unable to meet the adjusted requirements for membership at the South Church. The record nonetheless indicates that a son, Edward, was born to them on July 6, 1680, that another son, Josiah, was born on June 21, 1681, that both were baptized, but that Eunice did not become a member until September 9, 1681.[35] Fourteen children were born to Samuel and Eunice,[36] and to support this large family South Church gave Willard a salary of over one hundred shillings per week, plus certain additional expense allowances, and some years later in appreciation for his ministry presented him a special subscription amounting to three hundred and thirty six pounds.[37]

The year 1679 also witnessed the calling of the historic Reforming Synod—an attempt to head off what New Englanders feared was inevitable divine reckoning for mounting worldliness. To Willard and other Bay leaders the concurrence of a number of calamities—war, fires, shipwrecks, epidemics, and the new threats to their liberties by the Stuart government—were proofs that God had a controversy with New England. What were their provoking sins, and how could they be reformed? These were the burning questions calling for a special synod.[38] The response of the churches was unanimous, and on September 10, as the Synod convened, Samuel Willard, Edward Raynsford, John Hull, Thomas Savage, and Peter Thacher were on hand as the distinguished delegation of South Church.[39] Comoderated by John Sherman, father of Willard's first wife, and Urian Oakes, acting president of Harvard, the Synod produced a devastating diagnosis of New England's degeneration; its prescription for reform, however, was surprisingly external and formal. Willard was chosen a member of the committee to present this formidable *Result* to the General Court in October.[40] But he and the other leaders of New England were to discover that it required more than synodical edict to make these measures effective, however worthy they might be in themselves. Nonetheless, this codification of ideas did become a conspectus for their preaching during the next few decades.

Willard was also appointed to the committee mandated to draw up a confession of faith for consideration by the Synod the following year. Rather than producing a creed of their own, they recommended,

35. Hill, *op. cit.,* I, 141, 146, 244f.; Hill and Bigelow, *op. cit.,* p. 12.
36. Pope, *op. cit.,* p. 18.
37. Hill, *op. cit.,* I, 228n., 295.
38. Walker, *op. cit.,* pp. 411-412, 415-416.
39. Hill, *op. cit.,* I, 233.
40. Walker, *op. cit.,* p. 419.

practically unchanged, the adoption of the Savoy Confession of the English Puritans. The Synod dispatched this confessional work on May 11 and 12, 1680, and duly reported it to the General Court on June 11, which approved the document and ordered it printed for the benefit of the churches.[41] There is no evidence that the South or any of the other churches at this time formally adopted this confession as a local creed, but considering the part Willard played in getting it approved by both the Synod and the Court, it is reasonable to conclude that at South Church it possessed the weight of a formally ratified creed. Willard was a strong believer in consociation, and what had been approved by synodical action was for him morally binding. Indeed, the Westminster and Savoy creeds were the touchstones of his preaching throughout his career.

One of the deeply moving and solemn features of New England life in the 1680s was renewal of the covenant, strongly recommended by the Synod of 1679 as the Scriptural expedient for reformation. On the day appointed a church would gather for fasting and prayer (sometimes with a great confluence of neighbors), hear a sermon on the sins that the Synod had indicted as the causes of God's wrath, and then solemnly renew their covenant with God and one another, confessing their sins and pledging amendment of life by the grace of God. On March 17, 1680, Willard preached "The Duty of a People that have Renewed their Covenant with God" to Increase Mather's church. Having made trial of God for so many years, exhorted Willard, they had found Him good, gracious, and glorious, and had renewed their covenant with Him. But in so doing they had imposed a "strong and awful obligation" upon themselves to offer Him the sacrificial service of their hearts and lives; God expected more than words from them—He awaited a conspicuous reformation![42]

Three months later, on June 29, in a similar sermon on the "Necessity of Sincerity in Renewing Covenant," he warned his own church against the dissembling, flattery and lies so conspicuous in the Old Testament covenant renewals. "Their defect is our admonition," he declared, and they would not be able to "cheat" God with a rash, heartless covenant, nor would He be put off with "varnished hypocritical pretences." Yet having done their utmost, he assured them, "God loves and will accept of truth in the inward part, and whatsoever frailties are with you, yet this is pleadable in the greatest extremityes, Isa. 38.3." The intention was the important thing—was it "mere Ceremony and show" or "true and through [sic] reformation?" "He that

41. *Ibid.*, pp. 419, 421-422.
42. *The Duty of a People that have Renewed their Covenant with God*, pp. 6, 9, 10ff.

Covenants to forsake that Sin, which he hath a full purpose in his heart to keep and hug as his Darling, how is he like to stand to it?" He told them quite bluntly what they would be in for if they covenanted with God: "you promise that you will not run in the Current and Stream of the Times in the Pursuit of vanity, nor seek your own things, but the things of Christ." To do this you must take Christ as your "Undertaker and Surety," not with the careless presumption that says "let Christ answer for it," but by clinging to Him as covenant head, for "from him we shall fetch down Grace to animate, quicken, and strengthen our Souls to Duty."[43] At sermon's end the people renewed their covenant, pleaded mercy, promised greater regard for church ordinances, discipline, and Christian family life. They pledged themselves to reform their worship and service of all formalism and hypocrisy, and above all, to keep this sacred covenant.[44]

The response that year gladdened Willard's heart—no less than one hundred and twelve persons owned the baptismal covenant, fifteen became communicant members. Most of the former, many from prominent families, ultimately became communicant members as yearly new members were added to South Church.[45] Nonetheless, with the exception of the "harvests" of Solomon Stoddard at Northampton, New England would wait till well into the next century for that afflatus of the Spirit that was to sweep vast numbers of converts into the churches and profoundly transform the life of the common mass. Yet evidence of divine blessing upon the ministers' work, Cotton Mather noted, was seen "not only by the great *advancement* of *holiness* in the people, . . . but also by a great *addition* of converts into their holy fellowship."[46] And the year 1680 was Samuel Willard's greatest.

Willard as Preacher

It was as a "divine," as he liked to refer to himself, that Willard exercised his principal influence on his generation. Essentially and primarily a preacher, most of his published works were sermons. Only three occasional sermons had been printed before his settlement in Boston, but once he had been ordained as the Teacher of the South Church he burst into print, the number of his publications eventually being exceeded only by recognition-hungry Cotton Mather.

43. *The Necessity of Sincerity in renewing Covenant* (bound with *Covenant Keeping the Way to Blessedness*), pp. 134, 137, 142-143, 146-147, 149.

44. *Necessity of Sincerity*, pp. A2, A3.

45. Hill and Bigelow, *op. cit.*, pp. 104-107. In the next decade Josiah and Abiah Franklin became members, and on January 6, 1706, their son Benjamin was baptized at South Church.

46. *Op. cit.*, II, 331-332.

The seventeenth century was preeminently an age of the sermon, and the sermons reflect as no other literary remains the strong convictions and emotions engendered by the theological, political, and social upheaval of the time. Willard preached on all occasions then in vogue— Sunday morning and afternoon services, midweek "lectures," funerals, fasts and thanksgivings, and by invitation at the annual election for the General Assembly or the honorable Artillery Company. His sermons reflect the time, and spoke vigorously to it.

A preacher of the Word, he invariably took a Scripture text, analyzed the words and ideas in their context, formulated the truths in a series of doctrinal propositions, and in numerous "uses" applied the historic faith with contemporary relevance. "He was a *Judicious Textuary*," said Pemberton, "like *Apollos* a Man mighty in the Scripture."[47] As such he was a child of the Reformation age. Christian doctrine was "Heavenly Merchandize . . . ," he told the businessmen of the South Church, "delivered by God Himself." The Bible was the written Word of God, the "only touch stone" for faith and practice, and "whatsoever Doctrines are not according to it, are to be repudiated as false." He affirmed the perfection of Scripture as a "main article" of the Christian religion. It was an infallible guide. Divinely inspired, it was marked by unity: "every Truth agrees with the whole and with every other Truth."[48]

This divine high view of Scripture governed Willard's use of human authors, to whom God in His common grace had granted wisdom and insight. He permitted himself occasional general references, therefore, to "the philosopher," "the heathen Poets," "some Ethnicks," or Epicureans, Stoics, Platonists, and Peripatetics. Only rarely did he name individuals such as Pythagoras, Plato, Aristotle, or Seneca. As a Puritan divine he eschewed the latitudinarianism with which Anglicans ranged beyond Christian sources—at best such references were handmaidens or the foil for the truth. The profile of Puritan mentality emerges clearly in a quotation from classical antiquity: "A Philosopher reading John 1.1 cried out, This barbarous man hath shut up more in these few words, than all the Philosophers and Orators in their voluminous Writings."[49] The ancient fathers he cited with respect, though infrequently, to confirm an interpretation of the sacred text, but only with brief phrases such as "one of the Fathers commenting on it saith," "it is a worthy saying of Augustine," or "so Tertullian glosseth it."[50] He made virtually no reference to the scholastics, however, for scholasti-

47. *Funeral Sermon*, p. 66.
48. *Heavenly Merchandize*, pp. 8, 108-109, 113.
49. *A Compleat Body of Divinity*, p. 19.
50. *Ibid.*, pp. 387, 738; *Mercy Magnified on a Penitent Prodigal*, p. 381.

cism was associated with Roman Catholic domination when "Antichristianism" grew to a great height, and "the fogs of the bottomless pit grievously obscured the Sun-light of the Gospel."[51]

It was according to the insights of the Reformers and their successors on the Continent and in England that Willard preached the Scriptures. Puritans normally did not credit their sources, but Willard did occasionally indicate his mentors—among them Martin Luther, John Calvin, Emanuel Tremellius, Theodore Beza, and Johannes Piscator.[52] The margins of his published sermons on *Covenant Keeping* in 1682 acknowledge his indebtedness to such giants as Martin Chemnitz, Johann Buxtorf, Andre Rivet, Johannes Maccovius, Barthelmaeus Keckermann, William Gouge, Johann H. Alstead, David Pareus, John Owen, Samuel Stone, and Robert Bolton.[53] We may assume that he also thumbed the pages of standard reference works such as William Ames' *Medulla Sacrae Theologiae,* Zacharias Ursinus's *The Summe of Christian Religion,* and John Wollebius's *Christianae Theologiae Compendium.*[54] Besides these there was a spiritual brotherhood of English Puritans who served as mentors to New England preachers: Lawrence Chaderton, Arthur Hildersam, John Dod, John Carter, Samuel Crook, Julines Herring, William Perkins, Paul Baynes, Richard Sibbes, John Preston, and Thomas Goodwin.[55] And in America stalwarts such as John Cotton, Richard Mather, and Thomas Hooker for a generation already had been molding the New England mind.

The thought, the form, even the very phrases of these works are reflected in Willard's sermons, such mental and verbal assimilation being common at the time. Blended in the preaching of Willard were the fruits of Rhineland Protestantism, Genevan Calvinism, and the Continental Reformed thought generally, all of which, as the Westminster formularies show, had been appropriated by English Puritanism.[56] Willard's own commitment to this theology comes to light most notably in a series of Tuesday lecture-sermons on the Westminster Shorter

51. *The Checkered State of the Gospel Church,* p. 14.

52. *All Plots against God and his People Detected and Defeated* (bound with *The Child's Portion*), p. 226; *The only sure way to prevent threatned Calamity* (bound with *The Child's Portion*), p. 168; *Compleat Body,* p. 464; *Mercy Magnified,* pp. 63, 138, 376.

53. *Covenant-Keeping The Way to Blessedness,* pp. 2, 3, 4-6, 7, 12, 15, 29, 39, 19, 36, 45.

54. Ursinus's work was published in translation in London, 1633. On Ames and Wollebius, see footnote 35, Chapter 1.

55. Cf. Haller, *The Rise of Puritanism,* pp. 48-92.

56. Cf. Benjamin B. Warfield, *The Westminster Assembly and Its Work,* pp. 57-58; Heinrich Heppe, *Reformed Dogmatics,* especially "List of the Most Important Sources Quoted," pp. 713-716; L. J. Trinterud, "The Origins of Puritanism," *Church History,* XX (1951), 37-57.

Catechism begun in 1688.[57] These monthly homilies introduced a unique type of discourse in New England. The practice was not unknown in Germany, Holland, and England,[58] but Willard has the distinction of being the first "catechism preacher" in New England. "DIVINITY was his Favourite Study," explained Pemberton, and he "Excelled to an eminent degree in the Knowledge of the most abstruse parts of Theology. . . . His Knowledge in *Systematical Divinity* was celebrated by all. . . . But his knowledge appeared with a peculiar Lustre in his *CATECHETICAL LECTURES.*"[59] The sermons were heard with such "Relish" by the "most knowing and judicious" persons from the town and the college that, some years after his death, they were published through popular subscription as *A Compleat Body of Divinity.* "We need only say—*'Tis Mr. Willard's,"* declared editors Joseph Sewall and Thomas Prince, "and 'tis enough to Recommend it to their high Respect and diligent Attentions."[60] The sermons, described as "the work of a theological drill-sergeant,"[61] summarize the faith of New England in the seventeenth century.

Willard's preaching was widely acclaimed at the time. The catechism sermons and "his other excellent Performances," said Sewall and Prince, "have deservedly gain'd him so great a Fame & Esteem among us."[62] Samuel Sewall's *Diary* abounds with notes of appreciation. Ebenezer Pemberton, his colleague at South Church, observed that "His *Discourses* were all Elaborate, Acute and Judicious; smelt of the Lamp, and had nothing *Mean* in them." His ordinary sermons, he claimed, "might have been pronounced with Applause before an Assembly of the greatest Divines." In content they were solid, doctrinal, and practical. His delivery was effective and forceful.

The *Manner* in which he deliver'd his Discourses was agreeable to the *Matter.* In respect of both he spoke as become the ORACLES

57. Herbert W. Schneider, *The Puritan Mind,* pp. 98-99, is in error in imagining the setting of these sermons in the Old South Church on Sundays in 1724. Perry Miller, *The New England Mind. From Colony to Province,* p. 30, repeats the error in somewhat modified form when he says that Willard worked his way "on successive Sabbaths in the 1690's through the entire system." Joseph Sewall and Thomas Prince, the editors of Willard's *Compleat Body,* indicate in "The Preface" that these lecture sermons were delivered each month on Tuesdays.

58. Ursinus, author of the Heidelberg Catechism, preached catechetical sermons each Sunday after 1563. *The New Schaff-Herzog Encyclopedia of Religious Knowledge,* XII, 112. In 1566 the Reformed Churches in Holland adopted the practice. In England a number of divines had preached catechetical lectures.

59. *Funeral Sermon,* pp. 65-66.

60. "The Preface," *Compleat Body,* p. i.

61. Moses C. Tyler, *A History of American Literature,* II, 167-169.

62. *Compleat Body,* "The Preface," p. i.

OF GOD: With Gravity, Courage, Zeal, and Prudence, and with tender Bowels to Perishing Souls. His *Language* was always good; his Stile Masculine, not Perplexed, but Easy as well as Strong. And when the Matter required it, no Man could speak with a greater *Pathos* and *Pungency*.

He could speak in ways "suited to melt the rocky heart, to bow the stubborn Will, and to humble the proudest Sinner, and charm the deafest Adder."[63]

Willard's preaching was positive, but it also had a cutting edge. Religion, unlike science, could not simply "lay down what is Truth"; because of "the Pravity and Indisposition of our Corrupt Natures" error had to be uncovered.[64] Curiosity, he warned, was prompting New Englanders "to leave the worship and wayes of Gods institutions and run giddily after new Doctrines and Teachers."[65] Some, formerly orthodox, were gradually being drawn "to believe Lies instead of the Truth," by imposters who had a "wonderful art of palliating and settling off their false wares," and they needed to be fortified against these retailers of false doctrine.[66] "Never was there more need to Preach and Print in defence of those great Fundamentals of our faith and hope," he asserted.[67] In the interest of keeping New England orthodox, therefore, he championed the New England theocracy, vigorously opposed every antinomian tendency, resisted the infiltration of Arminianism, and did much to obstruct the inroads of Baptists and Quakers.

He epitomized the New England mind. It was not a fixed mind that remained completely unmodified by a century of New England experience; it was more complex, a mind in tension, in many respects an emerging mind. As they faced the new social, economic, political, and religious situations, some of the clergy attempted to withdraw and play safe. Some militantly combatted all change. Others more creatively related themselves to the new situations. Willard, in a measure, achieved a synthesis of these tendencies. He was conservative and protective in his attempts to preserve orthodoxy, and his assaults on the threats to orthodoxy were formidable; at the same time he was able to make necessary adjustments to new situations that would preserve the New England way, and confidently counseled the people to go forward.

63. *Funeral Sermon*, pp. 71-72.
64. *Compleat Body*, p. 647.
65. *Duty of a People that have Renewed their Covenant*, p. 12.
66. *Heavenly Merchandize*, pp. 43, 91-96.
67. *The Truly Blessed Man*, p. 6.

CHAPTER THREE

CHURCH AND STATE:
Under the First Charter

Rival political and ecclesiastical forces were stirring in a cauldron of unrest as Willard began his ministry. The founders' neatly contrived structure of virtually autonomous colonial government was being challenged by the new imperial policy of the restored Stuart government, and within the colonial government itself polarity was developing on local issues as magistrates and deputies aligned against each other. Annexation of the trade-conscious towns of Maine and New Hampshire was putting a strain on the coalition of church and state, and alien religious forces were contending against Massachusetts' ecclesiastical system. The unity of religion and politics was axiomatic in early Massachusetts, as the two admittedly separate but mutually interested spheres cooperated aristocratically in a system described generally as a theocracy. For a time the Bay leaders could count on the interest and cooperation of Puritan allies in England, but with the collapse of the Commonwealth and the altered religious and political complexion in the homeland, they no longer enjoyed these encouragements. Inevitably the impending changes in church-state relations that Massachusetts leaders eyed with dread came about under a succession of colonial and royal governors. And unavoidably Willard, as a prominent divine in New England's leading city, became actively involved.

The Administration of Governor Leverett

While Willard was in his first pastorate at Groton the severe and overbearing Richard Bellingham was serving for the ninth time as chief magistrate. Only brief allusions remain of the young parson's attitudes to what was going on in church and state. As Bellingham vigorously resisted not only the efforts of the royal commissioners to bring Massachusetts under closer imperial control, but also the attempts of the Baptists to establish their deviant worship in Boston, Willard came out strongly for firm governmental control. "Lenitie in Rulers," he declared in 1670, "brings ruine upon a people, whether in Common Wealth or in Churches." He exhorted his people to pray that rulers would be zealous against sin, and to "Incourage them in so doing, by rejoycing in acts of Justice, and severity, against such evils as grow and thrive among us."[1] Willard's diametrical opposition to Bellingham's unbending efforts as a member of the First Church of Boston to thwart the organization of the South Church, however, came out in a sermon in which he lamented the fact that there were some "ready to renounce Consociation and Communion one with another."[2]

Bellingham died in 1672, and John Leverett, the deputy governor, succeeded him on May 7, 1673, in a term vexed by the horrible King Philip's War. Willard delivered on June 5, 1676, the annual election sermon before the Ancient and Honourable Artillery Company on "The Heart Garrisoned." A refugee from the frontier, intimately acquainted with the peril, he might better have urged that the whole community be properly garrisoned. Specialized armies of Europe might follow the formal rules of warfare outlined by the famous jurist Hugo Grotius—but American Indians did not read Grotius, they darted out of the forests silently and with fiendish cruelty, brutally visiting havoc and destruction upon communities, lives, and property. Nonetheless, Willard's spiritualized treatment of a Christian soldier's life seems to carry an oblique call for greater preparedness. The soldier had no easy life: he had to make "recreation" of what others accounted death as he grappled with enemies "Fierce and Cruel." Among other things he needed prudence, prowess, fortitude, sobriety and fidelity. He spoke in the analogies of war with the knowledgeability of a member of a military family: fortify, cut off the supplies of the enemy, take care for reparation, keep a good watch, charge forward in every assault, call in help when strength fails, and beware of remissness after victory.[3] His hearers should have gotten the message.

Tension between the crown and the colonial government increased as Massachusetts came under fire for its religious limitation on the

1. *Useful Instructions,* p. 17.
2. *Ibid.,* p. 76. On Bellingham's opposition to the formation of Third Church, see Hill, *History of Old South Church,* I, 79, 91, 94-95, 141-142, 146, 173, 175, 177.
3. *The Heart Garrisoned,* pp. 7, 13-20.

franchise, the dominance of Congregationalism, the evasion of the navigation acts, in short, for its assertion of economic, political, and religious autonomy. Edward Randolph arrived in 1676 to assert the claims of the crown, to enforce the laws of trade, and to deliver the King's letter demanding explanation in London. William Stoughton and Peter Bulkeley were dispatched following some heartsearching discussions with the clergy, and Randolph returned with further charges to prosecute the English and Anglican interests. The softening explanations of the agents fell on deaf ears and they returned with many rebukes, and Randolph also returned.[4] Massachusetts was torn by party spirit over what to do: some were for firmness, others were disposed to yield to the encroachments of the king, and only Leverett's competent leadership kept the parties in check.

It was a severe loss for the colony, therefore, when Leverett died on May 16, 1679. Willard's funeral sermon was a jeremiad bristling with warnings against the divisive political spirit, threats about additional judgments if they did not reform, and counsel on the kind of leadership demanded by the times. Leaders like Leverett, "publickly both great and good," were not sufficiently appreciated at such a critical time, moaned Willard. Political contentions were doubly dangerous at such a time: with "secret plots and contrivances of Enemies abroad against us . . . heart divisions among us are exposing us not a little to be made a prey to others."[5]

What kind of leader was needed then? "I desire to be farre from being a stickler & busie body in matters of State, but only as a well wisher to the peace and prosperity of our Jerusalem," answered Willard; but he did have some definite ideas on the subject. Nine, in fact. First of all he had to be a man of authority and influence. In times of "epidemical" degeneracy, he must be godly, not "meerly moral." He must be "publick spirited," as well as skillful in discerning the times, for it was "not enough to be verst in general Maximes of State, but to know how to deal in the very change of a peoples manners." He must be zealous for God's glory, but intelligently so: "it is a point of Christian prudence in any Rulers, to know what cannot be done at present, & throw themselves upon unavoidable hazards, when they may better use other wayes to accomplish their dut[s] [duties]." He must be a man of undaunted courage, for "if he punish sin it is cruelty, if he curbe encroaching errors it is Tyranny, and he shall hear defaming on every side, and he had need therefore to be resolute." Besides all this,

4. For the general background of the renewed dispute with England see Palfrey, *History of New England*, Chapter VII; R. N. Toppan, *Edward Randolph*, IV and VI *passim*.

5. *A Sermon Preached upon Ezek. 22.30,31*, pp. 10-11.

he should be sensitive to the tokens of divine anger, a vigorous executor
of enacted orders, and finally, a man of fervent prayer—for wisdom,
counsel, courage, and success were to be "gained in heaven." In a word,
he summed up the matter, if "Rulers in Common-wealth and Church
are not such men, they are none at all."[6]

It was the people's duty, then, to make the right choice, he warned
in words loaded with meaning. Rulers were duty-bound to suppress sins
against the first as well as against the second table of the Mosaic law,
"unless we can say that Atheisme, Heresy, despising Gods Ordinances,
cursing, swearing, abusing Gods blessed Name, and profanation of his
holy Sabbaths, are no provoking sins." Knowing the difficulties the
colonial emissaries were encountering in England in behalf of their
charter and the liberty of self-determination, he more than suggested:

> I speak as to a people that are free; and it is a choice blessing to
> the people of God that they may have men of their own choice;
> and will be an aggravation of their sin and sorrows, if (having such
> a liberty) they abuse it to licentiousness.

Get rid of your factionalism and pray for rulers interested in reformation, he warned them, for it is in your own hands to fortify or ruin
yourselves.[7]

Willard revealed himself, therefore, as a representative seventeenth-
century Puritan on matters of church and state—religion and politics
were inseparable, the state must defend orthodoxy, and life within
society was to be stratified in aristocratic form. In the cleavage between
old-guard conservatism and the newer policy advocating accommodation to changing conditions, he emerged as a moderate. Holding aristocratic and theocratic ideas he did not inflame public reaction, but
counseled wisdom as well as courage. While he rejoiced in the freedom
that Massachusetts citizens still, though less confidently, possessed, he
feared royal and Anglican encroachments. In the face of the social and
religious changes that were coming about, he was intolerant of religious
heterogeneity, and championed the duty of the magistrate to exercise
his traditional power in maintaining both tables of the law, drawing as
he did so on the fund of ideas expressed repeatedly by predecessors.

The Administration of Governor Bradstreet

There was no one immediately in line to assume the governorship
when Leverett died, for Samuel Symonds, the Lieutenant-Governor,

---

6. *Ibid.,* pp. 13, 6-8.
7. *Ibid.,* pp. 9, 12, 13. Cf. Palfrey, *op. cit.,* III, 305-327, on the struggles of
the colonial agents in London.

had died more than a half-year before. Simon Bradstreet, a statesman who had been continuously in public service since his arrival with Winthrop, was called upon, and he functioned provisionally as chief magistrate until he was elected to the office in the next spring election. That same month, on May 22, 1680, Governor and Mrs. Bradstreet, bringing a letter from the First or North Church of Andover, were welcomed by Willard into the membership of South Church.[8]

In some respects he measured up to Willard's recommendations, but he lacked courage, resolution, and vigor, and was hardly equal to the task of steering the straining vessel of state in such stormy times. The public was grateful for his long record of political experience, however, including his diplomatic mission to the Court of Charles II in behalf of the charter, and he was a favorite of the moderate party. This party had begun to form in the commercial centers in the sixties, its members disposed, in the interests of trade, to take a calculated softer attitude toward the crown's imperial policy. Reflecting this moderate spirit was Willard's brother-in-law, Magistrate Joseph Dudley, whose wife was the sister of Eunice Tyng, Willard's second wife. Opposing them was the popular party, representing mainly the interior towns and districts, which clung more firmly to the primitive principles of Massachusetts. The election of deputy-governor Thomas Danforth, the acknowledged head of the popular party, gave added strength to Bradstreet's administration.

The great issue in matters of church and state that concerned political and religious leaders at this time was the movement against the charter. This was at least one of the reasons why the Synod of 1679, summoned by the administration, had reaffirmed the principles of close cooperation between church and state in Massachusetts. Their fears focused on the determination of the crown to enforce the imperial policy and on the encroachments of the Anglican interests. Both were a threat to the theocratic cooperation of the churches with the colonial government, and to the establishment of Congregational orthodoxy.

Toleration and the extension of the franchise were at the very heart of the matter, though economic interests also played an important role. The king's letter at the end of 1679 repeated his injunctions about the admission of members of the Church of England to the franchise and every civil equality, insisted that royal authority be recognized in military commissions and legal proceedings, demanded that the Acts of Trade and Navigation be obeyed, and announced that Edward Ran-

---

8. Hill and Bigelow, *Historical Catalogue*, p. 12. The letter is reproduced in Hill, *op. cit.*, I, 239. On the political background of Bradstreet's administration, see Palfrey, *op. cit.*, III, 329ff.

dolph had been appointed Collector of Customs for New England.[9] The Court anxiously made some minor concessions but continued a policy of stalling and temporizing on basic matters, and Randolph met opposition and hostility on every side. Bostonians commonly asserted, he wrote plaintively to the king, that they were not subject to the laws of England, "neither were those of any force till confirmed by their authority," and that "the Church party at Boston endeavored to debauch the merchants and loyal men." In all other colonies he was treated with respect, he said, but here he had been threatened to "be knocked at the head." News of "trouble at home" only encouraged the local faction to oppose him. "I expect hourly to have my person seized and cast into prison." Writing more letters, he assured his majesty, "will signify no more than a London Gazette."[10] He urged process against the charter of Massachusetts by a writ of *quo warranto*. But in September, 1680, the king, more angrily than before, demanded that fully empowered agents be sent to England.

Randolph, back in England the next March, and capitalizing upon the divisiveness and party spirit that Willard and others had warned about, pressed for the reduction of New England to strict dependence upon England under the immediate authority of a General Governor. No more opportune moment could be found, he argued. The governor, part of the magistrates, and many of the ministry were for dutiful submission to His Majesty's demands; the other part of them, "inconsiderable in estates or repute," outvoted the governor and his party at public meetings by their larger number, accounting him and his party betrayers of the liberty granted in the charter. Reappearing in Boston with greater powers than ever on December 17, 1681, Randolph presented a letter from the king that warned that unless agents fully instructed and empowered were sent over immediately the attorney general would be instructed to proceed with the *quo warranto* against the charter. When the letter was read to the General Court on February 15, 1682, John Richards and the politician Joseph Dudley were immediately chosen agents.[11]

The same day Willard preached a fast-day sermon at the Charlestown Church on "The Fiery Trial no strange thing." To New Englanders the Huguenot persecution begun anew in 1681 by Louis XIV was but another awesome token that the Protestant cause was in a more hazardous state than at any time since the Reformation. Knowing the

9. For the king's letter see Thomas Hutchinson, *A Collection of Original Papers,* reprinted as *Hutchinson Papers,* p. 519.

10. *Hutchinson Papers, 1677-1680,* X, 544-554.

11. Palfrey, *op. cit.,* III, 343-346, 349-352. Cf. Toppan, *op. cit.,* III, 110-113; *Mass. Records,* V, 333.

marked sympathies of the English monarch for Roman Catholicism, they considered the fortunes of the Protestant cause in France as significant for the Reformed cause in England. Unusual, unexpected, and without adequate reason as such trials were, Willard observed, they had been experienced by the saints of every age. God had warned them that their sins would be the cause of such chastisements by the hands of Satan and wicked men. The French onslaughts were not due to God's disapproval of the Protestant cause, however, nor were they an indication that He had rejected His chosen people. The Protestant churches had given God a great deal of provocation, and sometimes He willed that the truth should be sealed by the sufferings of His people. God designed to make His people more humble, holy, serviceable, and New Englanders, he warned, ought not to think it a strange or unlikely thing that they themselves might be brought under such a "fiery tryal." Their faction-ridden community seemed to be ready for it:

> yea we are likely enough to pull it down upon our own heads by our foolish divisions, and strange indiscretions: and ready enough we are to censure and charge one another in this kind; but there is another higher hand moving all these lesser wheels: . . . if therefore God should withdraw from us, and leave our publick affairs to miscarry in our hands, I would say it is of the Lord, that he might fulfil the words of his Ministers, that told and warned us of dayes of great calamity approaching.[12]

Four days later Willard preached the funeral sermon for Major Thomas Savage, another founder eminent in church and state, who had died the day before the Court convened to hear the king's letter. "I will not be curious in noting the day of his removal," Willard noted, "though I believe that it deserves its remark."[13] Savage had been commander-in-chief of the Massachusetts troops during King Philip's War, a deputy for many years, and an assistant. To Willard's mind the passing of this praiseworthy servant was another token of judgment, "a Presage of Evil Approaching." In references that clearly indicate the mounting strife between arch-conservatives and moderates, he claimed the "gap" had been widened by his removal, and replacement was becoming a problem. The times had so changed that "we are not now put to it to know whom to emply in our publick concerns in the Magistracy . . . and other places of weight, by reason of multiplicity of choice, as it hath sometimes been, but rather for want of choice." The situation was not hopeless, for "God hath a number yet, of choice and

12. *The Fiery Tryal no strange thing*, pp. 3-18.
13. *The Righteous Man's Death a Presage of evil approaching* (bound with *The Child's Portion*), p. 161.

faithful ones, yet their hands are thus weakened, and the sons of *Zerviah* begin to put out their heads and speak insultingly."[14] Once again Willard aligned himself with the party of moderation.

An election-day sermon three months later on May 22 further reveals Willard's mounting fears about political and ecclesiastical affairs. Although previous attempts to launch reformation had failed, this, he reiterated, was "the only sure way to prevent threatned Calamity." Brushing superfluous niceties aside, he immediately came to grips with the worsening situation.

> Such is the unhappy entertainment that plain-dealing and open-hearted reproofs do meet with in the World, that when they are most needed, they can be least born: the fouler the stomack, the more nauseous is the Physick: when the malady is come to a dangerous Crisis, and every symptom bodes a sad and sudden change, men are better pleased with a cheating quack that dissembleth the disease, and engageth all shall be well, than with an honest and faithful Physitian, who tells them the distemper is malignant, the issue dubious, and, without the application of some speedy and extraordinary means, desperate.[15]

When God commissioned His ministers to denounce, they had to deliver, and the people's responsibility was to respond. True, when one seriously considered their "Civil and Ecclesiastical" constitution with wholesome laws and sacred covenants, and reflected that according to the confession of unprejudiced strangers virtually nowhere could one find morality as high, it seemed hard to believe that an omniscient God should be against them. Some might even suspect that the incessant ministerial warnings were merely the "mistakes of an irregular (though well minded) zeal," or the "dumps and night visions of some melancholick spirits." But the fact is, "we are brought low in our outward affairs," Willard darkly observed, "and some sudden and doleful change looks as if it were at the door. . . . a few days may summe up and cancel our felicity, and we be left to sigh out our Ichoabod." Safety lay in unity. They had enough opponents abroad on the lookout for their weak spots without doing it themselves. Invective only "picks out the cement, and crumbleth away the mortar." Everyone who did not agree with them in every "punctilio" ought not to be denounced as the

---

14. *Righteous Man's Death,* pp. 158-159. The Biblical reference is to Zeruiah, a sister of David, whose three sons were officers over David's army, viz., Joab, Abishai, and Asahel (referred to in the books of Samuel, Kings, and Chronicles).

15. *The only sure way to prevent threatned Calamity* (bound with *The Child's Portion*), pp. 163-164.

enemy of God. "Men of the largest charity here, are the best friends of this Cause."[16]

He called for more covenant renewals by the churches, and for suppression of heresy by the representatives. This was their theocratic tradition.

> I have often heard (though I must needs confess not without some secret regrets) the Encomiastick titles put upon this Government, as if it were singularly a Theocracy, and carried in it a glorious specimen of the Kingly government of Christ.

And so risking "calumny," he tried to bolster this sagging theocracy by challenging the magistrates to live up to their reputation.

> I fear, if this government decline, or think it not their concern vigorously to extend their power in upholding the duties of the first Table, and secure them from the invasion of perverse men, these will be found no more than a few empty Hyperboles.[17]

Admittedly, their legislative power was limited to the charter provisions, but without exceeding this he urged them not to tolerate the dissemination of religious principles that breached the churches, nor to allow communions to be set up that were at variance with the churches they were supposed to defend—by which he meant not only Anglicans but also Baptists and Quakers. Unexecuted laws that were mere testimonies, he charged, were dangerous and disgraceful; they encouraged disregard of other laws and testified to their own cowardice. Laws against such notorious sins as "profane and scandalous Sabbath breaking," "beastly drunkenness," "desperate cursing and swearing," and "miserable idleness" needed to be vigorously enforced, and ministers needed to be faithful watchmen who analyzed and preached against the sins of the times.[18]

As to covenant renewal it was an illusion that, their civil and ecclesiastical constitution being what it was, they had nothing to fear from across the sea.

> It is an opinion which some seem strongly to be built upon, and it renders them strangely presumptuous, viz. That the foundations of this People are unmoveable; that our civil constitution and Church Covenants have so engaged the presence of God with us, that we ly out of the reach of forraign mischief.

16. *Only sure way*, pp. 179-189.
17. *Ibid.*, pp. 190, 192.
18. *Ibid.*, pp. 192-194.

Covenant renewals were called for, but genuine covenants: the Athe-
nians might chain the image of Minerva, but it was folly to imagine that
God could be bound as an idol by mere verbal covenants, as the ruins of
renowned places where His presence was once enjoyed testified, declared Willard.[19]

The three sermons, while they championed theocratic orthodoxy in
the spirit of the moderates rather than the rigid popularists, all struck
the note of dread of imminent changes in church and state. The events
of the next few months were to prove that Willard's fears were not
groundless.

Randolph's hostility to the colony could not be disguised. In a
stream of letters to England he encouraged *quo warranto* proceedings.
He advised the Bishop of London that part of the funds of the Society
for Propagating the Gospel among the Indians should be appropriated
for the support of the worship of the Church of England in Boston, and
that only marriages performed by ministers of the Church of England
should be deemed lawful. Never a master of suavity, he energetically
pressed his plans, with the result that the political affairs were in a state
of perpetual broil. He was delighted with the news that the Bishop of
London was about to send an Anglican clergyman to Boston, and
assured this prelate of his enthusiasm for both the political and ecclesiastical resettlement.[20]

Fear of an Anglican establishment was in part the motivation for the
reconciliation between the First Church and the South Church at this
time. Since its organization fourteen years before, and in spite of
repeated overtures from the South Church, First Church had refused to
grant it recognition. On April 23, 1682, the First Church finally
acquiesced in a proposal of reconciliation, and its minister, James Allen,
in company with Samuel Nowell, the magistrate, presented it in person
to Samuel Willard. The South Church agreed upon an equally courteous
reply on May 3, and Willard in the company of John Hull presented it
personally to James Allen. The First Church responded on May 7 in a
petitionary letter for forgiveness, and to the joy of the Christian
community the cordial relations were confirmed on September 7 with a
day of fasting and thanksgiving held by the two churches, Allen
preaching in the morning and Willard in the afternoon.[21]

Meanwhile, the colonial agents, John Richards and Joseph Dudley,
arrived in England on August 20, after a twelve-week passage, and

19. *Ibid.*, pp. 195-196.
20. Palfrey, *op. cit.*, III, 354-358, 363, 368-369. Cf. *Hutchinson Papers*, pp.
531-533, 538-540.
21. Hill, *op. cit.*, I, 244, 246; Love, *Fast and Thanksgiving Days*, p. 477;
Mather, *Magnalia*, II, 312-313.

dutifully presented their brief on the colony's obedience and its toleration of Anglicans, Quakers, and Baptists—a stretch of literal truth. But
the time had passed when such actions could suffice, for the design of
the king and his counselors to crush Massachusetts had matured, and
the agents were informed of the Privy Council's unanimous decision
that they should remain in England, and that unless they obtained
further powers without delay the colony would be proceeded against
by a *quo warranto* at the next term of the Court of the King's Bench on
December 20.[22] Randolph was ordered back to England to assist in the
prosecution of the writ.[23] Despondency gripped the colonists.

In the midst of this pervasive hopelessness news came of the defeats
suffered by the Protestant cause in Hungary and France. Boston's First
Church called a fast for January 25, 1683, and Willard preached. Less
than a year had elapsed since he had warned about these "fiery tryals,"
and he turned to Proverbs 21:30 to extract a "choice Elixer"

> to comfort the hearts of the People of God, and to keep them
> from fainting, when they see all the wit in the World, and the
> deepest politicians of earth and hell gathered into a combination
> against them.

The solace they desperately needed he found in the sturdy doctrine of
the divine decree. In every age, he said, there had been similar "con-
claves" that conspired to overthrow the divine purpose and subvert true
religion, but they had always proved ultimately unsuccessful. For His
own redemptive ends God permitted these political conspiracies to
prosper for a time—but not a hair's breadth beyond His decreed
bounds—for as long as time endured God would maintain His church.[24]
"The strongest Conspiracies, and most subtle combinations against
God's purposes, promises and People," he assured them, "shall be
altogether ineffectual."[25] The world's "great politicians" therefore
were fools, and their menaces should not cause those whose cause was
"twisted with Gods" to renounce their commitment.

> When you hear how Gods cause is the present suffering cause, and
> seems to go down the wind; so many Churches of Protestants
> dissipated in Hungary, so many thousands abjuring their Religion
> in France; so much bloodshed in one place, so much powerful
> adversary in another, be not now distressed.

22. Palfrey, *op. cit.*, III, 353-354, 369-370; cf. *4 M.H.S. Colls.*, VIII, 498.
23. Toppan, *op. cit.*, III, 207; Palfrey, *op. cit.*, III, 371.
24. *All Plots against God and his People Detected and Defeated* (bound with
Child's Portion), pp. 200-217.
25. *Ibid.*, p. 203.

The God whose glory was concerned was not sleeping. Be patient, wait for God's time to arrive, counseled Willard, and He will blast the adversary's counsels and "utterly dissolve hells conclave."[26]

That same month letters came to the General Court from the king and the colonial agents with bad news about the charter cause. Governor Bradstreet immediately convened the Court on February 9, which proclaimed a public fast for February 13 and adjourned till that time. After the fast the Court reconvened to compose letters to the agents, the secretary of state, and the king. Placatingly they asked the king not to vacate their charter, assuring him that they did not intend to act beyond its provisions, and that the agents were now empowered to deal on all necessary matters. They instructed the agents (perhaps with some apprehension about Dudley) to act jointly and severally in preserving the main ends of the founders' removal of the charter to New England, to consent to nothing that would alter the qualifications for legal admission of freemen, remove the seat of government to England, or change their political constitution of a Court composed of magistrates and deputies as the elected representatives of the people. Before adjourning, the Court appointed another day of fasting for their "sacred, civil, and temporal concerns."[27]

While New England awaited the issue of all this, the wealthy John Hull died on October 1, 1683. He had been mintmaster and treasurer of the colony as well as an eminent member of South Church, and Willard preached a funeral sermon on October 7, extolling Hull's saintliness as he lamented the passing of another of the colony's great ones. "This Government hath lost a Magistrate; this Town hath lost a good Benefactor; this Church hath lost an honourable Member; his Company hath lost a worthy Captain," Willard declared. But what was of greater concern, "God hath taken him from us, and by this stroak given us one more sad prognostick of misery a coming."[28]

On October 22, Joseph Dudley and John Richards arrived from England with intelligence that the *quo warranto* had been issued. Randolph arrived the same week, and the very next morning presented the documents to the governor and the General Court. A declaration of the king assured the colonists that their private interests and properties would be preserved if, before the prosecution of the *quo warranto,* the government would submit and resign the charter to his pleasure. He would then regulate the charter in a way that would serve him and the good of the colony, altering only what was necessary for the better

26. *Ibid.,* pp. 217-225.
27. Palfrey, *op. cit.,* III, 372-375; *Mass. Records,* V, 382-386, 388, 390-391; Love, *op. cit.,* p. 478.
28. *The High Esteem Which God hath of the Death of his Saints,* p. 18.

support of his government. In the midst of the consternation that ensued, a public fast was held, and Willard preached the sermon. The Reverend Peter Thacher recorded in his diary:

> 9 Nov. 1683. I went to Boston at the fast of the generall Court and Elders; Mr. Willard preached Prov. 16.3 which was his text. [Commit thy works unto the Lord, and thy thoughts shall be established.] then prayed. . . .

After the service, which included another sermon by Increase Mather and the singing of Psalm 46, the ministers met at Willard's house to consider the *quo warranto*. The ministers, said Thacher,

> considering of it together at Mr. Willards did conclude that if the patent was forfeited by law, then it was best to resigne it up to his majesty for such regulation as might make it most fit for his majesty's service, that soe the Essentials of the patent might be continued, and the patent continued.[29]

If Willard reflected the spirit of the moderates, a quite different stand was taken by Increase Mather. The governor and the majority of the assistants passed a motion on November 15 to submit to the king's pleasure, but the deputies refused to concur. To break the deadlock at Court a town meeting of the freemen was called for January 21, 1684. At the request of the deputies, Increase Mather, known to be a strong opponent of submission, made a vigorous speech against resignation, charging that it was against wisdom and a sin against God, and advising them to trust falling into the hands of God rather than men. One of the crowd left the hall "in a great heat,"[30] but a chorus of voices cried out, "We thank you Syr! We thank you, Syr!"[31] The proposal for submission was also stoutly rejected by the freemen. The policy of moderation had been shouted down.

Randolph had left for England shortly after the decision of the deputies, and on his arrival in London presented his report to the secretary of state and the Privy Council.[32] But in Massachusetts, Dudley and his associates still promoted the cause of submission, and the General Court sent a letter on May 10 to its attorney in London urging him to "spin out the case to the uttermost." Before the instruc-

---

29. The diary of Peter Thacher, quoted in Hill, *op. cit.*, I, 249, 250; Love, *op. cit.*, p. 478.

30. Toppan, *op. cit.*, IV, 244.

31. Increase Mather, *Diary, M.H.S. Procs.*, Second Series, XIII, January 21, 1683-1684; Cotton Mather, *Parentator*, pp. 91-92; Palfrey, *op. cit.*, III, 381-385; Hutchinson, *History of the Colony and Province*, I, 286.

32. "Narrative of the Delivery of his Majesty's writ of *quo warranto*," *Journals of the Privy Council;* cited by Palfrey, *op. cit.*, III, 385, 387.

tion reached England, however, all but definite action had been taken, and on June 21 the Court of Chancery made a decree vacating the charter.[33]

When the shocking news reached New England, the Court once more addressed the king with a plea for justice and forbearance, but before the papers could be dispatched from the colony, the Lord Keeper ordered a final judgment on October 23 vacating the charter.[34]

The winter was upon them and no word of it came to Boston until a vessel got through at the end of January. The governor and the Council appointed a fast day for March 12, 1685. Willard preached an "excellent sermon," said Samuel Sewall,[35] from II Corinthians 4:16-18: "For which cause we faint not; but though our outward man perish, yet the inward man is renewed day by day. For our light affliction, which is but for a moment, worketh for us a far more exceeding and eternal weight of glory; while we look not at the things which are seen, but at the things which are not seen: for the things which are seen are temporal; but the things which are not seen are eternal." Well might Willard endeavor to keep up their courage, for Massachusetts as a "body politic" was no more. It was a colony under royal control. Before the law of England it reverted to the status before James I made it a grant to the Council of New England. The ingenious system of church and state constructed by the founding fathers, maintained by their successors, and buttressed by a line of prominent preachers that included Samuel Willard, legally no longer existed. But New Englanders had little intention of relinquishing anything until forced to do so.

   33. *Mass. Records,* V, 436, 439; *Massachusetts Archives,* III, 38-44; Hutchinson, *History of the Colony and Province,* I, 289; Palfrey, *op. cit.,* III, 388-390.
   34. *Mass. Records,* V, 456-459; Palfrey, *op. cit.,* III, 391-394.
   35. Sewall, *Diary, 5 M.H.S. Colls.,* V, 67; Love, *op. cit.,* pp. 225, 478.

CHAPTER FOUR

CHURCH AND STATE:
Without a Charter

Massachusetts got a short breathing spell as Charles II, suddenly falling victim to a virulent disease, died on February 6, 1685, the day after he had been secretly received with the Church of Rome and given its last rite. His brother, James II, Roman Catholic Duke of York, acceding to the throne, issued a proclamation directing all persons in authority to continue in their offices till further order should be given.[1] Boston dutifully "proclaimed" him king in High Street on Monday, April 20, three weeks before the printed copy of the proclamation was received.[2] But though things continued outwardly the same, the minds of the leaders were filled with anxiety. On May 22, all the ministers of Boston's three churches observed a fast day with the magistrates at the home of Samuel Sewall. "Mr. Eliot prayed, Mr. Willard preached. I am afraid of Thy judgments—Text Mother [Mrs. Hull] gave," Sewall noted in his diary.[3]

Yet, trying as the year had been, and fearful as prospects for the future seemed (to add to their discouragement news came that the Duke of Monmouth's invasion of England proved abortive, and that persecution of the Huguenots had broken out again as King James' friend, Louis XIV of France, revoked the Edict of Nantes),[4] Willard that autumn endeavored to persuade the magistrates to reconsider their decision to have no thanksgiving day that year. He called on parishioner

1. Palfrey, *History of New England*, pp. 271-272; *Massachusetts Archives*, CVI, 339-341.
2. Sewall, *Diary, 5 M.H.S. Colls.*, V, 70.
3. *Ibid.*, 76.
4. *Ibid.*, 93, 97, 130.

Sewall to inform him that the ministers intended to observe a thanks-giving throughout the colony on December 3, even if civil sanction were not forthcoming. Bradstreet, playing it safe, presented the matter to the Council, but moderates and popular party members clashed over naming the "particulars" of the observance, and nothing came of it. On Sunday, November 15, Willard announced to his congregation what the ministers had decided,

> and propounded to the Church that we might have one on the First Thorsday in December; because had Fasted, and God had graciously answered our Prayers; so should meet Him in the same place to give Thanks for that, and any other Providence that hath passed before us. Silence gave Consent, no one speaking.[5]

Indirectly, the tightening of the cords of empire was already rending the unity between church and state.

Upon another matter, however, the Court and the ministers were in complete agreement: it was a serious time, not one for dancing. While they were debating about thanksgiving, Francis Stepney opened a school for mixed dancing in Boston, and scheduled it (of all times) on the weekly lecture-day. To the complaints of the ministers Stepney retorted that in one play he could teach more divinity than Willard or the Old Testament. He was ordered to close his school, and fined one hundred pounds, but he ran out of the colony before it could be collected.[6] Church and state at least saw eye to eye in legislating against sin.

But apprehension was the dominant mood of the time. Early the next year, on February 10, as Willard preached from Romans 8:1, Sewall sensed that his pastor seemed "very sensible of the Countries Danger as to Changes."[7] The changes were to involve some of Willard's own relatives.

The Presidency of Dudley

The establishment of an interim government on the urgings of Randolph resulted in the appointment of the ambitious and compliant Joseph Dudley as the chief executive in New England, much to the chagrin of the popular party.[8] He received the king's commission from

5. *Ibid.*, 105.
6. *Ibid.*, 103, 104, 112, 120-121, 145.
7. *Ibid.*, 121.
8. Toppan, *Edward Randolph*, III, 145-149; IV, 1-3, 12, 110; E. Kimball, *The Public Life of Joseph Dudley*, pp. 17, 33-34.

Randolph on May 14, 1686, two days after the disaffected freemen refused to reelect him to the Court of Assistants.[9]

Willard immediately indicated his disapproval of his brother-in-law's willingness to serve in the new government. On Sunday, May 16, Sewall noted, "Mr. Willard prayed not for the Governour [President Dudley] or Government, as formerly; but spake so as implied it to be changed or changing." The next day, Dudley and Randolph, with those who had consented to serve as counselors, presented their commissions to the General Court, referring to these officials now as "some of the principal gentlemen and chief inhabitants of several towns." Some of them spoke up after the meeting advising a protest, but Sewall, discouraging them, suggested prayer by the ministers instead. However, the next day he noted in his diary, "Mr. Willard not seeing cause to go to the Town-House to pray, I who was to speak to him refrain also." The night before in Willard's study, Captain John Phillips, father-in-law of Cotton Mather, had "a very close Discourse with the President to perswade him not to accept"—hoping, perhaps, that the colonial leaders themselves might continue the government.[10] But Dudley chose to accept the presidency. On Friday, May 21, the General Court abdicated, unanimously protesting the legality of the commission of Dudley and his Council.[11] The charter government came to an end with many tears as

> Mr. Nowell prayed that God would pardon each Magistrate and Deputies Sin. Thanked God for our hithertos of Mercy 56 years, in which time and calamities elsewhere, as Massacre Piedmont; thanked God for what we might expect from sundry of those now set over us.[12]

Unlike the former representative government, the new government was royally appointed with military, judicial, and executive power, embracing Massachusetts, Maine, New Hampshire and Rhode Island.[13] Among its members were Willard's father-in-law, Edward Tyng, and Wait Winthrop, a member of South Church.[14]

The political misery of Massachusetts was compounded by the introduction of Episcopal worship. Randolph on his return to Boston was accompanied by the Reverend Robert Ratcliffe, who came with

9. *Massachusetts Archives,* XLVIII, 193; Kimball, *op. cit.,* pp. 23-25.

10. Sewall, *op. cit.,* 138-139. Cf. Kimball, *op. cit.,* p. 25. The suspicion was expressed in a letter of Randolph to the Archbishop of Canterbury; cf. Hutchinson, *History of the Colony and Province,* I, 297.

11. Hutchinson, *op. cit.,* 290, presents the document in full.

12. Sewall, *op. cit.,* 140.

13. Palfrey, *op. cit.,* III, 484-485.

14. Hutchinson, *op. cit.,* I, 298n.; Palfrey, *op. cit.,* III, 494; Hill and Bigelow, *Historical Catalogue,* p. 290.

surplice and service book, duly empowered to set up the forms and ceremonies of the Anglican communion in the town. In order to give as little offense as possible, Dudley, knowing the temper of the people, saw to it that Ratcliffe had no part in the inauguration ceremonies. But on May 26, Ratcliffe waited on the Council, and Randolph proposed that he should have one of the churches of the town to meet in.[15] The request was denied, but the Council authorized him to occupy the east room of the town house where the deputies formerly met, until those who desired his ministry could provide a "fitter place"; and there he conducted service the following Sunday.[16] On June 15 the first Anglican Church in New England was organized, with nine persons present besides Ratcliffe and Randolph.[17] These unfamiliar proceedings led to "great affronts," Randolph wrote the Archbishop of Canterbury on July 7, "some calling the minister Baal's priest, and some of their ministers, from the pulpit calling the prayers leeks, garlic, and trash." [18] In spite of it Randolph and Ratcliffe tried to get each of the three churches of Boston to contribute twenty shillings a year for the support of Ratcliffe's ministry; but the Council decided that since his auditors alone raised fifty pounds a year for him he should look to them for his support.[19]

The Anglicans with their introduction of practices strange to Boston, repeatedly irritated the colonial leaders. In accordance with English practice the artillery company placed the cross of St. George in its flag, and Samuel Sewall resigned his commission as captain, citing John Cotton's arguments against the practice.[20] The officers of the frigates in the harbor so disturbed the Saturday evening quiet on September 27, as they celebrated the queen's birthday with music, cannon, and bonfires, that in the service the next morning, said Sewall, "Mr. Willard expresses great grief in 's Prayer for the Profanation of the Sabbath last night."[21] The Anglicans requested First Church (which was near the

15. "Massachusetts Council records under the administration of President Dudley," *2 M.H.S. Procs.*, XIII (Boston, 1900), 253; cited by Kimball, *op. cit.*, p. 33. Already on the previous October 30th (1685) in order to set up the worship of the Church of England in Boston, the Privy Council had ordered the shipment to New England of six large Bibles, Common Prayer Books, books on the canons of the Church of England, homilies of the church, copies of the Thirty Nine Articles, and tables of marriage. *Journals of the Privy Council;* quoted in Palfrey, *op. cit.*, III, 484n.

16. Sewall, *op. cit.*, V, 141-142.

17. Henry W. Foote, *Annals of King's Chapel*, I, 42-51.

18. *Hutchinson Papers*, 549ff.; quoted in Hutchinson, *op. cit.*, I, 297.

19. "Massachusetts Council records under the administration of President Dudley, 1686," *2 M.H.S. Procs.*, XIII, 262.

20. Sewall, *op. cit.*, 147, 156.

21. *Ibid.*, 152.

exchange) to ring their bell at nine o'clock on Wednesdays and Fridays to call them to prayers, but they refused, appealing to the liberty of conscience granted in the king's commission.[22] By fall the Anglicans were boldly attacking the Congregational way. On Friday, November 5, Sewall noted that "One Mr. Clark [of the English Church] preaches at the Town-House. Speaks much against the Presbyterians in England and here."[23]

What role did Willard play at the time? There is good reason to believe that he was working behind the scenes through Dudley. Dudley's conscience was going through a tug of war between allegiance to the power that had given him his position and loyalty to the traditions of the people among whom he had grown up. Part of the influence that worked for moderation and caution in Dudley must be traced to the ministers, and doubtlessly much of it was Willard's. Already on July 28 Randolph had complained to the Lords of the Committee that the

> proceedings of the Governor [President] and Council, whatever they write and pretend in their letters to your Lordships, are managed to the encouragment of the Independent faction, and utter discountenancing both of the minister and those gentlemen and others who dare openly profess themselves to be of the Church of England. . . . The frame of this government only is changed, for our Independent ministers flourish, and expect to be advised with in public affairs.[24]

He was even more specific as he wrote on August 28 to Sir Thomas Osborne (Lord Danby) that

> Mr. Dudley, our President, was not long since a zealous preacher amongst us; and though, while in London, he pretended to be of the Church of England, yet, since he is made President, courts and keeps private cabals with these factious ministers and others, who, in the time of Monmouth's rebellion refused to pray for his Majesty.[25]

Dudley was a schemer who knew the temper of the New England mind, and the ministers' power over the people. As a politician in home territory he was no fool. And Randolph, unable to cope with such odds, more than once expressed a longing for the speedy arrival of Sir Edmund Andros.

As the year drew to its close Andros arrived in Boston, bearing a

22. *Hutchinson Papers,* 552; cited by Palfrey, *op. cit.,* III, 501-502.
23. Sewall, *op. cit.,* 156.
24. Quoted by Palfrey, *op. cit.,* III, 496.
25. *Ibid.,* 502n.

commission for the government of all New England. Massachusetts was
no longer to have one of its own at the head, but an outsider.

The Administration of Governor Andros

While he was at his morning devotions on Sunday, December 19,
Samuel Sewall "heard a Gun or two," which made him think that "Sir
Edmund might be come," but he kept it to himself until a little later at
the Bradstreet home his premonition was confirmed. A frigate with the
"Flagg in the main Top" had been sighted in the harbor. Later that
morning at South Church, Joseph Dudley being present, Willard preached
from Hebrews 11:12, declaring that "he was fully persuaded and
confident God would not forget the Faith of those who came first to
New England, but would remember their Posterity with kindness." The
next day there was a colorful parade to the Town House, and Andros
officially assumed the broad powers of the new government, which
included a royally appointed advisory Council.[26]

The character of the new regime was presaged immediately as
Andros gathered the ministers together in the library to speak "about
accomodation as to a Meeting-House [for church services], that might
so contrive the time as one House might serve two assemblies." The
Boston ministers met the next day at the home of the Reverend James
Allen of First Church, with four leading men of each congregation, to
consider their answer. Nothing could have been more offensive, and
they agreed that they "could not with good conscience consent that
our Meeting-Houses should be made use of for Common-Prayer Worship." The following night Samuel Willard and Increase Mather called
on the governor and "thorowly discoursed his Excellency about the
Meeting-Houses in great plainess, showing they could not consent." In
the face of such firmness Andros seemingly thought it best to relent a
bit. "He seems to say will not impose," Sewall noted.[27]

Andros's attitude to traditional New England religious observances
exasperated Bostonians; his attitudes to Anglican observances gave
them cause for anxiety. Unlike former magistrates he did not attend the
time-honored Thursday lecture, but on Christmas Day (though Boston
went its usual way of disregarding the occasion with the shops open and
the people going about their business) Andros conspicuously made it a
point to go "to Service Forenoon and Afternoon" at the Town House,
"a Red-Coat going on his right hand and Capt. George on the left."[28]

26. Sewall, *op. cit.*, 159-160, 162; cf. *Massachusetts Archives*, CXXVI, 164.
27. Sewall, *op. cit.*, 162.
28. *Ibid.*, 163.

On January 25, 1687, he observed the Conversion of St. Paul, and "the Bell was rung in the Morning to call persons to Service." On January 31 services "respecting the beheading of Charles the First" were held at the Town House both forenoon and afternoon with the bell being rung again.[29] Boston was beginning to learn what it meant to have a royal and Anglican governor.

Irked by the incongruity of representatives of the Crown worshiping in make-shift arrangements while the Congregationalists met in three comfortable churches, Andros resolved, with the approach of the Easter season, to put an end to this provisional expediency. On Tuesday, March 22, "his Excellency" viewed the three meetinghouses, and the next day sent Randolph "for the Keyes of our [the Third] Meeting-house, that [they] may say Prayers there." This was the thing Willard and his colleagues had feared from the beginning, and they resolved to resist. A committee of proprietors was immediately dispatched to the governor with deed in hand to protest that the land and the church were theirs and that they couldn't consent to such use of it. But Andros had made up his mind to have the church and there was no power in the colony to prevent him. Brushing their protests aside he arbitrarily commandeered the place and on Friday of the same week, observed Sewall, "the Governor [had] service in the South Meetinghouse." Goodman William Needham, the sexton, against his will was commanded by the governor to ring the bell and open the door.[30] Samuel Willard's church thus became the first Puritan meetinghouse to echo to the ritual of the Anglican liturgy.

With a sense of satisfaction Andros informed the Lords of the Committee of Trade and Plantations on March 30 that he had arranged to have South Church for Church of England services at 11 a.m. and 4 p.m., commenting, "I shall continue this for the present."[31] But from this date until his deposition there was a continual clash between South Church leaders and the Anglicans over the scheduling of services. On March 27 the Anglican eleven o'clock service "broke off past two because of the Sacrament and Mr. Clark's long Sermon." Willard's afternoon service, scheduled for one-thirty, had to wait as exasperated South Church members milled around outside. It was "a sad Sight," said Sewall, "to see how full the Street was with people gazing and moving to and fro because had not entrance into the House." Once

29. *Ibid.*, 164, 166.

30. *Ibid.*, 171. Actually with the fall of the charter, all lands in Massachusetts now belonged to the king. Palfrey, *op. cit.*, III, 513-514.

31. *C.S.P., 1685-1688*, 350.

again on May 8, he observed, the Anglican sacramental service lasted "past one. . . . A pretty deal."[32]

Even Harvard College, the nursery for Congregational ministers, for a moment seemed doomed to Anglican intrusion. Sir Edmund and his Anglican chaplain attended the commencement at Cambridge on July 6, and Sewall noted apprehensively that "Mr. Ratcliffe sat in the Pulpit by the Governour's direction."[33] But their fears did not materialize, for Andros was busy enough with other pressing matters and in the main left the college alone.

The asperities were momentarily softened by the serious illness of Lady Andros, three months after her arrival from England. Willard offered prayers for her recovery at the morning service on Sunday, January 22, 1688, but about the time of the afternoon service she died. The funeral service for some reason was not held until February 10, and as darkness fell between four and five o'clock, the cortege moved down the muddy street lined with soldiers to the South Meetinghouse. The coffin was carried in through the west door and "set in the Alley before the Pulpit, with Six Mourning Women by it." Candles and torches lighted the crowded house as Puritan ministers, magistrates, and townsfolk respectfully attended the service. Afterwards the ministers "turn'd in to Mr. Willard's." The next day the mourning cloth was taken off the pulpit and given to Willard.[34]

Bickering over the scheduling of services broke out again in the spring. On Saturday, April 14, Andros sent Willard an order to begin his next morning's Lord's Supper service at eight o'clock. It was short notice for such an early hour, "yet the people [came] pretty roundly together," said Sewall, and they began "about ½ past 8." This was to be the last inconvenience, promised the governor, for they intended to build a church of their own. But the altercations continued for two months more, culminating in a hassle with the governor at the secretary's office on June 23.[35] Willard's committee was firm, and the contest ended in a draw—Andros agreeing to an early hour in order to hold the Anglican service first.

After the whole town had cried shame on them, wrote an anonymous New England divine,[36] the Anglicans finally built a church of

32. Sewall, *op. cit.,* 172, 177. Sewall also notes other altercations, *ibid.,* 179-180, 192.

33. Sewall, *op. cit.,* 181. On Increase Mather's fears, see *4 M.H.S. Colls.,* VIII, 700.

34. Sewall, *op. cit.,* 200, 202, 203.

35. Sewall, *op. cit.,* 210, 214, 216, 217, 218, 219.

36. "A Vindication of New England" (Boston, 1690), *Andros Tracts,* II, 44. Though often ascribed to Increase Mather, his bibliographer thinks it may have been the work of Charles Morton, of Charlestown, whom Cotton Mather may

their own. When Samuel Sewall for reasons of conscience refused to sell them some of his land, a site was obtained elsewhere.[37] Not until June 30, 1689, however, was the new church used for services, thus bringing to a close what later Anglican historians have confessed was one of the most arbitrary outrages on the common rights of property, conscience, and liberty perpetrated on the country by the English government.[38]

Willard and his colleagues also clashed with Andros over the appointment of thanksgiving days. The churches had originally designated such days, but years before the authority had been gradually transferred to the state. While the government was theocratic there was no problem, but with the fall of the charter tensions immediately developed over specifying reasons, and under Andros the matter came to a head. In 1687, while the governor was out of town establishing the royal government in Connecticut, the ministers arranged the annual thanksgiving for November 17, noting the "mercy of the harvest" and the "mercy of the king's declaration for liberty of Religion and confirmation of our properties."[39] The day before the contemplated thanksgiving Andros returned, and interpreting the proclamation as a usurpation of his prerogative, sent for the ministers and "so schools them that the thanksgiving is put by. . . ."[40] The governor and the Council thereupon declared December 1 a thanksgiving "for his Majesty's health . . . and his many royal favours bestowed on his subjects here, and for all other blessings and mercies of health plenty &c in these parts, and humbly to implore the continuance thereof."[41] Willard received an order for the thanksgiving,[42] but there is no record of how the day was observed.

The next spring Andros exasperated his recalcitrant subjects by designating Sunday, April 29, as a day of thanksgiving for his majesty's "apparent hopes & good assurance of having issue by his Royall Consort the Queen," who according to the latest intelligence "was with

have supplied with materials. T. J. Holmes, *Increase Mather. A Bibliography of His Works*, p. 615.

37. Sewall, *op. cit.*, 207.

38. Foote, *op. cit.*, I, 79, 82, 86. Francis Pitt Greenwood, *History of King's Chapel*, p. 39. Ninety years later King's Chapel willingly expiated this injustice by opening its doors to the Old South Church when it was dispossessed of its church during the revolution.

39. Quotation from the Salem Church records, in Love, *Fast and Thanksgiving Days*, p. 229. Cf. Sewall, *op. cit.*, 177; Palfrey, *op. cit.*, III, 542-546.

40. Sewall, *op. cit.*, 195.

41. Love, *op. cit.*, p. 231.

42. Sewall, *op. cit.*, 196. In Rhode Island some chose to disregard this new custom by keeping their shops open as usual. Love, *Fast and Thanksgiving Days*, pp. 231-232.

child."[43] A few days later he left town, expecting that the order would
be distributed to all the ministers. By some mistake Willard did not
receive a copy, and he took advantage of the omission to say nothing.
By the next Saturday evening someone saw to it that he did have a
copy of the order, yet, said Samuel Sewall, he

> read it not this day, but after the *Notes* said such an Occasion was
> by the Governour recommended to be given Thanks for. . . . Mr.
> Willard prays more particularly and largely for the King, but else
> alters not his course a jot.

Sewall was obviously pleased, and no other reaction is recorded about
Willard's defiance. James Allen of First Church, on the other hand,
offended some of his members by having the congregation sing the
suggestively loyalist words of Psalms 21 and 72.[44]

On August 15 news came by way of Salem from a Dutch vessel that
the queen had given birth to a son on June 10. That night from eleven
o'clock to one or two in the morning there was a noisy celebration with
drums, huzzas, guns, bell-ringing and bonfires. Not knowing what it was
all about, the people at first thought it was an alarm. Across from
South Church sexton William Needham, called out of bed for the keys
for a service, refused until they told him the occasion. Governor Andros
proclaimed Sunday, September 16, a day of thanksgiving, and Willard
"prayed for His Majesty morn and even, and said, wheras prayers and
giving of Thanks commanded, they did so, and prayd that might be a
Blessing." That night the town was filled with hilarious celebration. A
few weeks later at a private fast on October 16, Willard preached on the
meaningful words of Ezekiel 9:4—"And the Lord said unto him, Go
through the midst of the city, through the midst of Jerusalem, and set a
mark upon the foreheads of the men that sigh and that cry for all the
abominations that be done in the midst thereof."[45]

In other ways also the new order of things was imposed upon the
chafing Puritans. To make sure that everyone observed the martyrdom
of Charles I, the constables distributed a warrant to unheeding Boston
merchants at noon on January 30, 1688, causing "the Shops to be
shut." New Englanders who some years before had harbored the regi-
cides were understandably unenthusiastic, but the next year it was
proclaimed again as a day of "fasting and humiliation" for all, and with

43. Love, *op. cit.,* p. 232.
44. Sewall, *op. cit.,* 211.
45. *Ibid.,* 223, 234, 228, 232.

spiteful reminders about their former plea of ignorance the order was once more served on the shopkeepers by sheriffs and constables.[46]

Willard also spoke out against the new requirement of laying one's hand on the Bible in swearing, a practice Puritans traditionally abhorred as popish. He preached about "keeping a Conscience void of offence" on February 5, 1688. Three days later one of his parishioners was fined as a conscientious objector, and on April 11 another was fined for the same reason. Two days later Willard joined a number of other leaders, including the Reverend Messrs. Joshua Moody and Cotton Mather, at the Sewall home for a conference on the matter.[47] Willard spelled out the orthodox Puritan convictions against the practice in a short tract at this time, which reflected not only the maxims of the nonconformists, but the convictions of ancient church fathers and Reformed scholars, as well as the practices of Reformed churches both in Scotland and on the Continent.[48] Due to the censorship of the press under Dudley he could not get it published in New England, but with the aid of Increase Mather it was printed in London. In a preliminary way Willard postulated that all religious worship not commanded by God was forbidden, as were symbolical ceremonies humanly enjoined in religious worship. Such human impositions were an infringement of liberty of conscience. Indifferent things were to be avoided if they caused scandal, the practice of holy and good men being insufficient to warrant such practices. While the act of swearing itself was civil, belonging to the ninth commandment, the confirmation of this testimony by oath belonged to the third commandment, he contended, and thus was religious. The *use* of the oath for confirmation of truth was a civil matter, but its *form* involved divine address, making it religious. Whereas the ceremonies used in swearing might be merely civil, the appendages employed to strengthen or confirm the oath were distinctly religious, therefore ought to be tried by religious propositions. An oath, furthermore, being a solemn prayer and appeal, ought to be made to God alone; since that by which one swore became an object of worship, appealing to the Bible as well as to God made the former also an object of adoration. Thus, to lay the hand on the Bible in swearing was religious worship, not merely a civil sign, according to the intent of the law, the confession of those who did it, and the very fact that it was the Holy Bible itself that was appointed for this. For those whose con-

46. *Ibid.*, 201. Love, *op. cit.*, pp. 235, 480. The order is printed in *3 M.H.S. Colls.*, I, 83-84.

47. Sewall, *op. cit.*, 201, 202, 208, 210. Cf. Hill and Bigelow, *op. cit.*, pp. 226, 272.

48. *A Brief Discourse Concerning that Ceremony of Laying the Hand on the Bible in Swearing*, p. 6; "To the Reader," pp. 3, 4.

sciences considered this unlawful it was a scandal, and so it was better simply to lift one's hand.[49] Such was the Puritan position, but as long as the Andros regime remained in power it pressed the offensive practice.

A painful scene at the grave of Edward Lilley during the winter of 1688-89, graphically illustrates how the pressing of Anglican interests aroused Puritan hostility. Lilley had married Mehetabel, the youngest daughter of Theophilus Frary, a deacon at South Church. Lilley was sympathetic towards the Episcopal party and had contributed towards the building of its new church, but not being a member of the church, he had left the arrangements of his funeral to his executors. Ratcliffe, in spite of the unanimous disapproval of the family, came down with "Gown and Book" and sought to impose the reading of the Anglican service. The relatives asked Deacon Frary to speak at the funeral, and when he forbade Ratcliffe to "read Common Prayer at the grave" he was "bound to the good Behavi[r]" for twelve months. "What a case wee are all in," wrote Joshua Moody to Increase Mather in England after hearing about it from Willard; "what does the pclamã for liberty of Consc. doe, if such impositions are allowed! This is a very tremend[s] thing to us."[50] The issue precipitated a decision in Mehetabel's mind: a few Sundays later, on January 29, 1689, she was received by Willard as a communicant member into the fellowship of South Church.[51]

That same winter the Andros government had compelled the outward observance of Christmas, Moody complained to Increase Mather. "The shutting up shops on X[t]mas day, & driving the M[r] out of the school on X[t]mas Holydayes are very grievous."[52] Then on January 30 came another forced observance of the martyrdom of Charles I.[53]

Soon the whole matter was brought to a head.

Governor Andros's treatment of the churches and the religious customs of New England sought to deprive the colonists of all their former rights, civil and religious, and to set up in the colony the supremacy of the Anglican Church. New England, shorn of all legislative and executive power of its own, was being ruled as a conquered kingdom.[54] Increase Mather had been spirited away to England to

49. *Ibid.*, pp. 7-12.
50. Letter of Moody to Mather, January 8, 1699. *The Mather Papers, 4 M.H.S. Colls.*, VIII, 370, 371.
51. Hill and Bigelow, *op. cit.*, p. 14. Mehetabel had owned the baptismal covenant at South Church on April 30, 1680. *Ibid.*, p. 105.
52. *4 M.H.S. Colls.*, VIII, 371.
53. *3 M.H.S. Colls.*, I, 83-84.
54. Palfrey, *op. cit.*, III, 512ff., 522-524, 529ff. Cf. also Hutchinson, *op. cit.*, I, 303ff., and James Truslow Adams, *The Founding of New England*, pp. 413ff.

complain to the king, but no relief seemed forthcoming.[55] Popular disaffection was mounting as Andros returned from an unfortunate campaign against the French and Indians in Maine, and he moved to the fortress on Fort Hill. On the morning of April 18, 1689, as people came from the surrounding regions for the Thursday lecture, Boston was all astir. Armed men collected on the north and south ends of the city. An ensign was raised on Beacon Hill, and Randolph and other members of the governor's party were clapped into jail. In the Council chamber former magistrates conferred together until noon, then appeared at the gallery of the Town House and read to the assembled people a "Declaration of the Gentlemen, Merchants, and Inhabitants of Boston, and the Country Adjacent." It condemned the oppressions and misgovernment of the Andros regime, hailed the noble undertaking of the Prince of Orange in England which promised to save them from "Popery and Slavery," announced the seizure of those persons who had been, "next to our sins," the "grand authors" of their miseries, and called upon the populace to join them in prayers and "all just actions" for the defense of the land.[56]

Andros saw the handwriting on the wall, and by the hand of Edward Dudley (Willard's nephew) sent an invitation to Willard and the other ministers of the city to confer with him at the fort, but they declined. Over twenty companies of soldiers paraded in Boston by mid-afternoon, and the governor was sent a summons to surrender. After an abortive attempt to escape, he and his party capitulated. Writing to the Lords of the Committee for Trade and Plantations "from the common gaol" on May 29, Randolph reported that

> Five ministers of Boston, namely Moody, Allen, young Mather, Willard and Milburn, an Anabaptist minister, were in the Council-Chamber on the 18th of April, when the governor and myself were brought out of the fort before them, writing orders, and were authors of some of their printed papers.[57]

A revolution had been accomplished, and the government of the king dissolved. The Andros regime had been a trying one. Willard, more than any other minister, had experienced at first hand its vexations,

---

55. Kenneth B. Murdock, *Increase Mather*, pp. 187-189.
56. *Andros Tracts*, I, 11ff., 75ff.; *C.S.P., 1689-1692*, 33, 66ff., 92ff. Hutchinson, *op. cit.*, I, 309-321. Adams, *op. cit.*, pp. 427ff. Palfrey, *op. cit.*, III, 568-579. It is generally believed today that the document read by the leaders to the townsfolk had been composed in the main before this time, most likely with ministerial advice and assistance.
57. *C.S.P., 1689-1692*, 92. *Andros Tracts*, III, 234-235.

and, accordingly, participated fully in the proceedings that led to its overthrow.

The Provisional Government

The leaders of the revolution assembled the day after Andros was imprisoned, and formed a provisional government which they called the "Council for Safety of the People and Conservation of the Peace." It was necessary. Popular feeling was running high against everything associated with their former oppressors. A mob vented its pent-up feelings by defacing the Anglicans' new church, leaving it, according to one of them, its "windows broke in pieces, and the doors and walls daubed and defiled with other filth, in the rudest and basest manner imaginable."[58] Dudley, apprehended in his place of concealment in the Narragansett country, had to be protected against popular violence also.[59] The Council included a number of Willard's more prominent parishioners—Bradstreet, elected president at eighty-seven, Wait Winthrop, chosen commander of the militia, Peter Sergeant, John Joyliffe, Nathaniel Oliver, John Eyre, and Andrew Belcher.[60]

With the changed political situation came an immediate change in Willard's preaching. The heavy hand of repression was off, and ministers no longer needed to content themselves with oblique references to church and state. Less than a week after the uprising Willard mounted his pulpit to warn against the "extream danger" of "formal worship." God was a Spirit, and according to the Scripture that service which was most acceptable was spiritual. Andros might be in jail, but Anglican worship was still being conducted every week in Boston under the royal decree of religious freedom, and Willard felt the urgent need of buttressing adherence to Puritan principle. "Whatever else may be said to the unlawfulness of imposing upon men stinted forms of prayer and publick service to God," he declared, "there is this one thing that would perswade a serious Christian that desires to hold Communion with God . . . to be afraid of it," namely, that "of its own Nature it hazards being formal in it." It reduced the worshiper to a "spiritless frame," and rather than pleasing God such a churchgoer provoked Him to anger. A man might be "heartless and perfunctory in the other [kind of

---

58. *New England's Faction Discovered,* reprinted in *Andros Tracts,* II, 211-212; answered in *A Vindication of New England,* reprinted in *Andros Tracts,* II, 61-63.

59. Palfrey, *op. cit.,* III, 583-587.

60. Hutchinson, *op. cit.,* I, 324, gives the complete list of names. Palfrey, *History of New England,* III, 587. Cf. Hill and Bigelow, *op. cit., passim,* for biographical notes on the members of Willard's church.

service]," affirmed Willard, "but in this way he can hardly be otherwise."[61]

The political matter of immediate concern, of course, was the proper establishment of the government. Two conventions were summoned by the Council, on May 9 and 22, and delegates from the entire province, in spite of the cautions of the former magistrates, reconstituted the General Court along the old charter lines until orders should be received from England. On May 29, Boston with unrestrained joy proclaimed William and Mary king and queen, as a crowd from far and near hailed the Protestant accession to the throne and the passing away of the old order. Sir William Phips arrived that same day from England with the news that he and Increase Mather had persuaded the king to have Andros called back to render an account of his maladministration. Meanwhile the government was to operate along the former lines, though no assurances could be given that it would be officially reestablished by the Crown. Articles of impeachment were drawn up on June 27 against Andros, Dudley, Randolph and their party.[62] That same day the meetinghouses of Massachusetts rang with rejoicings as the colony observed its own appointed day of thanksgiving.[63] Once more the people felt free.

Actually things were far from settled. True, one of New England's own sons was the provisional governor, and on the British throne sat a Protestant prince, an orthodox Calvinist after the order of the Synod of Dordt. The prospects seemed fair to the citizens of Massachusetts. But King William mounted the throne at a time when political, commercial, social, and religious matters had become very complex. He was faced with the necessity of managing a coalition of numerous political and religious forces, and as a skillful administrator he soon proved himself to be less enthusiastic for creed than his New England subjects. Though they might hope for much from one who had been nurtured amidst toleration, they had to learn that however fair he sought to be, the settlement of religious and political issues depended upon the advice of counselors and the calculated interest of the empire. The Toleration Act of May 24, 1689, thus granted religious freedom to all loyal trinitarian Protestants who subscribed to the doctrinal articles of the Church of England.[64]

In New England itself the Anglican interests were far from quiet. The Anglicans sent a letter of complaint to London about the "griev-

61. *Compleat Body of Divinity,* p. 55. Sermon preached on April 23, 1689.

62. Hutchinson, *op. cit.,* I, 324, 328-331; Palfrey, *op. cit.,* III, 588, 590, 593-594.

63. Love, *op. cit.,* pp. 236, 480.

64. Palfrey, *op. cit.,* IV, 1-13.

ances" which the king's loyal subjects sustained in the new world. And Randolph from his Boston jail wrote accusing letters to the Lords of the Committee on Trade and Plantations and to the Bishop of London, hoping to block any consideration for recalcitrant New Englanders encouraged by "crafty" ministers. Increase Mather's book against Common Prayer worship, he declared, persuaded New Englanders that Anglicans were idolaters and unfit to be entrusted with government. [65]

Such was the character of the time as Willard chose to preach another vigorous polemic against "The Sinfulness of Worshipping God with Men's Institutions." Calvin in an earlier and different situation might speak of the tolerable ineptitudes of the Prayer Book, but Willard, remembering that it was the Anglican Church of Laud and the persecuting bishops from which their fathers had fled, would never concede this. Instituted worship required adequate authority, and to him, custom, tradition, or the example of holy and learned men was insufficient. What Willard condemned was *"things devised by men, and imposed as part of Worship, which are no where commanded by God."* It was a sin to "invent" them and tie them upon men's consciences, but also to "comply" with and "yield conformity" to them. Such worship dishonored God because it violated the second commandment, opposed divine prerogative and wisdom, cast reflection on Christ's prescription, and presumptuously obliged God to be present at humanly prescribed worship. Such tampering with worship provoked God, as the denunciations and judgments of the Old Testament showed. And actually, men harmed themselves by such worship, argued Willard: whatever was put into it was lost, they hazarded judicial divine withdrawal and risked the loss of all God's institutions.[66]

Once again Willard swept aside the argument of indifference: "indifferency" was gone the very moment such worship was *imposed.* The silence of Scripture argued not for indifference but repudiation. Every part of worship required Scriptural validation; there was no other argument.

> Although they may pretend that it is very profitable, that many have bin edified by it; that it is a very prudent way to secure the Interests of Religion, that many wise, holy, and learned men have pleaded for and practised it, that there is much decency in it, and

65. The letters, in the British Colonial Papers, are cited by Greenwood, *op. cit.,* p. 44. The address of the Anglicans (February, 1690), signed by the Rev. Mr. Miles, Foxcroft, and Ravenscroft, church wardens, is in *M.H.S. Colls.,* XXVII, 193. Cf. Palfrey, *op. cit.,* IV, 65-66. The work of Increase Mather cited by Randolph is his *A Brief Discourse Concerning the unlawfulness of the Common Prayer Worship* (Cambridge, 1686), published just before the Andros regime.

66. *The Sinfulness of Worshipping God With Men's Institutions,* pp. 4-21.

the thing in it self is no ways harmful: all this is fully answered with that one word, *God hath spoken nothing about it*, Heb. 7.14. *it never entred into his heart to enjoin it*, Jer. 7.31.[67]

New England should have been the last to be guilty of the sin of exchanging the purer worship of God for that which was "more mixt," said Willard. But, he asked with fine irony, "are there not they that have observed days of Humane consecration, and put a title of Holiness upon them, though they have expressed little of it in the manner of their observation?" He called them to remember the historic purpose behind their fathers' errand into the wilderness.

> Except we thus do, we shall directly vacate our Fathers design in Planting of this Wilderness. It is certain, that their Errand hither was to sequester themselves into a quiet corner of the world, where they might *enjoy Christ's unmixed Institutions, and leave them uncorrupted to their Posterity*.

If this design was unworthy, let it be buried with them and forgotten; but if it was worth forsaking the comforts and conveniences of a pleasant land for the hardships and difficulties and discouragements of an "Uncultivated Desert," to abandon this high commitment was a reproach. It would be nothing short of apostasy, for "these Churches have declaredly Covenanted with God, and mutually, *that we will serve the Lord with no other manner of Worship, but that which he hath appointed and established in his Word.*"[68]

One of Willard's parishioners, a certain Roger Judd, who had gone for the Anglican "mixt" worship, was dealt with in a way which illustrates how seriously the worship commitment of the church covenant was viewed. Judd became a communicant member of South Church on July 11, 1684,[69] but four years later when King's Chapel was built he developed a preference for Anglican worship. Samuel Sewall and deacon Captain James Hill were sent to "discourse with Roger Judd" on the evening of June 8, 1688, and numerous subsequent attempts were made to convince him of his duty to the church with which he had made a solemn covenant, but all without effect. Willard summoned Judd at length to a final meeting at the Sewall home on January 4, 1699, but he still proved intractable, claiming that he had affiliated with South Church only on the urging of Deacon Jacob Eliot and others, but that "now twas his Conscience to go to the church of England, and he had sin'd in staying away from it so long," and adding

67. *Ibid.*, pp. 23-24.
68. *Ibid.*, pp. 25-29.
69. Hill and Bigelow, *op. cit.*, pp. 13, 274.

that "if he was persecuted for it, he could not help it."[70] Willard, in reporting the case to the church, said in part:

> The summe of the offence is, that having declared his renouncing Communion with this Church and accordingly deserted it, he refused to give an account of it, when orderly Called to it, and declared that he neither owned himself subject to the minister nor the Church, which amounts to contumacy.[71]

Accordingly, on the Sabbath of January 29, noted Sewall, Judd was "cast out of the Church for his contumacy in refusing to hear the Church, and his contemptous behaviour against the same, and Mr. Willard the Pastor. Refus'd to be there."[72] The action taken was in accord with the provisions of the Cambridge Platform.

During the remaining months of the provisional government, as Increase Mather and his associates in London feverishly endeavored to salvage as many of their liberties as they could for the new charter, Willard quietly continued to dominate the ministerial scene in Boston. Through his parishioners on the Council he was in close touch with the official life of the province, but like the others he was waiting to see what the new charter would bring.[73]

70. Sewall, *op. cit.*, 490-491.

71. Record of the meeting of the church, January 22, 1699; quoted in full in Hill, *History of Old South Church,* I, 306-307.

72. Sewall, *op. cit.*, 492. Cf. "A Platform of Discipline," Chapter XIII, in Walker, *Creeds and Platforms,* pp. 224-226.

73. Sewall, *op. cit.*, 338, 352.

CHAPTER FIVE

CHURCH AND STATE:
Under the New Charter

The new charter granted on September 17, 1691, did not offer New Englanders all they had hoped for. It provided for a royally appointed governor, franchise on the basis of property rather than Congregational church membership, and guarantees for toleration of religious dissent. On the other hand, there were a number of concessions, such as freedom from the requirement of taking oaths on the Bible, and the legal confirmation of their defectively listed properties. Though independent government was curtailed, they retained the power to elect a General Court with power to levy taxes, set up courts, probate wills, and inflict capital punishment.[1] Increase Mather, in London, was given the privilege of nominating the new rulers, all of whom were approved by the king. Sir William Phips was chosen governor, and William Stoughton, lieutenant governor. Of the twenty-two councilors, five—Simon Bradstreet, Wait Winthrop, Samuel Sewall, John Joyliffe, and Peter Sergeant—were members of Willard's congregation.[2] Massachusetts, for the time being, was assured of orthodox leaders.

The Administration of Governor Phips

Sir William Phips and Increase Mather finally arrived in Boston harbor on Saturday night, May 14, 1692. Monday morning, as com-

---

1. *Acts and Resolves, Public and Private, of the Province of Massachusetts Bay,* I, 1-20. The provisions of the charter are extensively reviewed and evaluated by Palfrey, *History of New England,* IV, 75-84.
2. Hutchinson, *History of the Colony and Province,* I, 349-350. On the Third Church members see Hill and Bigelow, *Historical Catalogue,* 12, 267; 15, 290; 11, 259; 8, 241; 15, 288.

panies of soldiers lined the streets, the new governor and his councilors marched to the Town House, where their commissions were read and the oaths of office were administered.[3] At the order of the Court May 26 was observed as a day of thanksgiving for the new government.[4]

Willard's feelings about the new order at the time are not recorded, but on the basis of his previous pronouncements it may be assumed that he acquiesced with the inevitable. The new charter was apparently the best that the dexterous Increase Mather could have obtained, but, while Cotton Mather was ecstatic about it,[5] it was not universally received in New England. Elisha Cooke had refused to sign it in London, and upon his return home he immediately headed a party of reaction. At the first election one year later, in spite of Increase Mather's blast against old-guard malcontents, Cooke was elected by a narrow margin. Governor Phips exercised the power of veto the next day, and once again the embers of party spirit burst into flame.[6]

The situation was tense as Willard preached the next election sermon on May 30, 1694. While he was far from eager, he assured them, to appear on the stage at a time when no one could "speak without some off reflection [being] made upon him," he had none of that "sullen Humor" that shunned service for fear of affronts.[7] At this critical time he chose to portray the "fair face of a Well-ordered Government," reiterating the traditional doctrines of Puritan political orthodoxy. The basis of government was to be found both in natural law and in revelation, he declared, an affirmation interpreted by some today as an incipient shift from purely theological to rational-naturalistic principles. But it should be noted, he went on to explain, that while it could be discerned from the light of nature, Christians deduced it from the fifth commandment, a transcript of the law initially inscribed on the heart of man in the state of integrity.[8] Apostasy had robbed man of original perfection and produced those perverse principles which subverted order and produced chaos, necessitating civil government. To be without lawful government was always pernicious; "we ourselves had a Specimen of this," he said with a quick flashback, "in the short Anarchy accompanying our late *Revolution*." The responsibility of government was both negative and positive:

3. Sewall, *Diary, 5 M.H.S. Colls.,* V, 360.

4. Love, *Fast and Thanksgiving Days,* pp. 237, 481.

5. Cotton Mather, *Diary, 7 M.H.S. Colls.,* VII, 148.

6. Sewall, *op. cit.,* 378. Cf. Palfrey, *op. cit.,* IV, 82; Hutchinson, *op. cit.,* I, 345f.

7. Willard, *The Character Of a good Ruler,* "To the Reader."

8. *Ibid.,* pp. 1-2. Cf. Perry Miller and Thomas H. Johnson, *The Puritans,* p. 193; and Lindsay Swift, "The Massachusetts Election Sermons," *Pubs. C.S.M.,* I, 405.

to prevent and cure the disorders that are apt to break forth among the Societies of men; and to promote the civil peace and prosperity of such a people, as well as to suppress impiety, and nourish Religion.[9]

Willard especially emphasized that the character and qualifications of rulers determined the weal or woe of a people. Once again he berated the *"Narrow Spirit"* that sought private interest at the expense of public good. People did not exist for rulers, but rulers (under God) "for the Peoples sake"; accordingly they governed only *"Durante Bene Plecito."* Experience illuminated every word of Willard's appeal:

> When men can injoy their Liberties and Rights without molestation or oppression; when they can live without fear of being born down by their more Potent Neighbors; when they are secured against Violence, and may be Righted against them that offer them any injury, without fraud; and are encouraged to serve God in their own way, with freedom, and without being imposed upon contrary to the Gospel precepts; now are they an happy People. But this is to be expected from none other than men just and Pious.

The right to rule belonged to no one by natural right, and neither the light of nature nor the Word of God determined the particular form of government, "whether *Monarchical, Aristocratical,* or *Democratical:* much less, who are individually to be acknowledged in Authority." He obviously aligned himself with the democratic forces, however, provided the people chose good rulers.

> A good *Charter* is Doubtless Preferible to a bad one; it is a great Priviledge to be secured from being hurt by any but our selves: but, let *Charter Priviledges* be never so Excellent, Good Rulers only can make us Happy under them: and if they are not so, we suffer notwithstanding.

Addressing the rulers, he as much as reminded them that the seat of ultimate power was not in London but in heaven. God is "your Great SOVERAIGN," he declared, and the people of New England are

> the Subjects of his GOSPEL KINGDOM: If you do that which is Right to them, He will be Pleased, but if you should do otherwise, their APPEAL is open to Him, and there is a COURT that will be called, wherein their CAUSE shall be Heard, and Adjusted.[10]

9. Willard, *op. cit.,* pp. 2-3.
10. *Ibid.,* pp. 3-18, 16, 20, 22, 25.

Taken as a whole the sermon was another forceful blast against the ultraconservative reactionaries who were tearing Massachusetts to pieces by their bickering unwillingness to recognize continuity amidst expedient and necessary changes. Mentioning no names—everyone knew he had Elisha Cooke's party in mind—he tacitly reminded them that now was the time to end unrealistic personal political programs that would surely lead to a dead end. Theocratic principles could still be practiced if they used a bit of ingenuity and pooled their energies under the leadership of just and religious men, men of the Congregational way!

This time the election came off much more acceptably to the dominant political leadership of Massachusetts, and there was none of the bitterness and rancor that attended the previous year's contest.[11]

But the administration of Phips began to founder. Abetted by French Canadian Roman Catholic missionaries, Indian hostilities broke out anew on the frontier. The Oyster River outpost was attacked and many of its inhabitants massacred on July 17, and ten days later the savages ravaged Portsmouth, Exeter, Dover, and the rebuilt Groton, killing some and carrying others away as marketable captives.[12] With memories of that tragic day two decades earlier, Willard observed a "Solemn Day of Humiliation" at South Church on August 23, and preached an urgent jeremiad on "Reformation the Great Duty of an Afflicted People."[13] By the end of the year the quick-tempered Phips, valorous in military affairs but often inept in political management, maligned and charged by dissidents within the colony and perhaps also by the self-seeking Dudley in England, was summoned to London to defend his maladministration. The sun had set on the evening of November 17 as his ship sailed from Boston, leading Sewall to note that both his coming and his going were "in darkness."[14]

The Administration of Governor Bellomont

The government was put in the hands of Lieutenant Governor William Stoughton in the interim. It was a prolonged interval, for Richard Coote, Earl of Bellomont, though appointed as governor in 1696, did not arrive in Boston until 1699. Much of Stoughton's attention had to be given to the movements of the marauding Indians incited by the French from Canada. Willard's political involvements

11. Sewall, *op. cit.*, 390.
12. Palfrey, *op. cit.*, IV, 151, 152; Butler, *History of the Town of Groton,* p. 93; Green, *Groton During the Indian Wars,* pp. 63, 66. Sewall, *op. cit.*, 391; Mather, *Magnalia,* II, 68.
13. *Reformation The Great Duty of an Afflicted People.*
14. Sewall, *op. cit.*, 393-394.

were seemingly limited to offering periodic invocations at the meetings of the Council. He spoke out pointedly, however, on a day of prayer held at the Town House by the governor, the Council, and the Assembly, on September 16, 1696, as an expedition was being sent against the French in New Hampshire. Preaching on the theme "If God be with us who can be against us?", he "spake Smartly" against the negligence of the officials in not appointing a day of penitence for the doleful witchcraft episode through which they had passed, a fact that partly explained, he suspected, the continuance of judicial woes. The rebuke had its effect, and the Council proclaimed January 14, 1697, a day of prayer and fasting throughout the province for whatever mistakes the magistrates and the people had made during that demonic tragedy.[15]

On June 5, 1699, five days after Lord Bellomont arrived as governor, Willard spoke on "The Man of War" at the annual artillery election, making another urgent plea for greater preparedness. He spoke, he made it clear, as a "Gospel Minister," whose task was not to establish military points, but to deal with such matters as "tributary" to the Christian religion. He had the Bible to document his thesis that the "Employment of a Souldier is very Honourable," and because of human depravity necessary in the interests of "publick peace." Christianity was not opposed to war, he declared, denouncing the Socinian ethic—"that Christ, upon his Coming, had brought in a new Law, which forbids it." Personal revenge was forbidden, but the Christian religion at times could be defended only "at Swords point, and Canons mouth." Self-preservation was a principle of natural law contradicted neither by reason nor religion; the Münster Anabaptists illustrated the folly of forgetting it. He challenged them as Christian soldiers to beware of "that cursed Matchiavellian principle, *That too much Religion will make a man Pusullanimous.*" In closing, once again he pointed up the precarious safety afforded by emergency militia, the temptation in time of peace "to let their Fortifications fall, hang up their arms, and let them grow rusty and useless, and lay aside their Military exercises, as things superfluous." The fatal consequences of their cavalier attitude toward preparedness were patent:

> Peace hath bred Security, and times of Troubles have us unready; and the most of our Surprises and Defeatments by our Enemies, have deserved to be imputed to this. . . . Of how many of our surprized Garrisons, in which our people have been miserably butchered, may that of the *Poet* be asserted, *Invadunt urbem, somno—Sepultam.*

15. *Massachusetts Archives,* XI, 120-121. Sewall, *op. cit.,* 433, 440-441n. On the witchcraft episode see the last chapter.

Trust in God they must, but faith that nurtured negligence was not faith but "Presumption."[16] The Honourable John Walley, a prominent member of Willard's congregation, was chosen captain, and at the dinner that followed Lord Bellomont presented the commissions and the "Badges" to the officers, "saying that he approv'd of the choice."[17]

There are indications that in the changing late seventeenth century Willard actively espoused the ideal of a broadening church within the framework of orthodoxy. Religious tendencies described as a progressive movement came to greater expression at the time. The movement, which can be traced back to the Half-Way Covenant controversy more than thirty years before, was obscured somewhat during the intervening years by the all-consuming concerns of the charter struggle and the Andros regime, but the religious situation under the new charter fostered a more hospitable climate. This party of progress, composed mainly of young ministers and laymen associated with the Harvard College circle (tutors John Leverett and Ebenezer Pemberton, the treasurer Thomas Brattle, and the Reverend William Brattle of Cambridge Church), advocated no departures from orthodoxy on matters of faith, but did favor a broader attitude toward certain church practices. They supported elimination of public "relations" of spiritual experience by applicants for communicant membership, reading of the Scriptures without comment at Sunday services, use of the Lord's Prayer, baptism for children of all professing Christians who promised to nurture them in the faith, and selection of ministers by all supporting baptized male adults. While such innovations were vigorously opposed by the Mathers, Willard's sympathy for the movement was evidenced by his endeavor to secure Ebenezer Pemberton as a colleague at South Church.

These progressive ideas came to expression in the establishment of Brattle Street Church, the fourth in Boston. While introducing these changes in church order, it demonstrated its orthodoxy by subscribing to the Westminster Confession. The Reverend Benjamin Colman, completely in sympathy with these ideas, was secured as the first minister, and with careful forethought he was ordained in England by the Presbyterians before sailing for home. Colman began to preach for the new church immediately after his arrival from England on November 1, 1699. The church was organized on December 12, without the presence of a sanctioning council of ministers, but with hopes of a day of worship together in the near future. From the start South Church was

16. *The Man of War,* pp. 4, 7-14, 16-19.
17. Sewall, *op. cit.,* 497. Cf. Hill and Bigelow, *op. cit.,* pp. 11, 349.

cordial to the new congregation—the Leveretts and Brattles, besides a number of others, were all South Church people—and when the new congregation met in its new meetinghouse on Sunday, December 29, Sewall noted: "Our Meeting was pretty much thin'd by it."[18] The new church's overtures for a common recognition service were met with additional rebukes from ultraconservatives such as Increase Mather and James Allen of Boston, and John Higginson and Nicholas Noyes of Salem. But Willard, collecting the support of some of his leading laymen, was instrumental in getting the churches to agree to such a service, with the result that on January 31, 1700, all the Boston ministers—Allen, the two Mathers, and Willard—joined Colman at a special Fast Day service in the new church.

> Mr. Willard pray'd to pardon all the frailties and follies of Ministers and people; and that they might give that Respect to the other churches that was due to them though were not of their Constitution, and Mr. Cotton Mather in's prayer to the same purpose. Mr. Willard and C. Mather pray'd excellently and pathetically for Mr. Colman and his Flock.[19]

About the same time Willard's three-year effort to secure the South Church's approval of Ebenezer Pemberton as colleague pastor was finally successful. This young progressive Harvard tutor, an intimate friend of Colman, was a son of one of the founders of South Church. Baptized by Thomas Thacher in 1672, he became a communicant member at South Church in 1692. His mastery of logic and oratory won him recognition as one of the most talented tutors of his day, but it took long urging by Willard to overcome strong sentiments within South Church for either the Reverend John Bailey, the Reverend Simon Bradstreet, or Jabez Fitch (also a tutor). The church record intimates something of the tension that developed during the lengthy proceedings.

> At a Church meeting: Feb. 21 1699-1700
> Whereas there have formerly bin attempts used, and severall votes past, in and by this Church, in order to the procuring of another minister to take office among us; which have failed of

---

18. Sewall, *op. cit.,* 509. For the progressive movement in general and the establishment of the Brattle Street Church see: Palfrey, *op. cit.,* IV, 189ff.; Walker, *Creeds and Platforms,* pp. 472ff.; Hill, *History of Old South Church,* I, 304, 308ff.; Hill and Bigelow, *op. cit., passim;* Murdock, *Increase Mather,* pp. 358ff.; Herbert L. Osgood, *The American Colonies in the Eighteenth Century,* I, 322ff.; and Clayton H. Chapman, "The Life and Influence of Reverend Benjamin Colman," pp. 39-51.

19. Sewall, *op. cit.,* VI, 2-3.

their desired success through want of a comfortable unanimity in our proceedings; we do therefore joyntly agree to lay aside all former pretensions, that we may be no longer hindred in a free Choice; asking of God forgiveness of what hath bin displeasing to him, and his Gracious conduct, in our essays for a peacable and mercifull settlement.

Voted and agreed by the Church.

At the same time, was Mr. Ebenezer Pemberton elected, and with a free concurrence of the church, chosen to be their minister, in order to his settlement in office amon [sic] them; and the Honoured Capt. Sewall, Major Walley, Mr. Frary, Mr. Hill, Mr. Williams and Captain Checkly were chosen and desired to present the desires of this chosen to Mr. Pemberton:

Attests: Saml Willard
Teacher [20]

Pemberton finished the academic year at the college, and was ordained at South Church on Wednesday, August 20, 1700, in the presence of a great assembly, many ministers being present. Willard preached and gave the charge, Increase Mather and James Allen represented the clergy and the other Boston churches in the laying on of hands.[21] In securing Pemberton, Willard had strengthened the commitment of South Church to orthodoxy with a progressive outlook on minor matters of church order.

Meanwhile Willard had been active in securing a charter for Harvard College which would protect the interests of Puritan orthodoxy. Nine years of charter-mongering, with bitter recriminations between the House and Council, the colonial powers and the king's representatives, resulted at last in 1700 in a charter draft mutually satisfying to both Bellomont and the General Assembly. It contained no religious test, but it did provide that the Court should nominate a slate of college officers which would be subject to the approval of the Council, and that the Council would share visitorial power with the king. The control of the corporation was safeguarded by the appointment of those who were avowedly orthodox, all but three being clergymen. Increase Mather was named president, and Willard was made vice-president. Bellomont himself approved the new draft and, virtually capitulating to New England wishes, advised the Lords of Trade on July 15 to approve it, inasmuch as the restrictive clause excluding Church of England members had been dropped by the General Assembly. Bellomont thought that their desire to protect themselves against religious molestation was reasonable enough and that it was consonant with the liberty of conscience

20. Quoted in Hill, *op. cit.,* I, 314.
21. Sewall, *op. cit.,* V, 485.

allowed under the Act of Toleration. The draft became lost in the files of the king's solicitor-general, however, and Bellomont's death on March 5, 1701, prevented his own reminder to the king. Harvard therefore continued to function under the "Temporary Settlement" of the General Court on July 13, 1700, which provided that President Mather, Vice-President Willard, and the tutors should take the "oversight, care and government" of the college until "his majesties pleasure" regarding the college settlement should be known. This they did until the end of 1707, when the ancient charter was revived.[22] Harvard had been saved for the orthodox.

The responsibility of a caretaker government was again assumed by the aged lieutenant governor William Stoughton, who, failing in health, survived only four months. He died, unloved by many, at his home in Dorchester on July 7, 1701. Described by one contemporary as "pudding faced, sanctimonious and unfeeling,"[23] he was to Willard (though he vigorously dissented from some of his acts and attitudes) a leader notable for "Piety, Prudence, Learning, Integrity, love of Religion, love to his people, faithfulness to that Service in several capacities, and that in either England, zeal for the truth both in Doctrine and Worship, and noble Munificence," and with him "much of New England's glory" was entombed. "Under [his] mild conduct we enjoyed many desirable things," said Willard. Another gap has been made in our hedge, "& who shall thrust into, and make it up?"[24]

The successor was to be his own brother-in-law, Joseph Dudley! But while Dudley was intriguing in England to gain the appointment as governor, the Council of Massachusetts governed in an interim capacity.

In the Council chambers and at the college developments were taking shape which shortly demonstrated that Willard was destined to play a more significant role at Harvard than he imagined. Political and ecclesiastical resentments against Increase Mather, who had been president of the college since 1685, spurred a movement in 1700 to bring an end to his vacillations between the college presidency and the Second Church. The Court felt that it had pampered Mather long enough, and on July 10 both Houses resolved to establish a stipend of two hundred and twenty pounds for a resident president; a committee was appointed to inform Mather of his re-election and that the Court expected him to reside at Cambridge. Mather's church had always stood loyally behind him in refusing to grant him a dismissal, and he again offered the

22. Morison, *Harvard College,* II, 490-530, 537n., gives the history and documentation from the sources.
23. Quoted in Sibley, *Biographical Sketches,* I, 203. Cf. Palfrey, *op. cit.,* IV, 197-199 for a character sketch.
24. Willard, *Prognosticks of Impending Calamities,* pp. 31-32.

church's attitude as an excuse. But this time the Court called his bluff and ordered him to call a congregational meeting, sent an official delegation to argue for consent, and got it. Mather spent a stifling summer at Cambridge; the prospect of enduring a cold winter was too much to contemplate, however, and he returned to Boston, suggesting that they think of another president. The Court re-elected him, but decisively declared that "in case of Mr. Mather's refusal, absence, sickness or death, . . . Mr. Samuel Willard, nominated to be vice-president, . . . be . . . invested with the like powers and authority aforesaid in all respects."[25] Mather trudged back to Cambridge, but at the end of the term on June 30 he wrote another letter of resignation. The Court heard the letter on August 1 and immediately passed a resolution inviting Willard to accept the presidency. Willard delayed giving a definite reply until September, when he indicated that he would "do the best service he could for the College, and that he would visit it once or twice a week, and continue there a night or two, and perform the service used to be done by former Presidents."[26] By a clever ruse the Court noted that whatever the law said about the residence of the president, it said nothing about it for a vice-president, and both Houses resolved on September 6, 1701:

> That the Reverend Mr. Samuel Willard nominated for Vice-President of the Colledge . . . be desired to take the care and Over Sight of the Colledge and Students there according to the late Establishment made by this Court and to manage the affairs thereof, as he has proposed in his answer to this Court. Vizt. to reside there for one or two days and nights in the week, and to perform prayers and Expositions in the Hall and to bring forward the Exercise of Analyzing.[27]

The Mathers were grieved and angry. Increase confided in his autobiography: "The Colledge was through the malice of mr Cooke and Byfield put into the hands of mr Willard as vicepresident, who readily accepted the offer without so much as once consulting with me about it." Both the Council and the House, he firmly believed, had maneuvered Willard's approbation at a moment when members of the Mather party were absent from the chambers. He nursed his hurt feelings for a long time, noting in his diary in 1702: "The Colledge is in a miserable state. . . . [Willard] managed the Commencement . . . so as to expose himselfe to contempt and the College to disgrace."[28] In the judgment of others, however, Willard discharged his responsibilities with compe-

25. *Acts and Resolves,* VII, 271-272; quoted in Morison, *op. cit.,* II, 659-660.
26. *C.S.M.,* XV, lvi-lvii; quoted in Morison, *op. cit.,* II, 534.
27. *Acts and Resolves,* VII, 312; quoted in Morison, *op. cit.,* II, 534.
28. Quoted in Morison, *op. cit.,* II, 533, 535.

tence and filled his role with satisfaction, moderating regularly at commencement and presiding at fourteen corporation meetings.[29] His son Josiah served as a tutor for a time during his incumbency. Willard also composed a handy student guide, "Brief Directions to a Young Scholar Designing the Ministry," which proved to be so popular with the students that a number of years later it was printed from copies of extant manuscripts.[30]

Willard was a logical successor to Mather. Next to Mather, he was doubtlessly the most prominent minister in Boston and the whole province. Every whit as orthodox, he was more acceptable to the broader group. He had demonstrated his capacity for calm but courageous leadership during the trying days of the Andros regime when his own church had been conscripted for Anglican services. His reputation for discernment had been enhanced by his judicious handling of the witchcraft episodes at Groton and Salem. Unlike Mather, he was not personally ambitious in the government of the province and the college, and he had made no political enemies. Besides, he was a man of impressive family connections.

The Administration of Governor Dudley

The remaining years of Willard's ministry were spent under the governorship of Joseph Dudley. By dexterous manipulation of political strings Dudley had managed to get the appointment from King William in early 1702, but William's death made it necessary for him to wait for a new commission from Queen Anne, which was granted on the second day of her reign, March 10. Eleven years earlier Dudley had left Boston by way of a prison door; he now returned with a convoy of two armed vessels.

The very day of his arrival Dudley met with the Council to read his commission, and five days later he reconvened them to outline his program. Besides demanding a governor's residence, a regular and adequate salary for himself as well as for the lieutenant governor and the judges, and greater production for England, he demanded the rebuilding of Fort Pemaquid on the Maine coast. Willard himself had more than once urged greater attention to defense, and it may be assumed that he had communicated this concern to his brother-in-law. The representatives were not minded to be rubber stamps, however, and the passage of the program was obstructed by lengthy debates. Fortification of the

29. *C.S.M.*, XV, 366-377; cited by Morison, *op. cit.*, II, 539.
30. *Brief Directions to a Young Scholar Designing the Ministry, for the Study of Divinity*. The Preface was signed by Joseph Sewall and Thomas Prince.

remote post at Pemaquid particularly, they thought, was ill-advised and wasteful, and though the more propertied members urged its consideration, the representatives, reflecting traditional popular attitudes, resorted to the expedient of doing nothing.

While the cause of defense languished, the French and Indians were once more preparing for war. At a conference on the Maine coast at Casco in June the Indian chiefs reaffirmed their friendliness, but by autumn the frontier erupted with a series of savage attacks that began another terrible ten-year war.[31]

Willard's ethical idealism comes out in a catechism sermon touching on the question of how New Englanders were to react to this recurrent barbarism. Severity, necessarily, was one of the "unavoidable Effects of War," he observed, but "to slay Women and Children in cool Blood is a thing which ordinarily will admit of no excuse." The purpose of war was to subdue the adversary and secure one's safety from oppression, not to "lay the World waste, and to fill Places with nothing but images of Horror and Desolation."[32] An implicit condemnation of the Indian tactic, the sermon was also a caution against the temptation of succumbing to the same barbarism. In the light of all that Massachusetts suffered it required great inner spiritual discipline to follow it.

Less than a month later the western frontier was once more the scene of bloody carnage. Instigated by the French, the Indians made a surprise attack on Haverhill on February 8, 1704, killing some and taking others prisoners. Two strong parties of five hundred men each were immediately dispatched in pursuit, and the congregations of Massachusetts and New Hampshire met to pray for their success. But in spite of forced marches the distances proved to be too great, and as their provisions gave out they turned back.[33] On February 29 a band of two hundred and fifty French and Indians fell on the snowbound town of Deerfield, killing sixty and taking a hundred prisoners, including the Reverend John Williams, who lived to chronicle the gory tale. Willard's parishioners were on their way to church Sunday morning, March 5, as the news reached Boston, Sewall noted, "by which means our Congregation was made a Bochim."[34]

The General Court ordered a fast for March 15, and Willard preached an urgent sermon on "Israel's True Safety" before Dudley, the Council,

31. For the early days of Dudley's administration see Palfrey, *op. cit.*, IV, 204ff., 245-261.

32. *Compleat Body of Divinity*, p. 629.

33. Palfrey, *op. cit.*, IV, 261. Love, *op. cit.*, p. 277.

34. Sewall, *op. cit.*, VI, 96. Cf. John Williams, *The Redeemed Captive Returning to Zion* (Boston, 1707).

and the representatives. "They that have God for them," Willard assured them, "are abundantly secured from harm, by all that can be against them. [They] may undauntedly look in the face of all threatning troubles, and neither be terrified at the apprehension of the closest Conspiracies, nor dispirited at the most daring attempts that are made against them." But in what sense could God be said to be truly for them? Providentially? Yes; but more importantly, "Foederally." Willard accordingly harnessed the whole matter of their security to their covenant faithfulness. Externally considered, he explained, the covenant connects promises with conditions, so "then only can God be truly said *to be for us, when we are for him.*" Like the ingenious spiritual architects of the Congregationalist colony of Massachusetts Bay who in Old Testament fashion had built the social covenant on the foundation of the covenant of grace, Willard spoke of the covenant as referring to the "body of a People." Considered collectively in this sense, within the political framework, the promises and threatenings referred to this world and were temporary, and thus also the blessings and evils were "met withal here."[35] When they feared God, and when He gave them grace to repent and reform, they could know that God was for them. Consequently, they had more for them than there could be against them (II Chronicles 32:7, 8), for working in the interests of a federal people were all the divine perfections and attributes—his omnipotence, omnipresence, omniscience, wisdom, and sovereignty—and every aspect of defense was more than amply provided for.[36]

It was because they were not living up to this covenant that they were suffering the consequences! The very day they fasted God seemed to "*Smoke against our Prayers,*" and answered with the "*sad Catastrophe*" that befell Deerfield. Dudley, the Council, and the Assembly clearly had to do more than this. "*Fasting* and *Prayer* and making *Confession* unto God over these things, is a very necessary Duty," continued Willard, "and if rightly attended it will be the way to success." But if the good of this was not to be lost they had to repent and take measures to suppress the immoralities of the land.

> Then will he direct your Counsels, and prosper your Enterprizes. Then will he Spirit your *Militia,* and afford them safe conduct, and deliver up your Enemies slain at your feet. Then will he guard your Coast, and be a wall of defence to your frontiers.[37]

35. *Israel's True Safety,* pp. 5-6, 7-9. On the social covenant see Miller, *Orthodoxy in Massachusetts,* pp. 224-225; and *The New England Mind,* Chapter XIV, p. 415.

36. *Israel's True Safety,* pp. 11-17.

37. *Ibid.,* pp. 30-33.

The sermon's impact may be discerned in "A Declaration Against Prophaneness & Immoralities" issued by the General Assembly on March 24. But depravity is not controlled by declarations; implementation was difficult, and delinquency continued among the saints of New England. At the same time the war continued throughout the summer months, with numerous ineffective expeditions against an enemy that found ready retreats in the wilds, and Massachusetts was gripped with frustration and despondency.

Concurrently, Willard dealt lengthily with political themes in his catechism sermons on the fifth commandment, which summarized his thought on government—its establishment, form, right, rule, and duties. Reflecting his Puritan mentors and Reformed scholars throughout on the main points, he explained that government rested on the providence and prescription of God, and that its natural necessity had been augmented by human apostasy. It is sometimes averred that the Puritans inherited an Augustinian and medieval political philosophy, which asserted that if Adam had not fallen his descendants would have been just to each other without the supervision of the magistrate. Willard put the case quite differently. Since the fall the moral necessity of government was accentuated, for without it "there would be no living together for Mankind, but Humane Societie must disband; Murder, Adulteries, Rapine, and all manner of Oppressions would rage; and there would be less of Order in the Habitable World, than in Hell itself." [38] But man, declared Willard, was by nature "politikos" as a "Sociable Creature," and the magistrate was not brought in merely after the fall as a coercive power to whip lapsed humanity into civility.

There was no single obligatory "fixed" form of government, according to Willard; it was to be prudentially accommodated to the "genius" of a particular place. The question as to which of the three recognized forms—monarchy, aristocracy, democracy—was best, could not be absolutely or universally answered, for differing circumstances dictated different forms among diverse people. He recommended a "well-tempered" balance of the three. He had obviously moved with the times beyond the aristocratic Winthrop, though in countering certain reactionary democratic tendencies, he emphasized that magistrates should be men of quality.[39] The right of government, he continued, was *de facto* determined by the customs and constitutions of the various nations, either by succession or election. In general, he observed, in traditional orthodox terms, it was founded on "Compact." [40]

38. *Compleat Body*, pp. 618-619. Cf. Miller, *New England Mind*, p. 417.
39. *Compleat Body*, pp. 620. Cf. Stanley Gray, "The Political Thought of John Winthrop," *N.E.Q.*, III (1930), 685.
40. *Compleat Body*, p. 620. Cf. Miller, *New England Mind*, pp. 416-421.

And the rule of government (well might they remember Andros's regime) was never to be "arbitrary." It was to be administered by "wholesome and just laws," for "justice and judgment" was possible only where there were fixed and established laws (Deuteronomy 17:18).[41]

The rulers and the ruled were divinely established correlates, and Willard spelled out their duties in detail. Magistrates were to use their God-given authority for the common good. This meant, first of all, that they had to provide a body of good fixed laws. Obviously seeking to preserve as much of their theocratic way of life as he could within the framework of the new charter, Willard affirmed the permanent validity of the Mosaic law for human society, distinguishing its moral, ceremonial, and civil elements. The moral law was permanent as a transcript of natural law; the ceremonial law was now abolished; and the civil (or judicial) laws were abolished as appendices to ceremonial laws, yet as appendices to the moral law they required perpetual obedience. With this in mind, legislators were to frame laws that were righteous and good—righteous in the sense that they reflected the law of God and were elastic in their sanctions, and good in the moral and political sense that they promoted the well-being of the whole. On the question of legislation on things "indifferent," Willard carefully considered the thing in itself and its circumstances. To arbitrarily limit subjects in things lawful in themselves was oppression; but when things ordinarily indifferent became harmful, the case was altered. In summary, the best body of laws, as Willard saw it, was:

> When they provide that the true Religion may be established, the true Worship of God may be upheld, and no unscriptural Rites be imposed on Men; when they take Care, that all Orders of Men have their due Honour and Respect paid to them; due Distances be maintained between Superiours and Inferiours; that Men may enjoy their Rights, and be saved from violence and wrong; That the liberal Education of Children be encouraged; That those who deserve will be Rewarded, and Wickedness be punished: When by such Laws as these, they do as far as can be provided for a People's Felicity, they are very Good.

Times had changed, and toleration was now law, but Willard still preached historic orthodoxy. Rulers had the right and duty to legislate on worship and heresy, according to the dictates of reason and the Bible. They had no warrant to "Coin any New Articles" of religion or appoint "New Institutions" of worship,

41. *Compleat Body,* p. 620.

yet their Power is *Circa Sacra;* and they ought to provide that the House of God be built, His Worship upheld; the Ministers of his Sanctuary be supported; all Affronts against his Sacred Majesty be duly born witness against; and all Heretical Doctrines which are at any time broached, be suppressed.[42]

Secondly, rulers were charged with the equitable execution of laws. Laws that were only "Scarecrows" were soon disregarded, and so also the legislators' authority. To Willard it was supremely important, therefore, that only properly qualified judges should be appointed, men who were intellectually able, sensitive to divine accountability, respectors of truth rather than persons, and unbribable. They were conscientiously to refer everything to human and divine law, avoid rash judgments, defend the poor, give impartial hearings, work with recognized laws of evidence, allow defendants sufficient time to justify themselves, render sentences impartially, and see to it that sentences were executed. Like Winthrop, Willard believed that it was inadvisable to have fixed penalties for every case, that in some cases it was better to leave the matter to the wisdom and discernment of the judge. Judges were to administer justice, not pardon, and crimes such as murder were to be punished according to divine prescription without pity, that would-be criminals might be affrighted. There were cases, Willard conceded, where "extream Right would be extream Wrong," and in such instances the "supream Power" had a God-given prerogative to mitigate the severity of the sentence, or even to pardon, especially in those instances in which the law and sanctions were dictated solely by civil authority.[43] But Willard's penological ideas of fitting the punishment to the individual crime were not precursors of rationalism; they were drawn, as the numerous references indicate, from the letter and spirit of the Bible.

Thirdly, rulers were to provide for defense. Willard never doubted the legitimacy of war, defensive and offensive, domestic and foreign; to him self-preservation was a natural principle, and the need of preparedness was axiomatic. In this instance, however, he came out strongly for maintaining peace and order within the community: rulers, he declared, should obviate civil disturbances that breed in the "Bowels" of government by preventing discontent against their administration. Rulers were to defend the people's "just Liberties," Willard existentially declared; they were to impose no "heavy & unreasonable Taxes," and to keep all public officers within "due bounds." At the same time he once again denounced the "turbulent Spirits that love to Fish in troubled Waters, who are ready to blow up the spark of Discontent into a flame, and so raise Civil Wars in the heart of the Government." If after initial gentle

42. *Ibid.,* pp. 622-624.
43. *Ibid.,* pp. 624-627.

attempts to curb it, such discontent broke out in insurrection, it was to be suppressed in the interests of the "common good"; severity was to be restrained to the "ringleaders," for "extream Rigour" would only strengthen rebellion, whereas a general pardon and amnesty would tend "to make the Cement the stronger and more durable."[44]

Fourthly, rulers were to promote the prosperity of their subjects by protecting property rights against illegal invasions and preventing theft and robbery by proper penalties. There was to be no idleness; everyone had to have a lawful and honest "calling." Children were to be taught a vocation, and where "brutish" parents were negligent, the state was to do it. To prevent the squandering of precious time and money "Houses of Entertainment" were to be limited, sometimes closed.[45]

And lastly, rulers were to exemplify piety and morality in their own lives as keepers of both tables. They owed this to God, to their subjects, and to themselves, argued Willard. Good examples not only were often more influential than laws, they undergirded the entire system.[46]

Correlatively, subjects also had duties. They were to respect rulers according to their position in New England's stratified society, for the sake of their office, but especially when they were personally worthy. This meant that they should pray for their rulers, honor them with suitable demeanor, and also observe what New Englanders liked to call "due distance." It also meant actively obeying just and righteous laws, and in other instances passive obedience. Knowing doubtlessly the thoughts that this would trigger in the minds of those who had lived through the Andros regime, Willard as a Calvinist went on to explain that while historically *"Non-Resistance* and *Passive Obedience"* had been abused by "bigotted Patrons," there were forms of redress for maladministration. But redress was to be gained lawfully and orderly, not by plots and insurrections. They were to demonstrate their loyalty to rulers by oaths of allegiance, by willingly bearing arms, and by supporting government—even by cheerfully paying taxes. It was a matter of practical necessity, and he cited Biblical precept (Romans 13:7), but it must have been his most unpopular point. Denouncing the common cry about the "Intollerableness" of taxes, he conceded that they might well "grown" and seek redress if rulers "fleeced" them to gratify their own "lusts," but to regard all taxation as oppression, to pay only grudgingly, or to withhold fraudulently, would only provoke God to *give* them hateful rulers. Such "woful Parsimony," he warned, more than once set the stage for loss of liberty, estates, and lives.[47]

44. *Ibid.,* pp. 628-629.
45. *Ibid.,* pp. 629-630.
46. *Ibid.,* pp. 630-631.
47. *Ibid.,* pp. 631-634. Sermon CLXXXIV, February 8, 1704. Cf. John

Willard was not preaching into the air. The records show the stubborn unwillingness of the representatives to vote favorably on the repeated overtures of Governor Dudley and the Council for fixed salaries, adequate taxes, and allocations for defense. Six months earlier Dudley had tried again to get his program adopted, but to no avail; the issue only created new discord as he and the General Court remained deadlocked. If Willard hoped that by his sermon he could influence public opinion on this issue, however, he had something to learn. The next month (March 25, 1704) the House summarily replied to Dudley and the Council that they had "resolved not to raise any further money this session."[48] That June, Willard once more mounted his pulpit to rebuke the spirit of discontent and uprising against magistrates.[49]

On the whole Willard's political thought at the turn of the century reveals him to be no revolutionary, the strands of his thought being principles Puritans held in common with scholars in the generic Reformed tradition. The tone of some of his emphases, however, indicates the impact of the experiences of his generation, and some of these principles—that magistrates were limited by compact, that government was by laws rather than men, that subjects possessed the right of redress and that there were bounds to their obedience—were to play a decisive role in the great revolution later in the century.

The church was the other important correlate of social life, and Willard gave a succinct statement on it in another catechism sermon. His treatment of it was brief compared to his exposition of the political order; but none of his sermons dealt extensively with the order of the church. Throughout his ministry, as we have seen, he worked within the context of the orthodox theory of the church, fashioned initially in England under the influence of Henry Jacob and William Ames, refined and codified in the Cambridge Platform by the early colonial leaders, and slightly adjusted to the realities of waning religious ardor by the Synod of 1662, as well as by the minor accommodation which he himself had made on the matter of relating experience upon admission to communicant membership. In essence the Congregational way was Biblical, he believed, and it was to be preserved as the heritage of their fathers. Church and state were distinct, though related. It was "the Duty of every Christian in a Professing Government," he explained in his sermon on March 17, 1704,[50]

Calvin, *The Institutes of the Christian Religion*, IV, 20, 22-32. On limited prerogative see also *The Colonial Laws of Massachusetts, Reprinted from the Edition of 1660*, p. 33.

48. Palfrey, *op. cit.*, IV, 288-292.

49. *Compleat Body*, p. 655. Sermon of June 27, 1704.

50. *Compleat Body*, pp. 635-636. On Henry Jacobs and William Ames, and

to acknowledge his Relation to *both* States, so a Man may be a Ruler in the One, and a Subject in the other: And as none invested with *Ecclesiastical* Power are thereby discharged from the Subjection required of all Men, to those Powers under whom they live, so no Person in *Civil* Dignity, ought to exempt himself from the Laws of Christ in his Church.

The "Visible Church State," divinely ordained, comprised all who openly professed the true religion and devoted themselves to the service of God's revealed will. The Scriptures speak of "Churches" as "several Companies" of Christians, explained Willard, because God had instituted "particular Churches" as "orderly Combinations" of such believers to advance the cause of true religion among men. These churches had been given a divinely ordained ecclesiastical polity, with the keys of doctrine and discipline; and they were a correlation of rulers and subjects. But Christ, Willard declared, had appointed no earthly visible head for this church, and whoever presumed to become His vicar-general was anti-Christ.

The church state was "distinct" from the civil state, for though the same people were related to both, it was upon a "different account." The ends of the two were different: the state's concern was the peace and prosperity of men, that of the church their saving good. The means of achieving their ends were different: the state used the civil sword in behalf of temporal and outward interests, the church the sword of the Spirit in behalf of the souls and consciences of men. Their orders and officers were also different: those of the state were prudentially constituted, those of the church were divinely appointed. The important thing in Willard's thought was that both orders were appointed by God, and that they were designed to mutually assist each other.

But with the backbone of the theocracy broken by the new charter, it is not surprising that one finds Willard at this time actively endeavoring to preserve the cause of Congregational orthodoxy in another way. From the earliest days of his ministry he had strongly supported consociation, and now under the altered political and religious conditions of the time he was one of the prime movers in a new attempt to use this method to buttress the ancient Congregational system. The lessened influence of the ministers in the provincial government, and the enforcement of toleration for Episcopacy and other religious diversity under the new charter, dictated the need of greater unanimity and mutual conference among the Congregational clergy. The Ministers'

the orthodox theory of Non-Separating Congregationalism, see Miller, *Orthodoxy in Massachusetts;* and Raymond Phineas Stearns, *Congregationalism in the Dutch Netherlands.*

Convention of 1704 adopted a circular letter to the churches which outlined suggestions for strengthening decaying religion, involving more pastoral diligence in getting people to assume the full covenant relationship, and more pastoral cooperation in maintaining disciplinary standards, including a report to the annual Ministers' Convention. Willard, as moderator, signed the letter with twenty-five other ministers, and worked throughout the next year to gain support for the program. Nine delegates, representing five local associations, met at Boston on September 11, 1705, and two days later agreed upon the *Proposals.* The *Proposals,* drawn up under the moderatorship of Willard, urged that the ministers of the country form themselves into associations to consider periodically matters of importance to the common interest of the churches, and that delegates from these associations be formed into a standing Council, which would consult, advise, and determine matters which could properly fall under the consideration of an ecclesiastical council.[51] The *Proposals* were formally adopted by the Ministers' Convention on May 30, 1706.

But the scheme did not get far beyond the proposal stage. Ministerial associations were established, but nothing came of the recommendation about a standing council—it received no civil support for one thing, and it seemed too Presbyterian for some ministers and laymen. In Connecticut, however, where the situation was somewhat different under a government more favorable to the church system of the colony, the *Proposals* came to fruition in the Saybrook Articles of 1708.[52] Thus the labor expended by Willard on behalf of the *Proposals* was not wholly lost; one part of the program was put into effect in Massachusetts, and the heart of it lived on to bear fruit in the Congregational colony to the south.

It is obvious that the recommendations in the second part of the *Proposals* particularly would have led the Congregational churches of Massachusetts a long way from the earliest ideas of completely local autonomy. In taking the lead in this movement Willard evidenced an intelligent awareness of the fact that change (after eight decades) had to be faced. He believed in the Congregational system, and the *Pro-*

---

51. Walker, *op. cit.,* pp. 483-490.

52. For the text of the *Articles* see Walker, *op. cit.,* pp. 502-506. For the broader history of the *Proposals* see Walker, *op. cit.,* pp. 465-494; also Henry Martin Dexter, *The Congregationalism of the Last Three Hundred Years, As Seen in its Literature,* pp. 488, 491-494. John Wise's attacks against the proposals in his *The Churches Quarrel Espoused* (Boston, 1710) doubtlessly synthesized much of the spirit of resistance encountered when they were first recommended. Cotton Mather, *Ratio Disciplinae Fratrum Nov Anglorum* (Boston, 1726), pp. 184-185, commented that some "thought the Liberties of *particular churches* to be in danger of being too much *limited* and *infringed* in them."

posals did not give it completely away; he also recognized that changes in church and state made it necessary for them to employ what might seem to be "Presbyterian" tactics to preserve their churches and advise each other on such things as might be for the "Advantage of our holy Religion." While he was interested in preserving continuity with their ancient beginnings, he was also acutely aware that disorders which "plainly hurt the common Interest" had to be guarded against.[53] Seen in this light, Willard's interest in the *Proposals* is further evidence of the fact that his preeminent concern was to devise a system with the proper checks and balances which would preserve the cause of orthodoxy.

53. *Proposals,* Second Part, 4, 8; in Walker, *op. cit.,* pp. 488, 489.

CHAPTER SIX

ARMINIANISM

More basic for Willard than concern for the social order was his great interest in the salvation of the soul, important both for the continuing vitality of the church and the preservation of a righteous state. In fact, divine grace was a necessary precondition to every truly Christian endeavor. Nothing was more admirable to Willard than its wonders unveiled in the whole method of man's redemption, and his preaching jealously guarded the sovereignty of divine grace. But he never magnified grace to the point that he blinded his people to the beauty of holiness. Divine sovereignty and human responsibility were both parts of the eternal scheme, and though the paradox could not be comprehended by human minds it was to be preached as part of the Biblical revelation, for the secret of their harmony, he was sure, lay in the mind of God. Salvation for Willard was never a do-it-yourself project, yet he was second to none in urging the children of the covenant to do their duties. Balance was the all-important thing: "the way lyes very narrow between Antinomian and Arminian errors," he warned, "and therefore needs the greater exactness in cutting the threed true."[1]

Arminianism, named posthumously after the scholarly Dutch modifier of high Calvinism, Jacobus Arminius, was still considered one of the most dangerous of Protestant heresies. In a sense it was an ambiguous term. Arminianism seems to have developed in a number of places at the very time Arminius was advancing his ideas in Holland. An English presage of this theological trend can be detected in the late sixteenth century, and scholarly and social contacts with the Dutch strengthened it.[2] Arminian doctrines were extensively adopted by the Anglican

1. *Covenant-Keeping The Way to Blessedness,* p. 31.
2. A. W. Harrison, *Arminianism,* pp. 122ff.; Charles H. and Katherine George,

Church during the reign of Charles I, and as Puritan preachers were forced out of their positions for denouncing these errors and all hope for them was crushed with the dissolution of Parliament, the great tide of Puritan migration to America began. From the beginning, therefore, New Englanders identified Arminianism with the prelacy from which they had fled, and preachers carefully drilled their congregations on its dangers. When the temporarily victorious Puritans and Presbyterians in England gave the world a synthesis of Reformed doctrine in the Westminster Confession of Faith, New England heartily accepted it "for the substance thereof."

As Samuel Willard began to preach, Arminianism was once more ascendant in Restoration England. High Calvinism might be holding its ground in Holland and Scotland, but in England Arminians, Latitudinarians, and "reasonable" theologians had risen to positions of dominance.[3] The sects were seething with the heresy, and even Independents like John Goodwin, having embraced it, opposed the Reformed faith. New England was deeply concerned, for she still thought herself as one with the mother country. To New Englanders this theological world was the most important part of English life, and the leaders, knowing that correspondence with families and friends at "home" and that books that came with every ship from England exposed them to these winds of doctrine, understandably eyed this seething ferment of deviant ideas with dread. The fear of episcopal encroachment was ever present, and in 1679 the Reforming Synod frowned darkly at the evidences of "Will-worship" already observable in their Jerusalem. At the same time social forces and economic success in their heterogeneous society were creating a hospitable environment for sprouting a home-grown Arminianism.[4]

In coming to grips with it Willard found the covenant idea to be the most useful form with which to juxtapose truth and error. In fact, the doctrine of the covenant was basic to all of Willard's theological thought, but it came to notable expression in his early defense of orthodoxy against Arminianism.

The Protestant Mind of the English Reformation, 1570-1640, p. 67; Rosalie L. Colie, *Light and Enlightenment,* p. 15; Geoffrey F. Nuttall, "The Influence of Arminianism in England," Chapter 3 in Gerald O. McCulloh, *Man's Faith and Freedom,* p. 55.

3. Harrison, *op. cit.,* pp. 97-127, 129, 135, 161-162, 166-167; George, *op. cit.,* pp. 67-68; Colie, *op. cit.,* p. 7.

4. Cf. Bernard Bailyn, *The New England Merchants in the Seventeenth Century, passim,* for the success of the merchant class and the social changes that brought about religious alterations as the century progressed.

A Covenantal Frame of Reference

In a series of sermons in 1682 on "Covenant-Keeping the Way to Blessedness" he set forth the connection between God's promise and man's duty in the covenant of grace. The sermons were not "superva-caneous," wrote Increase Mather, for though many excellent treatises had been published on the covenant these discourses were doctrinally "Succinct, Solid, and Judicious," "Powerful and Seasonable" in their relevance, and an effective confutation of *"Arminian* tenets about Universal Redemption, Free Will, Apostacy from Grace, &c."[5]

From the day that God created man and placed him on the earth, explained Willard, echoing a long line of English Puritan and Conti-nental Reformed mentors, He has dealt with him in a covenant way, first in a covenant of works, and then when he had "utterly lost himself" by his disobedience in a "new & Gospel Covenant" with a glorious promise (Genesis 3:15). Like all covenants, God's transaction with His people was a "mutual Engagement," binding once it was made, and having conditions and consequents, the fulfillment of which was dependent upon the performance of the condition. The covenant of grace in no way annulled the covenant of works, but fulfilled it in such a way that the justice and righteousness of the first and the mercy and peace of the second "entertain each other with mutual embraces of perfect amity (Psal. 85:10,11)."[6]

The late sixteenth and early seventeenth centuries witnessed a refine-ment in federal theology, whereby the covenant of grace was conceived of more broadly as including God's purpose from eternity, or more narrowly as dealing with believers. Willard took it in the latter sense, following the lead of Westminster Presbyterians such as Samuel Ruther-ford, George Gillespie, and John Ball in speaking of two covenants: redemption and reconciliation. Though God was reconciled with the elect on the basis of the satisfaction given in the covenant of redemp-tion, the actual transaction between God and man was accomplished in the covenant of reconciliation. Both covenants spring from grace and design God's glory by the salvation of the elect through Christ, yet they

---

5. Willard, *Covenant-Keeping,* "To the Reader," an introduction by Increase Mather.

6. *Ibid.,* pp. 1-18. The standard history of the covenant theology is Gottlob Schrenk, *Gottesreich und Bund im älteren Protestantismus, vornehmlich bei Johannes Coccejus.* For the Continental influences on Puritan thought see Leonard J. Trinterud, "The Origins of Puritanism," *Church History,* XX (1951), 37-57; cf. also Heinrich Heppe, *Reformed Dogmatics,* chapters XIII and XVI. On the influence of English Puritan divines, see Perry Miller, "The Marrow of Puritan Divinity," *Pubs. C.S.M.,* XXXII (1938), 247-300; *The New England Mind. The Seventeenth Century,* pp. 374ff., 502ff.

47419

are distinct. They have different parties, God and Christ in the one, the Trinity and the mystical Christ embracing the church in the other. One is essentially a covenant of works with grace as its design, the other is grounded on gracious terms and conditions. One really had no mediator, the other of necessity made Christ the mediator. Yet the covenant of redemption, explained Willard, is the eternal background for the covenant of reconciliation, and a true believer "hath his eye alwayes upon it," for until provision was made for satisfying the claims of the law one could not hope for atonement.[7]

The covenant of grace as expounded by Willard, therefore, was the covenant of reconciliation, "that mutual engagement, in which God the Father, Son and Spirit on the one side, and His Church or People on the other side, stand engaged, in Conditions, and consequent Promises." He considered it not according to its efficacious inward and spiritual application to the elect, but more widely according to its visible and external dispensation in the ordinances, as a covenant with terms and conditions made with all those who, with their children, professed obedience to the Gospel-order and ordinances. Yet God gathered up His elect reasonable creatures out of the "rubbish" of the world in such a way, he said, that those who will not come in are left "inexcusable" and perish with greater condemnation; hence, "not only the Covenant of Works, but the Covenant of Grace too, will have to lay to the charge of all such as for abusing of it, Joh. 3.19."[8]

He touched the vital nerve of the Arminian controversy when he asked: what does it mean to keep covenant? If salvation by grace was one of the cardinal tenets of the Reformed faith, how could one assign a proper role to human effort and responsibility without infringing upon it? His answer was that the conditions of faith and obedience were not "Antecedent and Meritorious" but "connex and consequent." God did not command without giving grace; God "tells us what it is that He expects of us if we hope to enjoy Him, which (though it must

---

7. *Covenant-Keeping*, pp. 18-25.

8. *Ibid.*, pp. 24-29. Similarly in a series of sermons on *The Barren Fig Trees Doom*, p. 5, he said: "By the *Vineyard* we are to understand the *Visible* Church. It is not to be restrained to the Church of God's Elect, and Effectually Called: for though his Elect do til Conversion abide unfruitful, yet all his called ones do bring forth fruit unto him; but here is a Tree in the Vineyard that bears none, and is supposed never so to do: I know *Grotius,* to favour his *Arminian* notions, interprets the *Vineyard* to mean the *World,* and the *Fig-Tree* the Nation of the *Jews;* but, though a particular Church is sometimes resembled by a Plant, as a Vine, Psal. 80, and an Olive, Rom. 11. and the Members of it to so many Brances; yet the World is nowhere, that I know of, called in Scripture God's Vineyard, but the Visible Church is often, Isa. 5 begin 27."

be wrought efficiently by His Spirit, yet it) must be formally performed by us, Tit. 2.11,12."[9]

Such a careful scholar as Perry Miller has interpreted this to be a clever device by which a shrewd federal God incorporated the covenant of works into the covenant of grace, but Willard would have flatly denied it. "This obedience is vastly differing from that which is required in the Covenant of Works," he asserted. In the first covenant it was the antecedent condition and meritorious cause of man's blessedness, in the second it is only a consequent condition. In the first it was to be performed in man's own strength, in the second by the help of Christ. In the one perfection was required, in the other it is impossible, though God respects sincere striving after it. In the one the smallest defect meant death, in the other God covers many transgressions. In the one repentance did not count, in the other it is the way to pardon. Gospel obedience, therefore, was the fruit of faith, faith in exercise, trusting solely in the righteousness of Christ.[10]

A covenant was the best way for God to transact with fallen men, he said, for men could enjoy certainty through its terms, and God could also display His attributes, His infinite holiness and justice, and His sovereign mercy. But how far were those mercies conditional in the covenant promise? Puritans in both Englands had debated over the question whether the promises were absolute or conditional—though never in the Arminian sense of a conditional will in God that depended upon and was determined by the wills of men. John Cotton, for example, had asserted that the promises were absolute, while Peter Bulkeley stoutly affirmed that they were conditional—respecting the fact, of course, that the giving of the Spirit and regeneration were free and absolute. Willard came out strongly on the conditional side: as certainly as these mercies were conditionally propounded to Christ in the covenant of redemption they were conditional in the "visible and ministerial" dispensation of the covenant of reconciliation. "We cannot say unto any Man in particular, positively, and without any limitation you shall be saved." Like the apostles, they could preach salvation "but conditionally." But as Christ was proffered conditionally, so Christ as surety gave the power to perform the conditions.[11]

Since the covenant of grace rested upon the antecedent covenant of redemption between God and Christ in eternity, Willard explored this theme also in another series of sermons. The idea had been learnedly argued by federal theologians such as Francis Turretin and Herman

9. *Covenant-Keeping,* pp. 29-35.
10. *Ibid.,* pp. 39-42. See Miller, *New England Mind,* p. 384.
11. *Covenant-Keeping,* pp. 44-45, 50-54, 62. Cf. Larzer Ziff, *The Career of John Cotton,* pp. 41-42.

Witsius, but Willard treated the matter more popularly and reduced the speculation about this mystery to two things: the provision made for man's salvation in eternity, and the things He did in time to accomplish it. "All our speculations about the latter will be dark, short, and confused," he explained, unless they were traced back to eternity; without this "we shall neither know where our Salvation began, nor what Security there is in it, or how to act our Faith aright about it." Here was the "first Link of that Chain . . . which fastens all," and ignorance of it only afforded opportunity for "pernicious Errors" to take root. For His own glory God determined man's redemption in His eternal decree, and foreordained all the means to it from eternity, Willard explained in supralapsarian fashion. In this covenant Christ as the second person of the Trinity (not the "Christ mystical" of the covenant of grace) agreed to become the "Surety" and pay the "Price" for the elect, for the idea that all were redeemed sufficiently but only some effectively was, to Willard, nonsense.[12]

The question whether it would have been consistent with the rectoral holiness of God to pardon sin without satisfaction to His injured justice, Willard answered in the affirmative. He had ploughed through the arguments for the negative case offered by Grotius, Vossius, Voetius, Turretin, Heidanus, Owen, and Burgess, but took his stand rather with William Twisse. The necessity for the covenant of redemption, therefore, was "hypothetical" rather than absolute. "That Sin deserves it, is not to be doubted, but that God is naturally obliged to punish it so, and cannot be God unless he doth, needs further consideration." Holiness and justice were relative attributes, and punishment was to be reckoned as a work of divine efficiency, for which the rule was *"Omne opus ad extra est Contingens."* Being contingent, it was the execution of a free decree and therefore arbitrary. Perfections like mercy and grace proceed according to His good pleasure (Romans 9:18, 21-22). To those who asked why God determined to follow this way when, by virtue of His lordship, he could have pardoned without a mediator, Willard responded: who are we to call Him to account?[13]

All this covenanted in eternity explained why and how God saved in the covenant of grace. When men outwardly called willfully refused to enter the covenant of reconciliation it was their own fault, declared Willard, but those who do "actually close" with its terms do so not on their own power, but because of God. Here one could see the origin of those "absolute Promises" of the Scripture, he said, which the "Arminians so wholly deny." They were absolute because they had no de-

---

12. *The Covenant of Redemption,* pp. 3-52.
13. *Ibid.,* "To the Reader," pp. 65-92.

pending condition in the covenant of grace, for it would argue a contradiction for God to say, "I will Convert you, if you will Convert yourselves." These promises had their conditions and performance in the covenant of redemption, and were given in the Word of God to reveal the efficacy of that covenant and to assure believers of its certain fulfillment. To Willard it was logical that these promises were not of universal application, but were confined to the election of God. But this was not to induce a spirit of passivity: "Rest not contented till you have gotten some good Evidence that your Names were written in the Book of Life." They would be good spiritual frontiersmen, he seemed to suggest, if "following the stream up to the fountain" they searched for the evidences of sanctification that would lead them to conclude that they had been covenanted for and chosen in Christ. So everything depended wholly on the initiative and assistance of God, something obviously quite different from the Arminian scheme of things.

> If He should deliver us from the Law, so far as to make it a possibility for us to be saved by Grace, and yet leave us to Perish for want of the Evangelical Obedience, without which there is no Salvation, we were in a miserable state; for we can no more do this of our selves than we could the other: but it is far otherwise. That would be an *Arminian* mock Redemption; and it would be but to save us from one Hell, to throw us into a worse.[14]

And closing with another look at how "poor man" had been provided with the riches of grace in this covenant, Willard broke out into doxology.

A Quaker Arminian Attack

A vigorous Quaker missionary named George Keith overtly attacked this orthodoxy shortly after his arrival in Boston in 1688. He posted a challenge on June 21 to publicly debate the ministers of the town, but Willard and his colleagues (Allen, Moody, and Cotton Mather) had no intention of giving him the opportunity afforded by other villages to stir up controversy, and snubbed him with the terse announcement that they had neither the interest nor the time.[15] Angered, Keith replied on September 21 with ten pages of sharp criticism, and the next year published all the correspondence with a statement of doctrine in his

14. *Ibid.*, pp. 93-98, 115-119, 125, 135-141, 146-147. Willard's emphasis on endeavors can hardly be construed as going along with the tide towards Arminianism, as Perry Miller suggests; cf. *The New England Mind. The Seventeenth Century, passim*, and *The New England Mind From Colony to Province*, p. 66.
15. Ethyn W. Kirby, *George Keith (1638-1718)*, p. 52.

The Presbyterian and Independent Visible Churches Brought to the Test. The Boston ministers did not intend that Arminianism should spread through Massachusetts in this manner, and the next year Willard and his colleagues issued *The Principles of the Protestant Religion Maintained,* a spirited commentary on Keith's diatribe, particularly on the decrees, the atonement, and perseverance.

Keith declared that nowhere in the Scripture could it be found that God had reprobated any part of mankind before the foundation of the world, and charged the Boston ministers with teaching that God had made some in order to damn them. This was scandal, replied Willard and his colleagues, and it was not their doctrine; God made them for the glory of His justice, which was exalted in the damnation which they procured by their own fault. Keith seemingly did not know what he was talking about, they said, for he himself acknowledged an eternal counsel about them that perish and that Christ in His infinite justice permitted such to resist grace. They thought his assertion that God's prescience of the elect did not argue total reprobation of others was ridiculous, for if some were not elected, what was this but reprobation? They answered Keith's concern over reprobate infants going to hell for Adam's sin only by saying that they ought to commiserate them, yet they could not be helped beyond what God had purposed concerning them. These shared Adam's guilt and corruption as others, consequently they were by nature under condemnation of death; nowhere was it revealed that Christ's satisfaction applied to dying infants, but Romans 5:14 did speak of a sentence upon those who had not sinned actually.[16]

To Keith's claim that men are condemned only because they reject the light (John 3:19) the ministers replied that he should have also read verse 18: he that does not believe is condemned already. Very plainly the case was this, they said: in the first covenant men stand condemned for the breach of the law, either by imputation of Adam's sin, or by actual sins; when with the coming of the gospel Christ is offered as a way of life, and men despise Him and will not follow the light, this condemnation is added to the former, so that whereas formerly they were condemned by the law now the gospel condemns them too. Keith's conclusion that none suffer final rejection but those who reject the "Physitian," the ministers charged, made the condition of pagans (to whom Christ had not been offered) better than that of Christians.

16. *The Principles of the Protestant Religion Maintained,* pp. 74-76, 78-79. Cf. Keith, *The Presbyterian and Independent Visible Churches Brought to the Test,* pp. 76-78, 84, 88. On the Arminianism of early Quakerism see McCulloh, *op. cit.,* pp. 48-49, 62.

Men would be out of danger if Christ had but died for them and never told them of it![17]

They also crossed swords with Keith on his doctrine of universal redemption, which he sought to establish with the Scriptural designations "all," "all men," "every man," "the world," and "the whole world." The Boston ministers countered with the traditional argument that "all" did not mean all particular individuals but men of all sorts, all the elect. Keith had asserted that "all" must necessarily be as universal with respect to the death of Christ as it was with respect to the fall of Adam. Willard and his colleagues agreed, but not in Keith's sense, they said: for on this basis one would have to plead for universal salvation as well. Adam and Christ were paralleled in Scripture in many respects: Adam is a common head, so is Christ; Adam has natural seed, Christ has spiritual seed; Adam ruined all his, Christ redeemed all His; Adam's are called the world, and so are Christ's. But it had to be remembered that Christ's seed were a number selected out of the other, and though He saved "all" of His elect, they were not all the individuals of Adam's posterity, for Christ Himself spoke about those who were none of His sheep! Similarly "all" in I Corinthians 7:14 proved only that all of Christ's elect were dead and that He died for all of them, and Keith, they charged, perverted the apostle's intention in giving it a universalist interpretation. Furthermore his reference to the command of Christ to preach the gospel to all nations and the promise that this would be accomplished before the end of the world was no proof at all for universal grace, they said: many past generations had not been benefited by it, and it was slender logic to hold all mankind accountable because once in the end of the world it would be revealed to all the living. Keith's charge that the doctrines of election and reprobation made the effective use of the means of grace an absolute impossibility the ministers rebutted by the declaration that there was no more discouragement in their tenets than in his, for he also taught that only some of those who used the means were going to be saved, namely the elect.[18]

Willard and his friends also found Keith chopping at the pillar of perseverance, alleging that real beginnings of faith and sanctification could be lost. If he meant certain common preparatory works wrought in man, such as conviction of sin, they agreed. But these were not the beginnings of true justifying faith in God's elect, and Keith's citation of Scripture texts they found unconvincing. Hebrews 6:4-6, they said,

17. *Principles of the Protestant Religion,* pp. 79-83; cf. *Presbyterian and Independent Visible Churches,* pp. 88, 90.
18. *Principles of the Protestant Religion,* pp. 84-86, 88, 90; cf. *Presbyterian and Independent Visible Churches,* Chapter 6, sections 1 and 4.

referred to temporary faith, as did the parable of the seed falling in thorny and stony ground; Romans 11 related to the visible church, in which not all were true believers; the lamps in the parable of the virgins represented only outward profession, the vessels signifying the heart; and the threatening of Ezekiel 18:24f. was a conditional expression sometimes used by God to actually preserve His people by curbing their corruptions. Therefore, to suppose that the promise of preservation was hypothetical, that it depended upon human performance of a condition, was erroneous; part of the new covenant promise to believers was God's very keeping of His people from falling utterly (Jeremiah 32:40).[19]

Their work had not the least effect in silencing Keith, however, for he promptly replied with *The Pretended Antidote Proved Poyson,* dubbing the four ministers counterfeit defenders of the Protestant religion. Neither Willard nor the others made reply.

Preaching the Five Points

But literary warfare, however necessary, was never enough. And preaching, in the age of the sermon, was not only a means of edification and conversion, it was also for the defense of the faith. By the next decade New Englanders had to reckon not only with Keith, but with the Anglican interests now firmly established in Boston under royal protection, and with social forces in an increasingly heterogeneous society which were fostering a more optimistic attitude toward human nature. Willard met the rising Arminian tide with the sturdy doctrines of the generic Reformed faith—often word for word and phrase for phrase in the language of the mentors of the Puritan and the reformation age.

Predestination to him was a great theme to be preached. One New England scholar has asserted that after reading hundreds of sermons by New England Puritans he felt qualified to say that the cardinal Calvinistic doctrine of predestination was not stressed by them, and denied that they were predestinarian Calvinists, that for them salvation lay within the reach of every person who made an effort, that Christ helped those who helped themselves.[20] Not so Willard, nor perhaps many others. The decree of God, declared Willard, was absolute, not condi-

19. *Principles of the Protestant Religion,* pp. 110-112, 114-115; cf. *Presbyterian and Independent Visible Churches,* Chapter 8.

20. Morison, *Intellectual Life of Colonial New England,* p. 11. For another view, cf. Miller, *New England Mind,* pp. 402ff.; and Babette Mae Levy, *Preaching in the First Half Century of New England History,* pp. 32f.

tional; the conditions between things were not undetermined, but fixed, and the media of His decree. The decree was eternal, involved all things, foreordained them so that they passed from possibility to futurition, and was made freely according to His counsel and sovereign good pleasure, with His own glory its ultimate aim. Willard was no fatalist or necessitarian, however, for though the decree was unalterable and not frustrable, he declared, "yet this Will lays no forcible Necessity on the Creature; but only a Certainty as to the Event. . . . The Freedom of Causes by Counsel . . . [is not] . . . infringed by it, but ratified, because in it God purposes that Free Agents shall act freely." Look not too much at "instruments," therefore, he exhorted his congregation, but adore God's wisdom in all that transpires, and so bid farewell to anxiety.[21]

As one might expect, Willard's soteriological interest is evident in that he preached more on special than on general predestination. While heeding the reformers' caveat against over-inquisitiveness into the hidden ways of God, he felt that this was meant to minister consolation to God's people, and since not all were to be saved there was good reason "for everyone of us to give the more diligent heed to make sure that we be found among this number."[22] The method he recommended was the common one, the *a posteriori,* analytic, syllogistic method that reasoned from its evidences in one's life.

In underscoring God's determination of the means to this end, Willard deliberately involved himself in the great seventeenth century controversy between supra- and infralapsarians. The latter, he charged, mistakenly "fix the decree of Election upon the corrupt mass of mankind in the state of apostasy, making that the object of it, and so exclude all which went before from any consideration in Election." Aligning himself with the more speculative supralapsarians such as Perkins and Twisse, he declared that God considered men "only as *possible beings,*" and then determined the principal "media" of realizing His grand end:

> the creation or making of them; . . . the making of them men. . . .
> the creating of them upright; . . . the covenant made with
> Adam. . . . the permission of man to fall from his integrity. . . .
> the woeful state of sin and misery into which man is fallen by the
> apostasy. . . . the whole work of redemption wrought out by

21. *Compleat Body of Divinity,* pp. 91, 101-104. Cf. Philip Schaff, *The Creeds of Christendom,* I, 451; Heppe, *op. cit.,* Chapters VII and VIII; Westminster Confession of Faith, III; Benjamin B. Warfield, "Predestination in the Reformed Confessions," *Studies in Theology,* pp. 118, 121f.

22. *Compleat Body,* p. 249.

Christ. . . . the application of this redemption in calling, justifying,
adopting, sanctifying, and glorifying of them. . . ."

The means might be subordinate in execution, but they were coordi-
nate, for "God did not intend one before the other, but all together."[23] "A man upon a high Tower," Willard explained for the
average listener,

> sees an army of men passing by at one cast of his eye; but yet
> there is a succession in the Army; and they follow one another;
> God sees all things at once in the Decree in the infinite under-
> standing of his, but the things decreed by him are put into their
> several ranks and orders of being: the decree is in this respect
> compared to writing in a book, where things are written out in
> order.

That which was first in the divine intention was last in execution, "so
that by *Analysing* the works of God we find the order of his Decrees."[24]

What was the role of Christ in election? He was the means to bring it
about, not its meritorious cause. "He bought us with a price, and he
purchased heaven for us to be our possession; and redeemed us from
the curse of the law, and satisfied Justice for our offences; but he did
nothing to the purchasing of our Election: there was not buying of that
at all."[25] Christ was not the foundation of election, as Arminians
commonly declared, with grace in Christ being offered to all, making
belief or unbelief the decisive factor. The historical evangelical idea—
traceable through Wollebius and Calvin back to Augustine—was the true
view: Christ was elected as head, and believers were elected in Christ.

"Our adversaries" grant that God knows who shall be saved, personally and individually, declared Willard; but this necessarily implied that
He had foreappointed them, for all alike were naturally indisposed to
receive the offers of grace. The subjects of election, then, were a
"definite number" of particular persons, not hypothetically but absolutely foreappointed. How could one meet the opponents' charge that
this made God an unrighteous respecter of persons? Where a person is
under no obligation he cannot be so charged, he answered. Election was
like a bequest, an act of God's sovereign pleasure and grace, "and he
may bestow it where he will." It was a doctrine "ungrateful to none
that are converted." Not to love the doctrine, therefore, was a sign of

23. *Ibid.*, pp. 262-264. Cf. William Perkins, *A Christian and Plain Treatise on
the Mode and Order of Predestination and on the Amplitude of Divine Grace,* in
Works, II, 605ff.
24. *Compleat Body,* pp. 255-256.
25. *Ibid.*, pp. 264-265.

being unconverted. For believers it should be a cause for adoration and doxology: "How should it enflame, ravish, and engage our souls to him forever."[26]

Election to him logically implied reprobation, and Romans 9:22 and 11:7 proved it—so, though the Shorter Catechism did not touch on it, he followed the lead of the Larger Catechism and the Confession of Faith and developed the idea at length in his catechism sermons. John Goodwin, the English Independent, denounced reprobation as an act of injustice, the act of a judge who would see to it that execution would "not be done with hempen, but with silken Halters." To Willard it was an act of divine lordship, "the Predestination of a definite number of men for the manifestation of the glory of God's revenging justice in them." He predestined the means—desertion and condemnation—as well as the end. So it was not merely negative but also positive. Some divines, "to avoid the prejudices of men whose pride will not suffer them to acknowledge the sovereignty of God in this doctrine," he said, "go about to make this Reprobation to be nothing else but a leaving or not chusing of them"; but it was foolish to "mince" here. It did not make the case of deserted sinners any better: "if God leave them, under sin and guilt, they must needs come under condemnation." Yet Arminians, as people of ancient times (Ezekiel 33:10; Romans 9:19), Willard charged, "seek to load the doctrine with reproach, and tell the world that we teach that God made some men on purpose to damn them." But this was calumny: reprobation was not the cause of the sin for which the sinner is damned; God intended to damn none but for sin. "No man is doomed to hell and destruction, because he was reprobated, but because he was a sinner and deserved it." This is why the doctrine was to be preached, that sinners might be roused. But those uncertain of their everlasting estate were not to conclude themselves reprobates, for there was no Scriptural rule to do so. Nor should anyone become passive in the use of the means of grace, Willard declared: "there is *an who knows,* concerning you." But to the faithful assured of their election he also raised a monitory finger: "Remember there did but the Sheers go between you and others." It was a matter of doxology, therefore.

> Can Time and Eternity express Hallelujahs enough on my part to set forth the height, and depth, and length, and breadth of this love to me, in writing my name in the book of Life, who was a piece of clay in the hands of the potter, and he might, if he had seen good, have made me a vessel of dishonor.[27]

26. *Ibid.,* p. 265.
27. *Ibid.,* pp. 266-271. Cf. Goodwin, *Redemption Redeemed;* quoted in Harrison, *op. cit.,* pp. 153-154.

What God had sovereignly determined in eternity came to pass in time. There was creation, man made in the image of God, furnished with a stock of original sanctification, the bidding fair for happiness. "But behold," declared Willard, "the next News is, Man is fallen and undone." By this fall man lost all power and ability to keep the divine law and to be happy, he was deprived of his initial inherent sanctification, and no good thing was left remaining in him.[28] Willard therefore preached total depravity, and his Augustinian and Reformed heritage came out in nineteen sermons in a two-year period devoted to an exposition of this federal doctrine of original sin.

How was this apostasy and loss of primitive holiness brought about? The catechism's statement about the abuse of the freedom of the will was obviously too simple for Willard, so he led his auditors through an involved treatment of the differentiation divines commonly made between blameless and blameable causes. Blameless were the law of the first covenant, the decree of God, and the permissive providence of God. The law of God, rather than necessitating or causing the fall, only occasioned the fall as man opposed it. The foreordaining decree was an "antecedent" rather than a cause, for man's free will was not violated. The greatest difficulty, Willard had to confess, concerned God's permissive providence, for it was "not a meer suspension or cessation of divine acting, as *Arminians* and *Jesuits* dream; but hath an energy or efficacy in all those things that are done by the creature, by divine permission." So there was a "causal influence" in the action. But though God gave the trial command, ordered the temptation, provided the matter for the tempter to work upon, determined the event of the temptation, suspended His assistance, and influenced the act itself as a superior cause, yet God was morally blameless, explained Willard, for He did not command or persuade man by argument to sin (cf. Acts 2:23). The blame was to be attributed to causes instrumental (the devil—to whom he devoted two full sermons—the serpent, and the woman) and principal (Adam's abuse of free will). Since God intended to advance His glory in man's happiness by a covenant of grace rather than of works, He did not confirm him in his primitive state. Yet this had no compelling necessity on the fall: Adam, mutably good, sinned voluntarily in abusing his free will, transgressing in defect and excess.[29]

The act of our parents' first sin terminated with them, he explained, but its consequent guilt and pollution were "propagated" or mediated to all, so that all suffer sin and death. He preached not only the Augustinian idea that Adam's descendants were depraved because they

28. *Compleat Body,* pp. 155, 157-158. Cf. Canons of Dort, III, 1; Westminster Confession, VI, 2-4; Heppe, *op. cit.,* pp. 311-312ff.
    29. *Compleat Body,* pp. 177-189.

participated by union with him in the first sin, but the federal doctrine that they were guilty because they participated representatively in the first sin. Everyone was born under imputed guilt, and (contrary to the allegation of some that federal Puritans nullified the Augustinian idea with their contractual emphasis) everyone's whole nature was corrupt. Man, declared Willard, is a "creature utterly void of all goodness, and a seminary of all manner of abominations. . . . There is not the least part of any Theological good left in any of his posterity by nature." This explained why children from the cradle took so readily to evil: "Original sin is the mother, and this is the fruitful progeny of it." Just how this corruption was derived was one of the "deepest and most difficult" points of theology, Willard confessed, and all the arguments seemed obscure and unintelligible, but it was a Biblical "point of Faith" and consistent, he was sure, with the holiness and justice of God.[30] And so by their actual conduct men rendered their sinful state even more dreadful, he warned, for if "one sin is enough to damn you, how deep then will you sink, by the weight of such a company of sins as you are heaping up?"[31]

Men desperately needed to have this doctrine preached to them, for their consequent misery was, privatively, loss of communion with God, His favor and the benefits of it, and positively, subjection to God's wrath and curse, which included corporal and spiritual miseries in this life, death, and the pains of hell forever. God indeed manifested a common grace to the world, but unless sinners saw the misery of their condition they would not see the need and the preciousness of Christ. "Poor wretch!" he warned, "what dost thou mean? for a few nasty pleasures, to bring thy self into everlasting burnings?" In tones Jonathan Edwards was to use effectively a generation later Willard portrayed their fate: "you stand every moment upon the brink, and the least touch of God's angry hand, will turn you over: . . . the youngest and healthiest sinner of you all, may be in hell before morning." Yet Willard was not a sensationalist, nor a ranter striving for effect, much less a compromiser of orthodoxy appealing to the will of unregenerate man. God had prescribed the means as well as the end, and he earnestly pressed for human response to Christ. "Behold Him now coming to you in the offer of the Gospel, inviting you to come to Him, and promising you life if you do, Matt. 11.29."[32]

    30. *Ibid.,* pp. 194-212. Cf. Perry Miller's nullification thesis in his *New England Mind,* pp. 400-401.

    31. *Compleat Body,* pp. 212-216.

    32. *Ibid.,* pp. 216-245.

Moving on to the third great point of Reformed orthodoxy, Willard declared

> we are therefore here led by the hand, from the sorrowful and heart-breaking consideration of man's inexpressible infelicity by his apostasy, to the pleasant and soul-refreshing contemplation of his Anastacy, or restitution.

The fall was the foil on which God intended to draw "in most lively colors the portraiture of his rich grace" in the incarnate and redeeming Christ. But the atonement, explained Willard, was particular, not universal. Arminians proclaimed that God was minded to save through the death of Christ all who exercised their wills to believe, and the English Independent John Goodwin asserted that "squadrons" and "legions" of Scripture passages spoke of the "universality of Redemption by Christ."[33] Willard distinctly emphasized, however, that all mankind does not actually participate in the restitution (II Thessalonians 1:9; 2:11), for not only do a great many to whom this favor is offered reject it finally, God never intended or made provision in the Covenant of Redemption for the restitution of all. Reiterating many of the points he had scored against George Keith on the "all" passages of Scripture and on reprobation, he went on to state that to suppose that God had done all He could for their recovery, and that they damned themselves whether He willed or not, was directly contrary to scriptural passages about Him and the properties of the divine nature. The agreed price of redemption was for a numerous but certain number, not so many "in gross," but for "these and those by count and name." We have no reason to believe, said Willard, "that Christ would die for those for whom he would not pray. Joh. 17.9." Even the common distinction between sufficient and effectual redemption he thought was "very improper," "for though it is a great truth, that there is enough in the price that was paid to have purchased the whole number of mankind, yet to call that a Redemption which was never intended for, nor applied to the subject, is scarce intelligible." To him there was consistency among the constituent roles of redemption. "God's election, Christ's Redemption, and the Spirit's Application, carry on the same design; and consequently have the same subject." But this was not a cause for despair.

> Hope is the very life of endeavor; . . . and hope can gather spirits from the appearance of a meer possibility, a *Who Knows?* Say then to your own Souls, is there a way found out by the merciful

33. *Redemption Redeemed;* quoted in Harrison, *op. cit.,* p. 154.

God, in which sinners may be delivered from the wrath to come?
I will enquire after it, and seek to be found in it.

"Strive to enter," was the Saviour's advice, and "if you find your hearts
moved with an apprehension of your own great misery, and wrought to
a willingness to comply with the only remedy, in the Gospel way," he
exhorted, "be not discouraged, you are in a fair way to be one of that
little flock; Christ hath said, if you come to him, he will not cast you
off."[34]

A question of absorbing interest to Puritans was how a person
became a Christian. To them it was a dynamic and dramatic experience,
but it required careful definition, for by neglecting certain Scriptures,
deviants went astray in all directions. The sinner's regeneration and
conversion, Willard affirmed with the divines of Dordt and Westminster,
was accomplished by the triumph of divine grace in the soul, by the
irresistible grace of God. It followed logically from predestination and
depravity. Redemption itself put no one into the state of salvation, it
had to be applied and "made ours." God did this through the covenant
of grace, by way of compliance with necessary terms, but these terms
were wrought in man by the Holy Spirit through the instrumentality of
the Word. Though God used moral and persuasive means with His
reasonable creatures, the power to discern the excellency of the truth
and choose Christ came from the superior agent, "because in the doing
of it the blind mind must be illuminated, and the rebellious heart
subdued, Acts 26.18. And this they cannot do of themselves."[35]
Basic to this was the mystical union with Christ, rooted in the love
of God in the council of redemption, and subjectively realized within
the relationship of the covenant of grace by the Holy Spirit. It was a
"very mysterious, and most abstruse" doctrine (next to that of the
hypostatical union of the two natures of Christ), explained Willard, and
so in preaching it he waived the "divers niceties" of the scholars and
accommodated himself to "vulgar capacities." The Holy Spirit brought
this union about by illuminating the understanding with persuasive
arguments, planting saving grace in the soul, and motivating the soul to
embrace Christ by faith.[36]
A point of sharp dispute at the time was the role of human
preparatory work in all this. If enthusiasts would have none of it, and
Arminians allowed far too much to it, Reformed scholars generally

34. *Compleat Body*, pp. 246-248, 279-282.
35. *Ibid.*, pp. 424-426. Cf. Canons of Dort, III-IV; Westminster Confession of
Faith and Savoy Declaration, VIII, 8; IX, 4; XIV; XV; Heppe, *op. cit.*, pp. 510ff.
36. *Compleat Body*, pp. 428-431.

preferred to call such acts precedent rather than preparatory. True, such Puritan stalwarts as Perkins and Ames had also spoken about man's real preparation to conversion, and Willard acknowledged that there were many debates among the orthodox about whether this was a common or a saving work, yet he hoped that these controversies were "rather about terms, than the thing." All the orthodox agree, he observed, that a "new power" had to be put in man in order to believe in Christ, that in view of man's debility this could only be produced by the Spirit of God, that in this production He used means with reasonable creatures, and that He addressed Himself not only to those effectively called but also to others who develop "contritions, compunctions, convictions, &c" that never issue in the new birth. Some called this common preparatory work. But if preparatory work was understood to mean preparing and disposing the person for actual believing, this was "doubtless a saving work," declared Willard. Hence, he concluded,

> though there may be saving Qualifications in the Soul, before the *Act* of Faith be discerned, yet there are none before the *Habit* of faith is wrought. . . . And it is very certain, that all saving Qualifications are at once infused into the man, upon the great Work wrought by the Spirit in him, when he forms Christ in him, and endows him with the new Nature.[37]

Willard did not, therefore, as Perry Miller contends, go easily with the tide toward Arminianism in expanding the limits of natural ability by attributing to man a greater role in redemption.[38] He vigorously resisted it.

Some also "very mistakenly" considered the external call "Grace Sufficient," declared Willard. A blind man needed not a candle, however, but restored sight! And men spiritually dead needed more than illumination, they needed the Spirit's internal operation and the infusion of new life. The renewal of the will was the important work of the Spirit, Willard was eager to emphasize, for "eager Patrons of Free-Will" had filled the world with "unhappy disputes" about this work. He did not pursue at length the question whether the will and the understanding were two distinct faculties or one with distinct powers ("our knowledge of the nature of our own Souls is very shallow and confused," he confessed), but since judgment and election were two distinct operations of faith he inferred two diverse powers in the soul.

37. *Ibid.*, pp. 435-436.
38. Cf. Miller, *The New England Mind. From Colony to Province*, pp. 53-67, especially p. 66.

Both were depraved, however, and had to be restored alike. Thus in His renewing work the Spirit enlightened the understanding, gave the will an "irresistable spontaneity" to choose Christ, and put a "new spring" in the affections to embrace Him. Effectual calling was complete when man responded in the act of faith—faith as an effect of regeneration, not its cause. But even after one was in possession of this active principle synergism was out, for the Spirit always upheld, excited, and assisted the graces of the believer. Would you then not be deceived in your hopes, cautioned Willard, "take heed of building on a sandy bottom; . . . You see what it is to be a Believer."[39]

The fifth great point followed logically: "once in Christ . . . ever so." The Augustinian-Calvinist doctrine of the perseverance of the saints was a common target for Arminians, as Keith exemplified, and to it Willard devoted five catechism sermons in 1699. The people of God could have assurance of their eternal state and they were to strive for it, he declared. There was an assurance of state, based on the in-wrought condition that entitled one to the promise. But especially there was the assurance of knowledge, "when this state is discerned by us, and we can argue from it, to our safety." This assurance was gained by "self-reflection," in which the eye of the mind "doth not go *out* to the Promise, but *in* to find the application of the Promise." In this too the Spirit leads the soul to the Word.

> The Conscience draws its Assurance in a syllogistical way: it finds the first Proposition in the Gospel, viz. He that believes and repents shall be saved. It finds the second in the man, I have believed and repented. And draws the conclusion rationally, and surely, I therefore shall be saved.

The adjuvant instrumentality of the Word afforded certain ground for self-reflection in the first proposition of the syllogism, and the Spirit as the "supream Efficient" clarified this indited Word to the discerning understanding, enabled one to compare himself with it, and finally gave His own testimony to the soul. The result was full assurance of everlasting well-being. The assurance of one's good estate was never lost, but the confidence of one's assurance of knowledge varied as one's evidences were obscured by sin or self-examination was neglected. The highest assurance needed strengthening, yet even though there were doubtings there could be "infallible assurance," provided one made the

39. *Compleat Body*, pp. 441-449, 453-459, 461.

"endeavors" to secure it, for God worked not immediately but through means.[40]

This benefit of perseverance made all other blessings "happifying," for if a believer were to fall from grace he would lose all—"Justification, Adoption, Assurance, and everything." According to the catechism it was a privilege conferred upon them (I Peter 1:5); to Willard it was also a responsibility. "The Spirit of God, in persevering us, helps us to our duty of Perseverance." But far from conceiving of this synergistically, as Arminians did in making faith and grace mutually exclusive and limiting elements in salvation, he emphasized the divine role. Perseverance was, in sum,

> the fruit of the indwelling Spirit, in every Believer, by which he maintains the Life and exercise of all his Graces in him, so that they neither totally nor finally fail, but endure to the end of his Course, in despite of all that seeks to destroy them.

Grace was initiated, sustained, and perfected in the believer by the Spirit, who enjoined the use of means not as the "antecedent condition" of perseverance but as the means for promoting it. Grace was not self-sustaining: it was opposed by residual corruption within and attacked by formidable enemies without (Ephesians 6:12; I Peter 5:8); life therefore was a constant struggle.[41]

But though the believer might fall grievously, prompting those of "corrupt principles" to defend "the pernicious Doctrine of Apostacy of saints," he could fall from grace "neither totally nor finally," explained Willard. "Those who are once in Christ by Faith, shall never fall out of him again, because he will not suffer it to be so." Perseverance was grounded in Christ's covenant faithfulness—in His obligation to the Father in the covenant of redemption (John 6:39), and in His engagement to believers in the covenant of grace (John 3:16). This only encouraged licentiousness and carelessness, opponents of the doctrine charged. It was actually an encouragement, answered Willard. But he used the criticism to challenge the members of South Church.

> Ungodly men calumniate this Doctrine with this tendency. Let not your Example be produced to justify this Calumny. God expects that you Persevere. . . . And if you pretend to confide in this Security, and take no heed to yourselves, he may let you fall so far as shall cost you sorrow, though he do not leave you utterly to perish.[42]

40. *Ibid.*, pp. 504-507.
41. *Ibid.*, pp. 519-522.
42. *Ibid.*, pp. 522-523.

Thus perseverance, as Willard preached it, was no mere logical deduction apart from living faith. Doctrine and life, grace and faith, divine activity and human response, preservation and perseverance were closely and vitally related, though men's hopes ultimately rested only in the grace of God.

An incipient moralism was subtly supplanting New England piety as the social and religious revolution gained momentum by the turn of the century, and on May 23, 1700, Willard preached a sermon on "Morality Not to be Relied on for Life." Men owed moral obedience to God, he agreed, and with the assistance of the Spirit one could go a long way in improving his natural powers. And outward conformity to the law was not only a service to mankind, it might be an advantage to oneself, even to his eternal felicity. But morality alone still left one under the curse of eternal death, for it lacked the one important thing—covenant saving faith. Perfection was impossible for fallen man, and imperfect obedience was acceptable only in the new covenant in which the requisite was saving faith, faith that made one aware of insufficiency, and drove one to Christ for pardon and the strength to perform the new obedience as a "thank offering" to God.[43]

How careful ministers ought to be, therefore, in "preaching up moral duties," he declared.

> That it is their duty to preach them, and preach them upon their hearers, is certain; otherwise they cannot be faithful in *declaring the whole Counsel of God:* and yet if they so preach them as to revive the Covenant of Workes, to advance the Righteousness of man, and depreciate the Righteousness of Christ, they are far from being the *Ministers of Christ,* and are indeed the very betrayers of Souls to destruction, as far as in them lieth.

To him nothing did more to undermine Christianity than putting moral duties into a kind of legal dress and commending them as the "*Graces* of our Christian Religion." To do this without pointing out what was lacking was to be an "enemy of Grace" and a murderer of souls, and he would not have "such a Ministers account to give in the last day for a thousand worlds." Pride in man wanted to get credit for something, he warned, scoring the "flesh pleasing Doctrines that are at this day vended on this account." Social forces were obviously influencing religious life, and Willard was trying to stem the tide. "You live among men very Soberly & Abstemiously," he told his prosperous parishioners,

---

43. *Morality Not to be Relied on for Life,* pp. 7-24. On the revolution in New England thinking, see Joseph Haroutunian, *Piety Versus Moralism,* pp. xx, xxi, and *passim.*

you are no Drunkards, Gluttons, Gamesters, Fornicators, &c. You do no man any wrong in your commerce, you are diligent in your Callings, honest and conscientious in your traffick, zealous in the Religious observance of the duties of worship private and publick, and have the good word, and applause of your neighbors for these things: and if this be all that you can pretend to, you have your reward;... See then that now you get that one thing, else all will be lost, and your Souls perish forever.[44]

The foil for such preaching was the *haut monde* of the new world who lived lives of frivolous and wicked extravagance. Willard's Boston congregation was made up of many merchant families whose social level was rising with their economic successes. With the tightening of royal control on the province and the increase of officialdom the Anglican Church was growing, and many merchants were becoming sympathetic to the Church of England, some were even switching ties to join this communion. An inevitable concomitant was the growth of Arminian sentiment, and Willard fought to hold the line.

An Anglican Arminian Attack

George Keith, now an Anglican, precipitated another quarrel with Willard in 1703. The year before this former Quaker had returned to Boston as an equally fiery missionary for the Society for Propagating the Gospel in Foreign Parts.[45] The very first Sunday after his arrival he had declared to a "large auditory" at Queen's Chapel that one of his aims in coming was "to heal up the breach [among Protestants] if possible and be a Peace Maker,"[46] which he hoped to accomplish, it seems, by imposing upon New England the usages and polity of the Anglican Church! The next year he and his associates "chanced" to arrive in Cambridge at the time of the college commencement, and listened to the academic disputation on the question of predestination and free will. The thesis debated contained two propositions: that the divine decree was immutable, and that the reasonable creature enjoyed a liberty which was not destroyed by this. Ten days later Keith sent Willard an expostulatory letter in Latin, which Willard declined to answer as "rude & undigested talk, and a ripping up of some trite and vulgar

44. *Morality*, pp. 26-28. On the social influence of economic development on the religious life of the merchant class at the end of the century, see Bailyn, *op. cit.*, pp. 192-197.

45. Kirby, *op. cit.*, pp. 127-129.

46. Keith, *The Doctrine of the Holy Apostles and Prophets the Foundation of the Church;* quoted in Kirby, *op. cit.*, p. 129.

railleries against the Orthodox Doctrine." Written in Latin it could do
no harm, he felt, for learned men would recognize its weaknesses if it
fell into their hands. But when Keith printed an English translation of it
as *A Refutation of a dangerous & hurtful Opinion maintained by Mr.
Samuel Willard,* Willard yielded to the pressure of friends (apprehensive
about the popular rumor that Keith's arguments were unanswerable)
and published a *Brief Reply to Mr. George Keith.* Since Keith had not
only attacked him, but had "fouly represented . . . the Academy . . . as
. . . a Nursery of Error," hoping that it could be reformed to resemble
her mother in Cambridge, England, Willard sought to give a "fair
account" of the matter.[47]

Keith was a disingenuous controversialist who had long ago learned
to practice the Machiavellian rule *"fortiter calumniare, aliquid haere-
bit,"* said Willard; but the revilings of some men were a credit rather
than a reproach. His "refutation" was really a misnomer, it offered no
convincing demonstration. The thesis Keith objected to had been debated philosophically according to the principles of natural theology,
explained Willard, and all Christian academies agreed on the profitable-
ness of such logical disputations. As to the subject, the consistency of
the reality and immutability of the decree with unimpeded human
freedom was maintained by the greatest Protestant divines, asserted in
the confessions of faith, and even strenuously defended by Dominicans
against Jesuits. When Arminians like Keith obviously "seek to overthrow the Doctrine of the Absolute Decree, that so they may establish
an uncontrollable Sovereignty in the Will of man," said Willard, "we are
bound as industriously to withstand them." Reconciliation of the two
conceptions of the disputation was difficult, he admitted, but being
Scriptural they could be reasonably considered consistent, and it was
commendable to seek to demonstrate it.[48] Willard's arguments were
the same offered in his sermons—the decree was hypothetically necessary, not man's sin but his actions were determined, God concurred in
every operation of second causes as the immediate principle and whole
cause of every action and effect of the creature—and he pressed them
with logical skill and gleeful sarcasm. Considering all the facts, only one
conclusion was tenable: "the origine and cause of the Necessity of the
first sin, is more to be derived from God than from man himself," yet
the whole blame of sin is due to Adam, for in his apostasy he used his
own free will in voluntarily transgressing the command. Keith's eagerness to suppress this doctrine, said Willard, was a "notable engine" of

47. Willard, *A Brief Reply to Mr. George Keith,* pp. 1, 2, 6. Keith, *A
Refutation of a dangerous and hurtful Opinion maintained by Mr. Samuel Willard,*
p. 35.
    48. Willard, *Brief Reply,* pp. 2, 3, 7, 8.

Arminianism to subvert the truth and make the people of New England an easy prey to disseminators of "Pelagianism, Socinianism, and Jesuitism."[49] For good measure Willard threw in an appendix which blew Keith's charge of novelty to bits with a broadside from the writings of Anglican bishops Davanant and Prideaux and the creedal articles of the Church of England.[50]

Keith replied the following year with *An Answer to Mr. Samuel Willard,* a weak rebuttal in which he complained of unjust treatment and accused Willard of teaching Hobbism and Stoical necessity.[51] Willard doubtlessly recognized the futility of continuance and let his case rest without further reply. Keith on the other hand, confided that the controversy had had an excellent effect "in quieting the minds of many People in these parts and bringing them over to the Church."[52]

Arminianism continued to grow, as Jonathan Edwards observed a generation later. Yet this stalwart Calvinist and many others grew up in a tradition of orthodoxy that Samuel Willard, perhaps more than any other among the New England Puritans of the seventeenth century, had helped to preserve. Ebenezer Pemberton was right—Willard's whole ministry jealously guarded the honor of sovereign grace.[53]

49. *Ibid.,* pp. 9-16, 26-50, 52.
50. *Ibid.,* pp. 61-66.
51. Keith, *An Answer to Mr. Samuel Willard.*
52. Keith, *A Journal of Travels,* pp. 3-4.
53. Pemberton, *Funeral Sermon,* p. 68.

CHAPTER SEVEN

ANTINOMIANISM

It is difficult to determine which to New Englanders was the greater heresy, Arminianism or Antinomianism, for each went to an opposite extreme, and, as Willard observed, "the way lyes very narrow between [them]." Yet Antinomianism was particularly hateful to new world Puritans because it seized upon elements of inwardness in their faith and magnified them into positions akin to those held by odious sectaries and enthusiasts.

New England long remembered the vexatious controversy sparked by the magnetic Anne Hutchinson, and Samuel Willard had doubtlessly heard the episode recounted many times at the family hearthside at Concord. Peter Bulkeley had been one of the moderators of the Synod that condemned her, and Simon Willard had been a representative to the General Court that had disenfranchised and banished the ringleaders of the faction. At Harvard Willard had learned that Antinomianism was no upstart movement of New England origin. It plagued the Christian movement from the start, as New Testament writings revealed. The ancient Church had to grapple with Gnostic, Montanist, and Marcionite forms of it. The Middle Ages spawned the Friends of God and the Brethren of the Free Spirit. Calvin contested the Libertines, Luther and Melanchthon controverted Johannes Agricola, and the Marian exiles who had come under Continental influences on their return transplanted ideas out of which sprang up the Familists and other forms of Antinomianism in the later sixteenth and early seventeenth centuries. The error had roots that reached back through Christian history. The efflorescence of these ideas in England during the civil wars had been given perpetuity in the writings of John Eaton, Tobias Crisp, Robert Towne, Henry Denne, John Saltmarsh, Henry Pinell, William Dell, and others, and they lived on in a succession of sects such as the Seekers, Ranters, Levellers, Millenarians, and Quakers.[1]

Willard eyed Antinomianism as a distortion of essential elements in the Christian creed—such as revelation, justification, and sanctification—and in his preaching he carefully sought to preserve the balance of divine sovereignty and human responsibility, divine grace and human effort, objective revelation and ineffable experience.

Revelation

With the completion of the canon immediate revelation ceased, declared Willard, emphatically reasserting New England's historic orthodoxy. The ministers were justly apprehensive of "bottomlesse revelations" apart from the Word, convinced that "if they be allowed in one thing, [they] must be admitted a rule in all things, for . . . being above reason and Scripture, they [were] not subject to controll."[2] George Gillespie at the Westminster Assembly had neatly summarized the issue: "the written word of God is surer than any voice which can speak in the soul of a man. . . . that which we have seen described by the Antinomians as the testimony of the Spirit of the Lord, is a very unsafe and unsure evidence."[3]

But how were the ministers of New England to explain those moments when they themselves were seemingly inspired to interpret providences and to say and do things for the people's spiritual good? As a young minister at Groton, Willard posed the question in a fast day sermon. God warned His people about coming judgments through His "Ambassadors." "But Revelations cease, how then can they give us a true account of the minde of God, and his purposes of bringing judgments?" God gave a greater portion of His Spirit to ministers than to others, he answered. The Spirit extraordinarily directed their thoughts to consider His mind, revealing to them the sins of the times

1. See A. H. Newman, "Antinomianism," *The New Schaff-Herzog Encyclopedia of Religious Knowledge*, I, 196-201; Gertrude Huehns, *Antinomianism in English History*. The literature on Antinomianism and the controversy in New England is vast, but for brief summaries and bibliographies see Walker, *Creeds and Platforms*, pp. 133ff.; and Smith, Handy, and Loetscher, *American Christianity*, I, 115-123, 141.

2. John Winthrop, "A Short Story of the Rise, Reign, and Ruine of the Antinomians, Familists & Libertines, That infected the Churches of New England," in Charles Francis Adams, ed., *Antinomianism in the Colony of Massachusetts Bay, 1636-1638*, p. 177.

3. George Gillespie, "A Treatise of Miscellany Questions" (chapter xxi, 1649; Edinburgh reprint, 1844, 110); quoted by Warfield, *Westminster Assembly and Its Work*, pp. 256, 215.

and the mentality of the people, and enabling them to draw proper conclusions from comparison with parallel situations in ancient times, thereby verifying the promise of Amos 3:7. But these conclusions were to be drawn from Biblical premises, Willard was careful to indicate, for only thus were they a "sure word of Prophecie." Crying sins were answered with certain judgments, like sins brought like judgments, but always there was the explicit or implicit condition of repentance.[4] A definite distinction had to be drawn between ministers and ancient prophets as recipients of special communications, he observed several years later, but God did indeed touch ministerial hearts. How this was brought about was "difficult to apprehend," but many ministers could vouch for these "unaccountable applications."[5] It was his settled conviction, however, that with ministers as with believers in general the Spirit acted "in and with the means."[6]

In Bible times God indeed spoke extraordinarily to those whom he "made choice of," Willard explained in another catechism sermon, and these in turn imparted this revelation to others (II Timothy 3:16; II Peter 1:21), "but since the Canon is perfected such Revelation is ceased" (Galatians 1:8).[7] Man needed to have a rule even in the state of primitive integrity, how much more in the state of apostasy. Accordingly God dealt with him morally as a reasonable being with precepts, promises, and threatenings, in a covenant way (first of works, then of grace), the Old and New Testament Scriptures being the record of it. There was only one way of knowing salvation and the way of new obedience, and the Word of God, metonymically understood, was this sole and sufficient rule. Historically its communication was diverse in the various dispensations: in the patriarchal era it was by revelation through angels, inspirations, dreams, and visions passed down through the generations by tradition; from Moses to Christ God still instructed His people by revelation and tradition, but also in part by writing, as Moses and the prophets recorded the necessary parts of this revelation; but since Christ has appeared and revealed the gospel Himself and by His apostles, the canon is perfected and the whole mind of God as it concerns man's end is there revealed. God now deals with men only through His written Word. Only what God has revealed belongs to this rule of faith and life, and men are severally forbidden to add to it. God could still communicate this knowledge by immediate revelation, but He has chosen to limit himself to this sufficient Word. Therefore,

4. *Useful Instructions*, p. 47.
5. *Barren Fig Trees Doom*, p. 107.
6. *Compleat Body of Divinity*, p. 571.
7. *Ibid.*, p. 28. For a synthesis of the thought of the Reformation age on revelation and Holy Scripture, see Heppe, *Reformed Dogmatics*, pp. 12ff.

Willard exhorted the people of Boston, "Read much in it, Ponder much on it, and Pray much over both; [for] by this means we shall be directed aright, and kept from mistakes, and Soul Destroying errors."[8]

One of these soul-destroying errors was that one could know of his salvation by immediate revelation, without respect to the Scriptures, and that this could be as clear "as the voyce of God from Heaven to Paul."[9] Though the knowledge of what concerned one's "eternity" was the most desirable, this was never known by immediate revelation divorced from the means, Willard emphasized.[10] Convictions about one's election and justification did not come to the soul in lightning flashes, God created them in orderly fashion—through sermons which expounded the way of salvation to the mind, which in turn activated the will and the affections; and through lengthy self-examination induced by regular use of the means of grace. In fact, the secret of election might remain "underground a great while, before it rise and break out in effectual calling."[11] There were elements of inwardness in the Puritan tradition that obviously needed to handled circumspectly. Some thought that John Cotton, upon whom the Hutchinsonians doted, had come dangerously close to error in declaring that one might know of his spiritual state by an inner sense of life, like a woman in pregnancy; but Cotton had not stopped there—he went on to affirm that other signs were also required. Moving more explicitly in the tradition of William Ames, who had meticulously codified the tests of grace, Willard affirmed that the truly blessed man could gain such knowledge only by observing concomitant effects in one's life.[12] Over against the Antinomian boast that those who had the seal of the Spirit could judge the certainty of the election of others, Willard affirmed the orthodox conviction that the secret and internal new birth of the Spirit was known directly and infallibly only by God, and by the person himself "without immediate revelation," and the only assurance others could have of it was the evidence of "charity" which argued from "apparant fruits" to the secret and hidden root.[13]

Thus, by a self-imposed limitation God restrained His sovereign omnipotence, declared Willard. Choosing to reveal Himself through the written Word, He commissioned frail and sinful men to be His ambassa-

8. *Compleat Body*, pp. 10-33.
9. "A Catalogue of such erroneous opinions as were found to have been brought into New England," in Winthrop's "Short Story," reprinted in Adams, *op. cit.*, pp. 118-119.
10. *Child's Portion*, p. 90.
11. *Mercy Magnified*, p. A3 recto.
12. *Truly Blessed Man*, p. 100. Cf. Ames, *Marrow of Sacred Divinity*, pp. 131-132.
13. *Brotherly Love Described and Directed*, pp. 223-224.

dors and evangelical ordinances to be the medium of this communication.[14]

Justification

The preaching of salvation was distorted by over-estimating the function of faith, but also by over-emphasizing the sovereignty of grace. If Arminians erred in the former, Antinomians did in the latter by exalting divine grace to such a height that they lost sight of the relevance of faith. To Willard the doctrine of justification by faith was one of the main articles of religion, and a right conception of it was as necessary in making a "sound and stable Christian as any one thing in Religion." But it had become such an "apple of contention" and a "ball of controversy" that there was "need for care to be well established in it."[15]

Willard's high view of the doctrine reflected the Reformed consensus. But there was a literature extant which sought to scuttle this historic principle. "To be justified by faith, is to be justified by workes," averred New England's earlier Antinomians. "The faith that justifieth us is in Christ, and never had any actuall being out of Christ. . . . We are competely united to Christ, before, or without any faith wrought in us by the Spirit. . . . To say that we are justified by faith is an unsafe speech, we must say we are justified by Christ."[16] The "free justification by Christ alone," rhapsodized John Eaton, "cannot bee beeleeved or enjoyed by this justifying faith, but by looking into the gaping wounds of Christ."[17] Reflecting on this ineffable experience, Henry Pinnell wrote, "now (and never till now) did I know what Justification is. . . . I understood the notion of it long since, I mean Notionally. . . . but it was infinitely short of this, for this was so glorious, excelent and transcendent that it is impossible for me to express it."[18] The republication of Tobias Crisp's *Christ Alone Exalted* in 1690, and the recrudescence of Antinomianism in England,[19] gave the orthodox fresh concern, for in seeming to magnify the grace of God this doctrine was as dangerous as it appeared plausible.

14. *The Best Priviledge,* pp. 13-14.
15. *Brief Discourse of Justification,* p. 7, and "To the Reader."
16. "Unsavoury speeches confuted," in Winthrop's "Short Story," reprinted in Adams, *op. cit.,* p. 125.
17. John Eaton, *The Honey-Combe of free justification by Christ alone* (1642); *The Discovery of the most Dangerous Dead Faith* (1622-1644), p. 76; quoted in Huehns, *op. cit.,* p. 41.
18. Henry Pinnell, *A Word of Prophecy,* p. 12; quoted in Huehns, *op. cit.,* p. 50.
19. Crisp's sermons, preached in the years of the civil war (1642-43), were

The doctrine of justification, "not a little undermined & depraved in the present age," declared Willard in 1698, needed to be "defended by all such as love the honour of our Lord Jesus Christ."[20] Justification belonged to the second part of the Spirit's applicatory work; a believer was united with Christ in effectual calling and put in possession of the redemption wrought by Christ, and experienced justification as one of the purchased benefits. It included pardon for all one's sins and acceptance as righteous in Christ.[21] Antinomians, however, confidently spurned all petitions for pardon. "The child of God need not nor ought to ask pardon for sin . . . it is no less than blasphemy for him to do so."[22] "A man must take no notice of his sinne, nor of his repentance of his sinne."[23] "If a man know himself to be in a state of grace, though he be drunk, or commit murder, God sees no sin in him."[24] Willard took issue with such loose attitudes toward repentance. No sin of the justified person could ever bring him into judgment, he explained, but the justified person was under a covenant of grace that had sanctions. God required obedience of His people, though they were not under law but grace. By their sin they provoke Him, and "they shall smart for it."[25] It was quite wrong to say that God was never angry with His children;[26] sometimes God hides His face from them until they are brought to the brink of despair—and this was not legal prosecution but according to the covenant of grace. Don't expect pardon, he told New Englanders, until by "thorough and soaking Repentance" you renew your covenant by faith in Christ. Unless you discover the justice as well as the grace of God, "your foundation is sandy, and your conscience will deceive you."[27]

God accepted believers as righteous by virtue of the evangelical righteousness of the covenant of grace procured by Christ's perfect obedience to the law. Christ's righteousness was the meritorious and

printed in 1646, and reprinted by his son in London in 1690. Cf. Daniel Neal, *The History of the Puritans,* III, 28.

20. *Compleat Body,* p. 463.

21. *Ibid.,* pp. 461-463. For the orthodox teaching of the Reformed tradition reflected in Willard, see Heppe, *op. cit.,* pp. 543ff.

22. An antinomian tenet summarized by Thomas Gataker, *Antinomianism Discovered and Confuted* (London, 1652), quoted in *New Schaff-Herzog Encyclopedia of Religious Knowledge,* I, 198.

23. "A Catalogue of erroneous opinions," in Winthrop's "Short Story," quoted in Adams, *op. cit.,* p. 115.

24. Gataker, *op. cit.;* quoted in *New Schaff-Herzog Encyclopedia of Religious Knowledge,* I, 198.

25. *Compleat Body,* pp. 463-466.

26. *A Declaration against the Antinomians* (1644); quoted in Huehns, *op. cit.,* p. 8.

27. *Compleat Body,* pp. 466-467.

material cause of the believer's justification. Christ mediatorily satisfied
the condition and the penalty of the first covenant, thereby procuring
pardon by His passive obedience and eternal life by His active obedience. Briefly stated, justification was a divine contrivance whereby
justice and mercy shone together in the fulfillment of all the provisions
of the covenants of suretyship, works, and grace.[28]

It was by imputation, Willard was careful to emphasize, that Christ's
righteousness became the believer's. Antinomians sometimes boasted of
identification with Christ in terms that virtually affirmed an infusion of
Christ's grace and righteousness, so that God could see no sin in the
believer at all. "The power of the spirit . . . finds him nothing but a
lump of sin, and makes him the righteousness of God in Christ,"
declared Paul Hobson; "in all your lowest acts Christ acts as well as in
your highest."[29] But without this principle of imputation, Willard
claimed, the "whole Fabrick" of justification would fall, and it was
necessary to "fight" for it against "Armies of Adversaries." Reason
itself dictated that the righteousness of Christ had to be imputed, he
argued: an individual's actions and passions terminate in himself, and
cannot be done or suffered by another. Justification was conferred
"whiles in many things we offend all."[30]

When was the believer justified? In their eagerness to magnify
sovereign grace and strip from man any possibility of work righteousness in faith, Antinomians pushed justification back into eternity and
equated it with the decree of God. "A man is united to Christ and
justified without faith, yea from eternity," it was said.[31] "God tied
himself irrevocably then to lay iniquity upon Christ, even from all
eternity," Crisp declared; "then he did it in his own determinate
counsel."[32] The issue was not a scholastic supralapsarian puzzle, it
touched a vital area of the Christian faith, and Willard carefully explained that "in the days of eternity" in the covenant of redemption
there was a transaction between the Father and the Son whereby the
elect "were appointed to obtain pardon and eternal life through this
merit of [the Son]"; at Christ's resurrection there was another time
"when there was a solemn act of Justification past for, or in behalf of
all these . . . Rom. 4:25"; but there is a time in which the elect are
personally without grace and children of wrath (e.g., the Ephesians

28. *Ibid.*, pp. 470-474. In this, as in his other positions, Willard reflected the
Reformed consensus; Heppe, *op. cit.*, pp. 546ff.
29. Paul Hobson, *Practical Divinity*, p. 17; quoted in Huehns, *op. cit.*, p. 44.
30. *Compleat Body*, pp. 474, 476, 477.
31. Summarized by the English heresiographer, Ephraim Pagitt, *Heresiography*
(1662), p. 124; quoted in Newman, *op. cit.*, I, 201.
32. Crisp, *Christ Alone Exalted*, p. 345.

before their conversion, years after the resurrection), and he concluded
that they were actually justified at the moment of faith.[33] Willard
sought to resolve the issue, therefore, not by proposing an antithesis
between justification in eternity and justification in time, but by
making the prevailing distinction between the eternal appointment,
Christ's procurement, and the temporal application of justification at
the moment of faith.

The value and function of faith was clear: it was the instrumental
cause of justification. "To affirme there must be faith on mans part to
receive the Covenant is to undermine Christ," cried the Antinomians;
"there can be no true closing with Christ in a promise that hath a
qualification or condition expressed."[34] Thus they sought to "spoile
man of all matter of glorying."[35] But it was clear, declared Willard,
that a "reception" of Christ's righteousness was required to enjoy
justification. In effectual calling "wee accept of and imbrace Jesus
Christ as he is offered to us in the Gospel," and Christ's benefits and
His person go together.[36]

The task of preaching then was to urge people to believe. The
Antinomians were wrong in asserting that "none are to be exhorted to
believe, but such whom we know to be the elect of God, or to have the
Spirit in them effectually."[37] Willard kept divine initiative and human
responsibility in balance. "Jesus Christ is in the general promise offered
to every one in particular, that is priviledged to hear it, upon a Gospel
condition," he declared; thus every creature should be exhorted to
believe. One may safely argue, "I am herein concerned, I may come if I
will, the invitation is made to me, why then should I neglect to accept
it, or shut myself out by unbelief?" True, God must "both *perswade
and Enable them*" to do it, but they must do it; "and if they refuse it,
it is an article against them."[38] Carefully steering between the Cha-
rybdis of Arminianism and the Scylla of Antinomianism, he underlined
the fact that faith was not a work but a necessary instrument that
appropriated the righteousness of Christ. It was one of the graces
inwrought by the Spirit; it was never alone, but it alone justified.
"Faith is the only Grace in us, which is fitted to receive the Lord Jesus
Christ, and His Righteousness on the Gospel offers."[39] Two things had

---

33. *Brief Discourse of Justification*, pp. 69-71.
34. "A Catalogue of erroneous opinions," in Adams, *op. cit.*, pp. 106, 107.
35. Robert Towne, *The Assertion of Grace*, p. 123; quoted by Huehns, *op.
cit.*, p. 41.
36. *Compleat Body*, p. 478.
37. "A Catalogue of erroneous opinions," in Adams, *op. cit.*, p. 102.
38. *Brief Discourse of Justification*, pp. 89, 103; *Compleat Body*, pp.
478-479.
39. *Brief Discourse of Justification*, p. 107; *Compleat Body*, p. 481.

to be remembered: "the sinner never struck one stroak to the procuring of his own Justification, or to his deserving to have this Righteousness of Christ imputed to him, it is all Christ's"; but the "freeness of Imputation" did not eliminate the "condition of believing which is required in the Gospel Covenant."[40] God made the condition as well as the gift. Here then was a gospel that could be preached, and he did it with urgency.

> Consider, This Righteousness of Christ is freely held forth and offered unto you in the Gospel; yea, the Lord Jesus Christ is earnestly soliciting and wooing you to accept of it: it will therefore be your own fault if at last you shall go without it: God himself provided it, Jesus Christ hath wrought it out, and there now wants nothing else but your cordial accepting of it to make it yours.[41]

How could one know that he was justified? By soul scrutiny: "Have we received it by Faith?"[42]

Sanctification

Faith alone justified, but faith never stood alone, declared Willard. [43] It evidenced its genuineness in a sanctified life. A Christian was to perfect the graces of God within by the same sovereign grace that justified him; he was saved from the power as well as the penalty of sin.

At this point also Antinomians joined issue. It was "a fundamentall and soule-damning errour to make sanctification an evidence of justification," they charged; wherever this was championed by the ministers, "in that Church there is not sufficient bread."[44] Sanctification was "nothing at all esteemed by God."[45] "Whoever you are, that go by signs and marks, drawn from sanctification," declared Crisp, "you will be puzzled, if you deal faithfully with your own spirits"; the important thing was the "voice of the Spirit of God to a man's own spirit" and the voice in the spirit of man "as an echo."[46]

All the orthodox acknowledged, Willard asserted in his sermons on covenant keeping in 1682—and it was to be maintained as a "grand

40. *Brief Discourse of Justification*, pp. 78, 72.
41. *Ibid.*, p. 130.
42. *Compleat Body*, p. 481.
43. *Brief Discourse of Justification*, p. 107.
44. "A Catalogue of erroneous opinions," in Adams, *op. cit.*, pp. 119, 123.
45. "A Declaration Against the Antinomians and their doctrine of Liberty .... These being the Antinomian Conclusions as Understood ... ;" quoted in Huehns, *op. cit.*, p. 8.
46. *Christ Alone Exalted*, II, 78, 93.

Pillar" over against "Antinomianisme" which would "exterminate New-Obedience from this Rule"—that besides the promise on God's part there was a duty on the believer's part, faith's evangelical response to divine mercy. Such obedience was the fruit of faith, "Faith in exercise, animating, quickening and improving all the Graces of Sanctification to their proper actions." Far from being legal work, its evangelical nature was exhibited in love for the divine commandments and endeavors to conform to the whole known will of God, contrite consciousness of failure and reliance on grace for acceptance.[47] This sanctification, he explained in a catechism sermon later, was a divinely bestowed benefit which changed a believer's life by renewing the image of God in him by an infusion of graces, affecting the whole man (soul, spirit, and body) in the process. It was a subjective experience which involved effort on man's part, the Spirit assisting him.[48] It quite definitely included repentance. "There are those who . . . charge those that press it on their People for being Legal Preachers," he explained,

> but such will find their hopes to deceive them, and finally fall short of the Salvation they promise themselves; For tho' it be a Truth, that everyone that truely Believes in CHRIST shall be saved; yet it is alike true, whosoever really Believes in CHRIST, hath also Repented, and turned from Sin to God. And would we not lose our expectation at last; let us carefully see to this.[49]

In repentance the Spirit makes sin bitter to the believer, gives him a new power to resist it, and furnishes him with the resurrection power of Christ so that once again he serves God with new life. All this comes to expression in grateful obedience to God, so that

> we love God and His Laws, . . . our Joy or Delight acquieseth in Him and in His Law. . . . we . . . count it our Honour to . . . pay Obedience to His Commands . . . [and] our desires are prest in longing after Strength or ability to serve Him.[50]

The norm of sanctification, therefore, was the law of God. Antinomians explicitly denied this "Ruling Use of the Morall Law unto Christians under the Gospel,"[51] commonly referred to in the Reformed tradition as the third use of the law. Eaton rhapsodized that Christians

---

47. *Covenant-Keeping*, pp. 2-5, 34, 39, 40-41. Cf. Heppe, *op. cit.*, pp. 565f.
48. *Compleat Body*, pp. 491-493, 495.
49. *Ibid.*, p. 801.
50. *Ibid.*, pp. 497-498, 801-802, 804-805.
51. John Sedgewick, *Antinomianisme Anatomized*, or a glasse for the Law-lesse who deny the Ruling Use of the Morall Law unto Christians under the Gospel (1643); cited by Huehns, *op. cit.*, pp. 37, 40, 173.

were not only emancipated from the "schoolmasterlike government and pedagogical whipping" of the law, but also from the law as a moral guide.[52] "It remains a Rule, so farre as we are in the flesh," declared Thomas Collier, "I mean in the knowledge of Christ after the flesh, but as God writes his Lawes in the hearts of his people . . . so shall they live above the Law in the Letter, even of the Gospel, yet not without it, for they have it within them . . . and so they are a Law to themselves."[53] This is exactly what Willard and his colleagues feared. The liberty of the Christian, warned Willard, "is not (as vain men would have it) a freedom to live as they list; a liberty discharging them from holy Obedience to the commanding power of the Law of God." They were indeed freed from bondage to the law, but not from its "regulating power" as the "directory" of Christian life.[54]

With the echoes of the pamphlet war between Presbyterians and Independents in England rebounding all over New England, Willard preached a sermon on evangelical perfection, reemphasizing that it was "purely Antinomian" to assert that "the Law Moral no longer binds them under the duty of conformity to it, but that upon their believing in Christ they are freed from any such engagement." Why did the children of God have the "title of Obedient" if there were no duties? They were to glorify God and enjoy Him, and the evangelical commands of the covenant were designed to enable them to enjoy this blessedness. By keeping them believers were to press on to perfection.[55] Justification by faith in Christ did not make void the law but established it, he asserted in another sermon that same year. An "accurate and distinct enquiry" into the matter, he believed, was necessitated by the disputes of the time, for while "some in pretence of honouring free Grace, despise the Command, and open a door of Licentiousness; . . . others to avoid this, verge as much to the Contrary extream, and bring in a New-Covenant of Works."[56] This Neonomian reaction to Antinomianism affirmed that after conversion man's sincere imperfect good deeds were accounted as satisfying the law through the merits of Christ.[57] Willard wisely sought to avoid both extremes by giving both the law and the gospel their dues. In answer to "invectives" spread around that because New Englanders were not Arminians they must be

52. *Honey-Combe of free justification*, pp. 85-86; cited by Huehns, *op. cit.*, pp. 39, 40.

53. *Marrow of Christianity*, p. 68; cited by Huehns, *op. cit.*, p. 53.

54. *Child's Portion*, p. 23.

55. *Evangelical Perfection* (bound with *The Fountain Opened*), p. 177. On the English background, see Olive M. Griffiths, *Religion and Learning*, pp. 99ff.; Miller, *The New England Mind: From Colony to Province*, pp. 219f.

56. *The Law Established by the Gospel*, "Christian Readers."

57. Griffiths, *op. cit.*, p. 101.

Antinomians, and that because they gave the law its proper authority they undermined the gospel, Willard laid down the emphatic thesis: "THAT THE DOCTRINE OF EVANGELICAL JUSTIFICATION IS SO FAR FROM VACATING THIS LAW, THAT IT DEFERS TO IT THE GREATEST HONOUR THAT CAN BE THOUGHT OF." Christ grants righteousness through faith, having satisfied the demands of the law, but the gospel still requires believers to render obedience, and nowhere encourages men "to live as they list." He found the whole decalogue reinforced in the New Testament, especially in the Epistles. Holy living was so often referred to in the Scriptures because sanctification was the divinely intended consequence of justification. The Spirit, along with faith, puts sanctifying graces into believers. He leads them to Christ for grace and strength, He puts a holy fear in them and offers motives to excite it, and helps them to renewed acts of repentance and faith when they fall short. Thus the law returns to its original function as the believer, animated by grace, renders new obedience to his Redeemer under the guidance of the law. Once this was understood, he said, the orthodox in New England could not justly be charged "either with NEONOMIANISM or ANTINOMIANISM."[58]

Sanctification to him meant also the imitation of Christ, for responsiveness to Christ had as its ultimate aim resemblance to Christ. They erred greatly, he explained, who thought of Christ only as a pattern, but, taking his cue from the previous generation's codification of Antinomian errors, he reiterated that those who thought they could have the benefit of Christ's earned righteousness "and will not imitate him," deceived themselves.[59]

Willard found sacramental reinforcement for all this in the Lord's Supper. As they came to the holy table he urged them to make this covenant new obedience part of their self-examination. By this they would prove their faith and love.

> Have we made free choice of the Law of God for the Rule of our Life? . . . Do we regulate our Lives carefully by the Law? . . . Do we try ourselves by this Rule? . . . Do we take pleasure in doing the Will of God? . . . Do we shun the Temptations to Sin? . . . Do we mourn under the constant sense of our Concupiscence?[60]

New England moved into the eighteenth century with the feeling that one of the favors of God to His "New English-Israel" was the fact that the Antinomian errors which had bred such contentions among the

58. *Law Established by the Gospel*, pp. 6-7, 13, 17-22, 25-27, 29-32, 39.
59. *Compleat Body*, p. 362. Cf. "A Catalogue of erroneous opinions," in Adams, *op. cit.*, p. 96.
60. *Compleat Body*, p. 880.

nonconformists across the sea produced no such vitiating effects on this side of the Atlantic.[61] Their greater success may be explained in part by the ministerial earnestness in grappling with the major issues, evidenced so conspicuously in Willard's preaching. "How thoughtful [he was]," eulogized Pemberton at his funeral, "least Grace should be abused in Wantonness! And how careful in all his Dispensations to guard against this Mystery of Iniquity, and to set out the Glory of Divine Grace, and the Beauty of Holiness in their proper Lustre and admirable Harmony."[62]

61. Cotton Mather, *A Pillar of Gratitude*, p. 23.
62. Pemberton, *Funeral Sermon*, p. 68.

CHAPTER EIGHT

THE BAPTISTS

The emergence of the Baptists, "Anabaptists" as they were derisively labelled in Willard's generation, was another threat to the religious establishment of Massachusetts. Arising out of the same ferment of ideas that had given birth to a similar movement earlier within English Independency, these Puritan left-wingers challenged New England orthodoxy at three fundamental points: infant baptism, liberty of conscience, and the relation of church and state.[1] From the first Massachusetts eyed them as a menace to the success of her enterprise. Ever since their rise a hundred years earlier Anabaptists had been "incendiaries" of commonwealths and "infectors of persons" in religion, declared the General Court in 1644 (Willard's father representing Concord), and

1. For a convenient summary see Smith, Handy, and Loetscher, *American Christianity*, I, 143-146. The Puritan context of the English Baptists has been stressed by Winthrop S. Hudson in "Baptists Were Not Anabaptists," *The Chronicle*, XVI (1953), 171-179, and in "Who Were the Baptists?," *Baptist Quarterly*, XVI (1955-56), 303-312. On the other hand, Ernest A. Payne, while distinguishing Baptists and Continental Anabaptists, argues a connection in "Who Were the Baptists?" *Baptist Quarterly*, XVI (1955-56), 339-342. James D. Mosteller argues that they stand in the same tradition and represent the same general type of Christianity: "Baptists and Anabaptists," *The Chronicle*, XX (1957), 3-27, 100-114. Similarly Robert G. Torbert indicates that the Baptists were spiritual descendants of some of the Anabaptists and appropriated some of their heritage: *A History of the Baptists*, pp. 35-55, 59-83, 219. For New England Baptist emphases on baptism, liberty, and separation of church and state see Isaac Backus, *A History of New England*, I, 41ff.; David Benedict, *A General History of the Baptist Denomination in America and other Parts of the World*, p. 368; Champlin Burrage, *The Early English Dissenters*, I, 365; Robert G. Torbert, *op. cit.*, p. 221; and R. E. E. Harkness, "Principles of the Early Baptists in England and America," *Crozer Quarterly*, V (1928), 440-460.

accordingly decreed banishment for every obstinate opposer of infant baptism and theocratic magistracy.[2]

Safe in Rhode Island, the renegade Roger Williams encouraged the Baptist cause with a barrage of acrimonious pamphlets against the New England order, but Massachusetts resolved to stick to its guns.[3] When John Clark, Obediah Holmes, and John Crandall held an unauthorized religious service in 1651 at the home of an aged Baptist in Lynn, they suffered the consequences: whipping, fines, and imprisonment. Clark published such a damaging account of the episode in his *Ill Newes from New England* on his return to England the next year, that Sir Richard Saltonstall, one of the first magistrates of Massachusetts, dispatched an anguished letter from England to pastors John Cotton and John Wilson, but the ministers in a prompt reply whitewashed the whole proceeding.[4] The very next year Henry Dunster, Harvard's first president, refused to present his son for baptism and shortly thereafter came out openly for believer's baptism.[5] He was dismissed, but the cause of orthodoxy had suffered a severe blow. As their numbers grew the Baptists became more confident. It was not until 1663 that the first Baptist Church in Massachusetts was organized on the frontier at Rehoboth, but in the spring of 1665 Thomas Gould (who had been suspended from the Charlestown Church in 1656 for refusing baptism for his infant child, walking out during baptisms, and holding private services in his own house) boldly organized his own schismatics and recent immigrants into a Baptist Church in Boston itself. Heedless of churchly admonitions to attend properly ordered worship, he was finally excommunicated, and the provoked magistrates (as soon as the King's commissioners had left) sentenced his fellow Baptists with disenfranchisement, fines, and imprisonment. On his release from prison the intrepid Gould retreated with his associates to Noodles Island in the harbor, where they reestablished their meetings.[6]

To stem the Baptist advance a public disputation was held at Boston's First Church in the spring of 1668, but it was ineffective. Increasingly alarmed over the threat to ecclesiastical and civil order as well as the dissemination of heresy, the General Assembly finally

2. *Mass. Records*, II, 85.

3. Cf. Williams, *The Bloudy Tenent of Persecution* and *The Bloody Tenent yet more Bloody*.

4. John Clarke, *Ill Newes from New England*. Cf. Backus, *op. cit.*, I, 173-200.

5. Backus, *op. cit.*, I, 228-229; Jeremiah Chaplin, *Life of Henry Dunster: First President of Harvard College* (Boston, 1872), Chapters 9-15; Torbert, *op. cit.*, p. 222.

6. Henry Melville King, *Rev. John Myles and the Founding of the First Baptist Church in Massachusetts; Diary of John Hull, A.A.S. Trans. and Colls.*, III, 219; Backus, *op. cit.*, I, 284-285, 288ff.

sentenced their leaders to banishment—but they refused to move.[7] The Court did not give up, however, for when a group of citizens petitioned moderation at the fall session, it levied fines on the petitioners. When the next spring rigorous Governor Richard Bellingham received a letter from the eminent English divines Goodwin, Owen, and Nye, urging Massachusetts in the interest of their common cause in England to suspend punishment of dissent, the Court still stood resolutely by its decision. When the more moderate John Leverett succeeded Bellingham in 1673, however, external pressures were relaxed, and William Hamlit wrote reassuringly to a friend in 1674: "The church of the baptized do peacably enjoy their liberty."[8] Sadly, the orthodox John Hull noted in his diary the next year: "This summer, The Anabaptists that were wont to meet at Noodle's Island met at Boston on the Lord's Day."[9]

Willard, with his fellow clergymen, eyed these developments with dismay and concern; and shortly after settling in Boston he discussed these disorderly "Anabaptist" meetings with the Rev. Joseph Rowlandson and the Rev. Thomas Shepard at a conference at Sewall's home. If ministers and magistrates only agreed and cooperated, they thought, the magistrates would see the necessity of handling them. Unless all the children of the country were baptized they felt that religion would come to nothing.[10]

But the Baptists became bolder. They built a house in Boston in 1679 which was not designated as a place of worship until its completion. The more rigorous Simon Bradstreet had succeeded Leverett as governor, and the leaders of the Baptist society were haled before the May meeting of the Court to answer to a hastily enacted law against unauthorized use of such houses for worship. But the Baptists countered that they had built the house before the enactment of the law, and they had occupied it on the strength of the king's 1679 demand for liberty of conscience. Nonetheless, the Court ordered the marshal to nail up the doors of the meetinghouse. Not to be outdone, the Baptists met in the church yard. As soon as the doors were opened, they again met inside, despite new Court orders.[11] Not daring to defy the king any further, the Court gave up further attempts at suppression by force.

7. *Diary of John Hull, A.A.S. Trans. and Colls.*, III, 226-227; *Mass. Records*, IV, Part II, 1661-1674, 373-375; Backus, *op. cit.*, I, 300-301.

8. Backus, *op. cit.*, I, 304-305, 314-317, 319-320, 327.

9. *Diary of John Hull, A.A.S. Trans. and Colls.*, III, 238.

10. Sewall, *Diary, 5 M.H.S. Colls.*, V, 30.

11. Backus, *op. cit.*, I, 382-384, 388-391; Hutchinson, *Hutchinson Papers*, II, 259.

Zion's walls had been breached, and reviewing the generally deterio-
rating situation the Reforming Synod sadly lamented:

> such Anabaptists as have risen up among us, in opposition to the
> Churches of the Lord Jesus, receiving into their Society those
> that have been for scandal delivered unto Satan; yea, and im-
> proving those Administrators of holy Things, who have been (as
> doth appear) *Justly* under Church Censures, do no better than set
> up an Altar against the Lord's Altar. [12]

They resolved to continue the battle, but with other tactical weapons.

The Battle of the Pamphlets

The skirmish began in 1680 with Increase Mather's publication of
The Divine Right of Infant-Baptisme, in which he charged that none
had scrupled against the traditional Scriptural doctrine of infant baptism until "those execrable persons in *Germany* . . . led the dance," and
denounced their limitation of membership to baptized believers, the
acceptance of an uneducated ministry, insolence and other irregulari-
ties. [13]

Immediately shoemaker John Russel, the Baptist minister at Wo-
burn, responded with *A Brief Narrative*[14] in which he asserted that it
was God who had moved them to covenant together as a church, and
thus in spite of abuse to names, liberties, and estates, they continued to
grow. His argument in brief was that they were not opposed to
government itself, for they had bravely fought in the Indian War;
neither did they deny other congregations the right to be called true
churches, though they did affirm that only visible saints should be
baptized and that baptism itself was a nullity; nor were they against
learning as such, yet they did not believe that the Spirit was locked up
within the narrow limits of college learning or that office in the church
should be reserved only for those so trained. In a preface six English
Baptist ministers observed that it seemed strange that, unlike their
counterparts in England, New England Congregationalists should exercise the very severity from which they themselves had fled earlier.
Surely for Protestants to persecute those who were under the same
divine rule, they chided, was more unreasonable than Catholic cruelties.
If New Englanders would rid themselves of prejudice, cease abusing

12. Walker, *Creeds and Platforms,* p. 428.
13. Increase Mather, *The Divine Right of Infant-Baptisme,* pp. 15, 26, 21.
14. London, 1680.

power, and practice the Saviour's golden rule, they would have more compassion for these Christian friends.[15]

This scribbling complaint the Massachusetts clergy would have preferred to ignore, but they could no longer do so. The attitude of English dissenters had to be reckoned with as well as that of the king's counselors, and in New England itself sentiment against suppression was growing. Silence would have been misconstrued as admission of guilt, deceiving the simple, and three thousand miles away the report would have been received with the same credulity afforded the Baptist letters. Someone had to set the record straight, and the task was given to Samuel Willard.

He wrote as "an Historian in point of Truth and error," he explained, and, satirically advising Baptist cobblers to stick to their lasts, set out in his *Ne Sutor Ultra Crepidam* to correct misrepresentations. They were quite wrong in accusing the government and churches of New England of persecuting orthodox saints, contrary to the spirit of the Congregational pioneers, Willard declared, echoing Nathaniel Ward and Urian Oakes.

> I perceive they are mistaken in the design of our first Planters, whose business was not Toleration; but were professed Enemies of it, and could leave the World professing they died no Libertines. Their business was to settle, and (as much as in them lay) secure Religion to Posterity, according to that way which they believed was of God.

Let "Anabaptists" who had neither "scot nor lot in that charge" set up their own settlements, he sneered, "and we shall not so molest their Churches, as they have shamefully done by ours." They did not deserve to be called brethren who refused to recognize Congregationalists as "visible Christians," and denounced their baptism as "Male administration" and a nullity. And if, as they pleaded, the doctrine of baptism had been so long controverted, why were they now so stiff about it?[16]

Point by point he subjected the Baptist construction to devastating criticism. Like all heretics, he said, they pretend that God was the explanation of their organization, but God did not instigate irregular and unlawful actions. If merely entering into a covenant together made

15. The Preface was signed by Wiliam Kiffen, Daniel Dyke, William Collins, Hansard Knollys, John Harris, and Nehemiah Cox.

16. *Ne Sutor Ultra Crepidam*, pp. 1, 2, 4-6. Cf. Nathaniel Ward, *The Simple Cobler of Aggawam*, p. 3: "all Familists, Antinomians, Anabaptists, and other Enthusiasts, shall have free Liberty to keep away from us, and such as will come to be gone as fast as they can, the sooner the better." Also, Urian Oakes, *New England Pleaded With* (Cambridge, 1673), p. 54: "I look upon an unbounded toleration as the first born of all abominations."

a church, then "every combination of Enthusiasts, Ranters, Socinians, &c. may become Churches of Christ." Furthermore, excommunicated deniers of the historic doctrine and practice of infant baptism, ring-leaders of schism, and fomenters of trouble were hardly fit material for a church, yet these are the people, taunted Willard, who complain about the rugged spirits of their oppressors. "Experience tells us that such a rough thing as a New England Anabaptist is not to be handled over tenderly."[17]

As to the alleged persecution in estate, liberty, and name, New England's legal prosecution followed the historic Christian principle which was the practice "of the Reformers of old" and the "constant judgment" of the church "since the Apostles," namely, that Christian magistrates were duty-bound to suppress error. Working within the framework of generic Reformed thought Willard explained that they had no intention of lording over conscience, but "if we tarry till all men are agreed about what is truth before we oppress Error, we shall stay till there is no need of it." Yet in spite of opprobrium, scorn, and insolence the magistrates had never been violent, but proceeded "far on this side of the Law"—even the sentence of two ringleaders to banishment had not been implemented. Such men left alone, however, would under-mine churches, ruin order, destroy piety, and introduce profaneness. Was God really the explanation for the increase of such folk? asked Willard: many things happened by permissive providence, and there was also a prophecy about evil men and seducers waxing worse![18]

He proceeded to spell out the bill of indictment against them. One: they were schismatics, for their churches had been formed by undis-missed people like Thomas Gould and Thomas Osborne, and previously unaffiliated immigrants who joined schismatics shared their sin. Two: they were scandalous in calling such to minister holy things and receiving the undismissed and excommunicated into their fellowship. Three: they were disorderly in welcoming those under censure for moral evils and excommunicated impenitents into their fellowship. Four: they were disturbers of the peace, as their earlier factious conduct, the manner of their complaint, and their misrepresentations of the case showed. Five: they were underminers of churches, drawing Congregational members into their own communions, vilifying the churches, scoffing at the ministers, alienating the people, nullifying infant baptism, and referring to Congregationalists as unbaptized. Six: they were neglecters of orderly worship, refusing to worship with

17. *Ne Sutor Ultra Crepidam*, pp. 7-8, 10.

18. *Ibid.*, pp. 11-12. Cf. Heppe, *op. cit.,* pp. 691-694, for the Reformed consensus on the role of the magistrate.

established churches when inoffensive scruplers were always permitted. Seven: though they had not been called idolaters, unwarranted alteration of divine institutions was indeed a sin against the second commandment. Eight: though not charged as enemies of civil government, they were contemptuous of authority. And as to their citation of loyalty, it should not be overlooked, observed Willard, that the enemy first attacked their settlement at Swansea, and "any man would fight, rather than have his throat cut; it was not for Religion, nor Civil Government, but for lives and estates."[19]

As to the ministry, Russel did not think the Spirit worked only in college, continued Willard: "nor we neither; nor yet Ministerial gifts to be (ordinarily) acquired in a Shoemakers Shop." Every Christian had the Spirit, but it was clearly "Enthusiastical" to think that this qualified him to teach and instruct a congregation. If Russel was fit to be a minister, scoffed Willard, "we have but fooled ourselves in building Colledges, and instructing our Children in learning."[20]

It was a question of church order too. Willard agreed with Mather: what could be more pernicious than the idea that only baptized adults constituted the church as visible saints? This principle undermined all the churches in the world except their own, for it implied that the only visible saints were the "Anabaptists."[21] And so, reaffirming the principles of the Congregational way enunciated by early nonconformists such as Cartwright, Whitaker, Baynes, and Parker (with which Congregationalists in England still concurred), Willard asserted that congregations were liable to the censures of civil magistrates when disorders arose.[22]

Actually, much of Baptist belief was akin to the Puritan brand of Calvinism, but to New Englanders the points of difference were sufficient to mark them as heretics, as threats to the established order. And so Willard did not let the matter rest with this pamphlet skirmish, he carried his polemic into the pulpit, joining battle with them especially at the three points of infant baptism, the ministry, and the alliance of church and state.

19. *Ne Sutor Ultra Crepidam*, pp. 14-24.

20. *Ibid.*, p. 26.

21. *Ibid.*, p. 27.

22. *Ibid.*, "To the Reader." Cf. Walker, *op. cit.*, "A Platform of Discipline," Chapters III-V, X, XIII-XIV, XVII; Westminster Confession of Faith and Savoy Declaration, Chapters XXI-XXII, XXIV, 205f., 207f., 209f., 217ff., 224ff., 227ff., 388f., 390f., 393f. Cf. also Perry Miller, *Orthodoxy in Massachusetts*, Chapter VII.

Infant Baptism

One year after the publication of his *Ne Sutor Ultra Crepidam* the coals of controversy were still hot, as Willard's sermons on "Covenant-Keeping The Way to Blessedness" indicate. "Who can but acknowledge that times are then bad and sad, when a due and sober witness-bearing against the prevailing evils of the time and places, is stigmatized for persecution," he asserted.

> ... the Church of Christ ever accounted Her self engaged to condemn and suppress [heresy] both by Preaching and Writing against the Doctrines, and sharpening the Church censures against the persons of such as vented, & pertinaciously persisted in them; purging out such Leaven from the lump: Nor did the Professours of the Truth ever call this Persecution, till now of late. . . . it is a great pitty that it should now be esteemed the Glory of any Churches that they can bear with them; yea, cherish and defend them: The Covenant (I am sure) obligeth to the contrary.[23]

The ordinances of the church had to be kept from depravation and rejection, and *"Anabaptisme* is a dangerous underminer of Gospel-Order and Ordinances," he warned South Church. Many, reflecting the growing indifference and heterodoxy, thought lightly of neglecting these duties, but "If God were so exact with *Moses,* that he strictly engaged him to follow the pattern given him in the mount. . . . surely then He will charge breach of the Covenant upon all such as dare to mutilate or curtaile any of his Gospel-appointments."[24]

Standing squarely in the federal tradition of generic Reformed thinking he argued for baptism of infants on the basis of the covenant of grace. Only those who manifest "repentance towards God, and Faith in Iesus Christ" were to be baptized, asserted John Clarke; only those so baptized were "Saints by Calling & fitt matter for a visible Church," said Thomas Gould; infant baptism thus was a "nullity."[25] Not so, declared Willard. Parents, recognizing the covenant tie as well as the natural tie with their children, were to look after their religious interest. The church had the God-given duty of acknowledging them as God's by "applying the Ordinance of Baptisme" to them in infancy and looking after them in "riper" years. Infants were not to be baptized on the ground of presumptive regeneration ("we know that for the most part it is otherwise"), but because of the appointment of God, who used this

23. *Covenant-Keeping The Way to Blessedness,* p. 102.
24. *Ibid.,* pp. 98-99.
25. Clarke, *op. cit.;* Nathan E. Wood, *The History of the First Baptist Church of Boston (1665-1899),* p. 65.

as a means for their conversion. As for those who never reached years of discretion, Willard like Cocceius and Heidegger optimistically declared: "we believe He doth it in a secret way for those that dy in infancy."[26]

But these privileges were matched by equally great responsibilities. Covenant children set apart for divine service in baptism could keep or lose covenant mercies. "If you depart from God, break his commandments, keep not his Covenant, this will be a witness against you," he warned the fold at South Church.[27] One should never trust in externals, for "there is a Circumcision of the flesh, and of the heart, a Baptisme of Water and of the Holy Spirit." This, to Willard, was a much more effective way of propagating holiness than the flimsy method of the Baptists. And it was to be preserved at all costs. Their fathers' errand into the wilderness, he reminded them in words echoing Danforth's, was the securement of "the free, pure, and uncorrupted libertyes of the Covenant of Grace" for themselves and their children, and it would be horrible ingratitude to slight it.

> Beware you do not wilfully overthrow the foundations which your Fathers have laid. . . . if you put your hands into the Wall to pluck down the Wayes of Christ, a Serpent will bite them: If you destroy what your Fathers have built, expect that God will destroy you, at least make you feel the smart and bitterness of it. If *Jericho* could not be built without a Curse, then certainly Jerusalem cannot be undermined without a Curse.[28]

Thus he spoke in 1682.

When the new charter, in line with the Act of Toleration, brought legal toleration for the Baptists in 1691, Massachusetts, as much as possible, sought to retain its ecclesiastical law. Willard for one did not believe that changed legal status involved toleration of Baptist doctrine. That same year in a series of sermons on "The Barren Fig Trees Doom" he charged Baptists with setting themselves against Christ in denying church status to covenant children. "Are we wiser than he? or shall we dare to control him? Shall he say, I have planted these in my Vineyard, and shall we say they are in the Wilderness?" The underlying reason for such mistakes was misunderstanding about the church, he declared. There was the "Church of the first born" and the "visible Church." Referred to as the called and converted, the church did not include

---

26. *Covenant-Keeping*, pp. 104, 111-112, 114. Cf. Wollebius, *Compendium*, p. 105; Heppe, *Reformed Dogmatics*, p. 623.

27. *Covenant-Keeping*, pp. 112-113, 120-122.

28. *Ibid.*, pp. 117, 124-125. Cf. Samuel Danforth, *A Brief Recognition of New England's Errand into the Wilderness.*

every visible believer (Romans 9:6), but referred to as all in external
covenant with God, it did (Psalm 50:5). While only the converted
actually experienced the inward saving benefits of Christ, all visible
professors shared in the common privileges of the visible church.[29]
Willard emphasized as much as any the *Corpus Christi* (in distinction
from the *Corpus Christianum*), but whereas Baptists, emphasizing the
sequence "believe—be baptized—be saved" (Mark 16:18), restricted
membership to those who voluntarily entered the church by believer's
baptism at the age of accountability, Willard in Reformed fashion
stressed the covenant relationship and the privilege of infant baptism as
one of its blessings.[30]

Willard's catechism sermons were summaries of the main arguments
generally employed in the polemics of infant baptism. The New Testament sacrament of baptism, supplanting Old Testament circumcision,
was a holy ordinance instituted by Christ, appointed with sensible signs
and seals to represent and apply His covenant benefits and to signify
one's initiation into the covenant with God. Etymologically considered,
baptism was proper by sprinkling or immersion, but though immersion
might have been more frequent in the early church it was "superstitious" to insist upon it, and history indicated that aspersion was used in
colder regions. The quality of water rather than its quantity appointed
the sign, and aspersion answered the purpose. Surely the apostles must
have sprinkled the three thousand baptized in one day (Acts 2:41), and
considerations of health and modesty also argued for the general
practice.[31]

Baptism was to be administered in the name of the triune God,
implying the authority of the three persons and consecration to each
one as engaged in the salvation of the elect. Such baptism in itself was
hypothetically rather than absolutely necessary, but Christ's command
made it a preceptive and moral necessity, so that all who knowingly
neglected it despised divine authority. That which was signified and
sealed in baptism was union with Christ with its accompanying mutual
obligations. Baptism sacramentally illustrated the Spirit's removal of sin
through communication to the believer of the cleansing and regener-
ating blood of Christ, but its efficacy was not limited to the moment of

29. *The Barren Fig Trees Doom*, pp. 31-34.
30. See the Cambridge Platform in Walker, *op. cit.*, pp. 204-205f.; Heppe, *op.
cit.*, pp. 624, 664f., 667f.; cf. Franklin H. Littell, "The Claims of the Free
Churches," *The Christian Century*, LXXVIII (1961), 417; and also his *The
Anabaptist View of the Church*, pp. 83-86.
31. *Compleat Body of Divinity*, pp. 842-843, 845-846. Cf. Heppe, *op. cit.*,
pp. 620ff.; Benjamin B. Warfield, "The Polemics of Infant Baptism," *Studies in
Theology*, pp. 389-408.

observance, since sin was removed progressively. Therefore, urged Willard, believers should seek the signified grace and "improve" it to holiness, thereby promoting salvation.[32]

Asserting that infants, as children of obedient believers within the visible church, were entitled to baptism according to Christ's institution and that their infancy did not morally obstruct participation in the ordinance, Willard drew the common theological distinction between *jus in re* and *jus ad rem*. The former was a primary consideration in infant baptism and furnished the basis for the latter, he explained. According to the New Testament record God received the children of parents who were members of His covenant by profession. Christ's order for gathering the church had perpetual validity: when preaching the gospel resulted in profession the seal of baptism was to be placed upon them and their children as the badge of discipleship, and this was to be followed by instruction in covenant duties. Such children not only had a right *in* baptism, they had a right *to* it, analogous to circumcision. "This is a Principle not to be parted from," Willard asserted,

> nor can all the Adversaries of it ever be able to undermine it, unless they can blow up the Gospel. . . . And as long as this abides a Truth, our Argument standeth strong, and it will so abide true as long as the World stands.

Infants eight days old did not understand circumcision, and were incapable of the act of faith or its open profession, yet to God this was not an impediment to it or reason for its delay. In the same way, argued Willard, Christian infants were as capable of receiving the New Testament parallel signifying and sealing the righteousness of faith.[33]

Lack of explicit Biblical statements for infant baptism or instances of it did not invalidate it if it came within the precept, Willard continued in traditional fashion, else women might also be forbidden the Lord's Supper. The nation of Israel comprehended infants, and to exclude them from the "all nations" of Matthew 28:19 was against common sense. In apostolic practice households were baptized with the converted heads of families (Acts 16:15, 33; I Corinthians 1:16). It was "meer banter" to question: "How do you know there were infants in those Houses?" "How do you know there were not?" retorted Willard. If infants were capable of regeneration, the infusion of grace, federal holiness, and the heavenly inheritance signified in baptism, they were also able to receive the sign. Of course, they were not to trust in an

32. *Compleat Body,* pp. 846-851.
33. *Ibid.,* pp. 854-858. Through a printer's error in pagination numbers 856 and 857 are omitted.

external and automatic sacrament: they were to depend on the grace
and Spirit of God to receive all that was signified by living faith.[34]

It was a great pity, he observed, that that which was intended to be a
unitive aspect of the Christian religion had become a divisive factor and
a "ball of contention." Precursors of the antipedobaptists were to be
found in the "first Ages" of the church, but in these latter times "they
have much more abounded, and given no small disturbance to the
Church of God," withstanding the "Orthodox Doctrine," and denying
the "Visible Christianity of the greatest part of the Professing Churches
in the World." Granted, many of these folk were godly and acted on
conscience ("tho' erroneous"); nonetheless the many disputes and "un-
suitable heats" had resulted in undue separation. This necessitated the
reiteration that to withhold baptism from infants was an injury to them
and an affront to Christ.[35]

The Ministry

The denial of infant baptism and the development of an irregular
ministry in New England, as Willard saw it, were linked together. It was
ministerial ambition that led Thomas Gould to gather a private meeting
at his own house, and Thomas Osborne had withdrawn to join Gould's
schismatic gathering not first of all out of dislike for infant baptism,
"but that the Church gave no liberty to private Brethren to prophesie,
that they limited the Ministry to learned men, and that he did not find
his own spirit free to come." Their religious convictions were a ruse for
self-aggrandizement, therefore.

> ... these men (having privately exercised their gifts in Meetings
> with applause) began to think themselves wronged that their light
> was put under a bushel; and finding no remedy in our Churches,
> threw on a cloak of Anabaptisme, and so gained the thing they
> aimed at, in a disguise.

Similarly John Farnum, thought to be so godly by the Baptists, soon
after affiliating with the Dorcester Church evidenced his dissenting
spirit when, unable to get his way, he renounced their communion for
that of the "excommunicated," laying down as one of the four conditions for rejoining the Congregational church the right to prophesy. All
these joined Gould and Russel in the formation of a fellowship in which
they could exercise their gifts without reservation.[36] Haled before the
court for such schismatic practices, they spread out a confession of

34. *Compleat Body,* p. 858.
35. *Ibid.,* pp. 855-856.
36. Willard, *Ne Sutor Ultra Crepidam,* pp. 14, 16, 20, 26.

faith, which, echoing John Clarke, clearly stated: "when the Church is mett to gather they may all prophesie one by one that all may learne & all may be Comforted."[37]

The practice had roots in England. "Prophecying," adopted in England in 1571 mainly as a clerical exercise, had been gradually taken up by laymen, but not without resistance from the more ecclesiastically minded Puritan element who feared the repetition of the lay religion that went wild among the radical Anabaptists on the Continent earlier. In the chaotic days of the English revolution Presbyterians particularly objected that it was ecclesiastically out of order and that it tended to become "extempore" by virtue of the lower educational level of the participants. To the enthusiasts of Cromwell's army, however, the Holy Spirit counted more than education, and among the proliferating sects such ideas enjoyed a heyday.[38]

> Even *How* the Cobler dares the Pulpit climb. Belike he thinkes the difference is but small Between the sword o' th' Spirit and the Awle. And that he can as dextrously divide The word of truth, as he can an Hide.[39]

Samuel How's early treatise on the sufficiency of the Spirit's teaching had been reissued in England by a prominent Baptist named William Kiffen in 1655, and these ideas now being echoed in New England caused the clergy of Massachusetts no small concern. "An undervaluing of the Ministry," Willard had warned the folk at Groton, "[and] an elevating [of] ... private gifts, &c. ... hath led men by degrees to those great Apostacies, whereby their light (which would have shone clearly in its proper Orb) hath spent it self in a blaze, and gone out in a stinking snuff."[40] He was too orthodox, of course, to question the great Reformation principle of the priesthood of all believers, which, ideally conceived, let every Christian rise to his full stature as prophet and priest; but he made it quite clear that this did not negate the fact that not everyone was officially a preacher and a teacher, that for the sake of order some were divinely set apart and appointed to serve in this capacity. This office Willard magnified throughout his ministry,

37. Quoted in Wood, *op. cit.*, pp. 65-66. Cf. Clarke, *op. cit.*

38. G. F. Nuttal, *The Holy Spirit in Puritan Faith and Experience*, pp. 75-84; Haller, *The Rise of Puritanism*, p. 267.

39. Thomas Hall, *Vindicae Literarum*, p. 68. Samuel How was a cobbler who gave expression to these spiritual convictions in *The Sufficiency of the Spirits Teaching without human Learning: or a Treatise* tending to prove humane Learning to be no help to the spiritual understanding of the Word of God (London, 1639).

40. *Useful Instructions*, p. 58.

reflecting the Reformed doctrine of the ministry traditionally championed among the Puritans.[41] As "Ambassadors of God" ministers were engaged in the "greatest work"; it was a "noble employment" upon which Christ had conferred "dignity." Truth was the same, whether spoken by a minister or another, "yet it may come with more efficacy from such an one, than from another; not from any virtue in him, but from the grace of God, who will thus own his own appointments." Though they were men of like infirmities with their parishioners, when God put His Spirit into His ministers, what they spoke "that he saith," and therefore those who despise the ministry despise God. Ministers, on the other hand, deriving their authority from Him, must follow His directions.[42]

Integral with such a high conception of the ministry was his conviction on the necessity of a proper call. It was a scandal that Baptists should call excommunicated persons like Thomas Gould to minister in holy things. They did not improve their reputation when in 1699 they received with open arms Samuel (Axel) May, who as an alleged Presbyterian preacher at first drew even the Mathers into his sizable following, until he was exposed as a bricklayer with plagiarized sermons and a fictitious certification.[43] Clearly and simply in this context Willard stated the orthodox position. All Christians had a general call to teach according to the grace they received, but this was quite distinct from the special call given to ministers. "Official teaching," teaching by "precept," was reserved for those whom God called to the ministry, "and notwithstanding gifts, men must wait for this till called to it according to the Gospel Rule, Rom. 10:14. *How shall they preach, except they be sent.*" So, however helpful and important Christian experience might be, to qualify for official teaching it was necessary that he be officially called by the church.[44]

41. Cf. Calvin, *Institutes,* IV, 1 and 3 *passim;* Heppe, *op. cit.,* pp. 673-681; Wilhelm Pauck, "The Ministry in the Time of the Continental Reformation," and Winthrop S. Hudson, "The Ministry in the Puritan Age," in H. Richard Niebuhr and Daniel D. Williams, eds., *The Ministry in Historical Perspectives,* pp. 110-147, 180-206; John T. McNeill, "The Doctrine of the Ministry in Reformed Theology," *Church History,* XII (1943), 77-97; Walker, *op. cit.,* pp. 142-143, 145, 217.

42. *The only sure way to prevent threatned Calamity* (bound with *The Child's Portion*), p. 176; *Barren Fig Trees Doom,* pp. 94-95; *Mercy Magnified,* p. 347; *Barren Fig Trees Doom,* pp. 102, 225, 277, 95; *Compleat Body,* pp. 326, 328, 345.

43. Cotton Mather, *Diary,* I, 313-314, 315, 318, 323-324, 328-329, 337-338.

44. *Truly Blessed Man,* pp. 415-416. Cf. Heppe, *op. cit.,* pp. 673-675, for the differences between Independents and Reformed on the matter of who does the calling.

To fill worthily such an office one had to be adequately trained, and Willard was second to none in championing the idea of a learned ministry. Willard himself, according to Pemberton, was an "uncommon Scholar" in whom the "Gifts of Nature . . . were advanced and rendered more bright by great Improvements of hard Study,"[45] and it is not surprising that he vigorously opposed enthusiastical notions. A minister had to have the gifts of grace, but also prudence, acquaintance with history, and the ability to judge rationally between causal and super-natural events,[46] declared Willard. God's messengers sometimes re-ceived "deep and powerful" impressions from the Spirit, he once declared before the magistrates, but immediately went on to assure them "I am far from pleading for, or justifying anything that looks like Enthusiasm."[47] To avoid impertinent handling of the Scriptures, a preacher, he explained to South Church, had to have a competent knowledge of grammar, rhetoric, and logic; and to do it right took a great deal of time and study.[48] Only the ancient apostles, prophets, and evangelists possessed immediate and extraordinary inspiration—all others attained these gifts only "by study, reading, industry, [and] being trained up in the Schools of the Prophets"; they needed time to study their sermons, and they had no business coming before their people with "indigested Discourses."[49] Preaching was applicatory as well as doctrinal, so one had to be skilled in "cases of Conscience," one had to be able to evaluate people's religious condition and individual differences of temper; and all this required knowledge and discretion.[50] In sum, their great task was to preach the Word by exegeting the Scriptures, declaring the articles of the Christian religion, confuting the errors of the times, establishing the truth, and doing their utmost to win souls and build them up in the faith.[51]

But social forces were obviously aiding the Baptist cause. The wilderness, a new generation, a steady influx of less committed immi-grants, as well as the character of the times created a different mental and spiritual attitude toward preaching. People were beginning to tire of the technical and involved sermons that had been New England's diet for years, and were hankering for a simpler fare that required less concentration, a sort of precursor to the hot-gospel harangue of the Great Awakening a generation later.

45. Pemberton, *Funeral Sermon*, p. 63.
46. *Heart Garrisoned*, p. 13.
47. *Only sure way to prevent threatned Calamity*, p. 174.
48. *Heavenly Merchandize*, pp. 111-112.
49. *Compleat Body*, pp. 326, 370, 637.
50. *Truly Blessed Man*, pp. 423, 426, 430.
51. *Compleat Body*, p. 815.

To aggravate this situation New England was beginning to face a minister shortage as their aged godly ministers died and an insufficient number of young men aspired to fill their places. Furthermore, a new anti-clerical spirit was developing, Willard complained, as "the sons of Zerviah begin to put out their heads and speak insultingly."[52] A growing "Korah-like" spirit rendered the ministers "low and contemptible"; they were condemned by some, contemned by others, and (if works proved anything) scarcely believed by any.[53] Absence from church was excused with the retort that they only heard "what we already know as well as the Preacher"; when they did attend, they left to "carp . . . scoff . . . flout . . . and deride." In this situation, declared Willard, imposters thrived, peddling their wares, "undermining & scandalizing the true and faithful servants of Jesus Christ."[54] People were running after "novelties," Willard complained at the end of the century, counting "the cheapest Ministry to be the most eligible," preferring ignorance to the best gifts and graces, and "cry[ing] down the Schools of the Prophets" as needless.[55]

Willard became acting president of Harvard College in 1701, and sometime before his death six years later he composed a small tract giving brief directions for young men preparing for the ministry.[56] It was a mere thumbnail sketch compared to William Perkins' *Of the Call to the Ministrie,* the *Art of Prophecying,* and a host of other seventeenth-century manuals, but it was eagerly perused by students at the time; to us it is interesting as the earliest American production on the subject. It exemplified the intellectual tradition of the seventeenth century, and as such suggested no departures; it outlined the pattern of his own training—the inherited structure of the medieval trivium and quadrivium pressed into the service of divinity.

Here in a nutshell was Willard's idea of the fundamentals of ministerial training. Since every good and perfect gift comes from the Father above, let the student pray much and shed high opinions of himself in order that he may work more industriously. The source of theological truth is the Word of God, so let him diligently read the Scriptures in the original, getting at "the Import of the Words, the Sense of the Axiom, and the theological Truth contained in it" through the skills of grammatical, logical, and theological analysis. The theological truths of the

52. *Righteous Man's Death* (bound with *The Child's Portion*), p. 159.
53. *Covenant-Keeping,* pp. 102-103; *Only sure way to prevent threatned Calamity,* p. 180.
54. *Heavenly Merchandize,* pp. 86, 93.
55. *Truly Blessed Man,* p. 350; *Best Priviledge,* pp. 22-23.
56. It was published three decades later as *Brief Directions to a Young Scholar Designing the Ministry, for the Study of Divinity.*

Bible were to be digested into a methodical system of divinity, this systematic ("Common Place") divinity being the student's first concern as the foundation for safe and profitable pursuit of other theological studies. One should read the "most approved Systems," for until one was soundly principled in the fundamentals of theology he was exposed to every wind of doctrine and baffled by "cunning Sophisms of Imposters." He should then proceed to "Casuistical" divinity, the application of doctrine to practical heads, for the purpose of knowledge was "eupraxy," and an able minister had to be skilled in resolving difficult cases of conscience. "Polemical" divinity had to be mastered in order to be able to refute error. He was to study the most approved authors ("where there is least Danger of being seduced"), yet he was not to pin his faith on the authority of any: all but Scriptural authors were to be accounted fallible. This was no head-in-the-sand policy, however; the student should also outline the noted ancient and modern heresies that had "pestered" the church, in order that recognizing them in his reading he might not become infected unawares. The best way to read a book, advised Willard, was to put significant notations in the margins: notable theorems, weighty arguments, cases to be handled, erroneous doctrines and assertions, and references to remarkable providences and Scripture truths. He recommended that each student prepare for himself a large "Common-Place Book" listing topically all the doctrinal, casuistical, and polemical treatments of the subjects that could be found in one's own library, as well as errors and their confutations. Occasionally he should practice on a particular "common-place" of divinity. He should also confer with others, especially with orthodox and able ministers, about "dark" and difficult points. All the while, of course, he should also study other disciplines such as philosophy, history, and especially ecclesiastical history.

As they slipped into the eighteenth century, whatever changes had been witnessed in the seventeenth, Willard was not disposed to make concessions to heterodoxy in preparation for the ministry.

Church and State

The zealously guarded alliance of church and state was another point of tension. Baptists had little quarrel with the secular enforcement of outward morality, but to them (as to Continental Anabaptists) promotion of privileged interests in religion and compulsion of individuals within the Christian community on matters of faith were anathema. They applauded Roger Williams' protest against enforcement of the "First Table" and persecution on matters of conscience. John Clarke, echoing the persecuted English Baptists, epitomized the early New England Baptist consensus:

> no such believer, or Servant of Christ Iesus hath any liberty, much less Authority, from his Lord, to smite his fellow servant, nor yet with outward force, or arms of flesh, to constrain, or restrain his Conscience, nor yet his outward man for Conscience sake, or worship of his God, where injury is not offered to the person, name or estate of others, every man being such as shall appear before the judgment seat of Christ, and must give an account of himself to God.[57]

"Wee desire to give unto god that which is gods," confessed Thomas Gould, "& unto Ceasere that which is Ceaseres & to every man that which belongeth to them."[58]

At the funeral of Governor John Leverett in 1679 Willard vigorously reaffirmed the pronouncements of predecessors as, lamenting the "great Gap" made by heresies, he insisted on political intolerance of religious dissent. It was incumbent upon rulers to suppress such provocation: "they both have Authority, and it lyes upon them in duty to suppress it."[59] The impudent boldness with which many propagate their corrupt doctrines, he lectured the magistrates at election time in 1682, "calls for your vigilant and resolute industry in the suppression thereof." Recognizing that speaking in this way he exposed himself to criticism, he came out strongly nonetheless for New England's historic position.

> If men, upon pretence of Conscience (and who will not pretend it, if they may find it a shelter against Justice?) . . . may be suffered . . . without any restraint to run to and fro, Disseminate their erroneous principles, make breaches in Churches, undermine and seduce silly souls, set up their Posts by God's Posts, enjoy as free and publick liberty to carry on their own wayes, as those Churches of Christ whom you profess to countenance and de-

57. Clarke, *op. cit.*
58. Quoted in Wood, *op. cit.,* p. 66. For the Anabaptist point of view see Littell, *Anabaptist View of the Church,* pp. 64-65, 89, 91. Cf. also Moehlman, "The Baptist View of the State," *Church History,* VI (1937), 24-49, *passim.* To enforce conformity, said the English Baptists, was "wholly against the mind and merciful law of Christ, dangerous both to king and state, a means to decrease the kingdom of Christ, and a means to increase the kingdom of Antichrist": Leonard Busher, *Religious Peace: or, a plea for liberty of conscience* (1646), p. 2; quoted in Haller, *op. cit.,* pp. 205, 409.
59. *Sermon Preached upon Ezek.,* pp. 11, 9-10. Cf. Winthrop, "A Model of Christian Charity," *Winthrop Papers;* Ward, *op. cit.,* pp. 3-12; Norton, *Heart of New-England Rent,* p. 54; Higginson, *Cause of God and His People,* p. 12; Oakes, *op. cit.,* pp. 54-56; Torrey, *Exhortation unto Reformation,* p. 21; "A Platform of Church Discipline," in Walker, *op. cit.,* pp. 234-237.

fend, and that by total silence, and all connivance; if thus you can tolerate the dishonour of Christ, let me boldly say, I believe he will soon and signally testifie his dislike of it.[60]

He called upon the ministers to back up the magistrates, even though, thrown on the defensive, they seemingly had to justify their right to battle for orthodoxy in a community undergoing social change. Even though the times resent it, Willard challenged them, be true watchmen, men of knowledge, fixed principles, and holy convictions: "beware of being Idol-Shepherds."[61]

The change one decade wrought can be seen in Willard's next election sermon twelve years later. The political affairs of the colony had been significantly altered during the disturbing eighties, and the new decade had brought a new king and a new charter that provided liberty of worship for dissenters. Willard's election sermon of 1694 still blessed God for rulers who sought New England's weal by endeavoring to advance "religion" and "righteousness" as "Custos utriusque Tabulae," but the tone is different. A good ruler, Willard explained, will "do his utmost that the true Religion may be countenanced and established, and that all Ungodliness, as well as Unrighteousness, may have a due Testimony born against it at all times."[62] But he no longer denounced; there were no sharp pronouncements. New England was slowly coming to terms with its pluralistic self. Baptists in some instances had also been quite cooperative, as, for example, the Reverend William Milborne who had joined the four Congregational ministers of Boston in the Council Chamber when Andros and Randolph had been summoned during the revolution. Subtle changes of attitude did not alter basic convictions; they did modify the manner of their promotion.

As the world's timepiece turned to 1700 Willard preached a series of sermons on the peril of the times. Increase Mather introduced their publication with an observation that in the Protestant and Reformed English nation religion came to expression in various forms—Episcopal, Presbyterian, Congregational, and Antipedobaptist, but since these did not differ in the fundamental articles of faith there were among all of them "some with whom Godliness in the Truth and Power is to be found."[63] We may presume that Willard agreed with Mather's sentiment.

60. *The only sure way to prevent threatned Calamity*, pp. 191, 192-193.
61. *Ibid.*, pp. 194-195.
62. *Character of a Good Ruler*, pp. 7, 12-13.
63. *Peril of the Times*, "To the Reader."

How far Willard had moved beyond animated polemics to a charitable difference of conviction may be seen in his funeral sermon for Lieutenant Governor Stoughton in 1701. While he still extolled usefulness to the public and promotion of God's glory, suppression of sins and encouragement of righteousness and piety, the vehemence evident in the sermon at Leverett's funeral two decades earlier is nowhere to be seen.[64]

He had not abandoned his orthodox convictions, however. Do civil rulers have power to make laws about religious worship and heretical doctrines? he asked two years later in a catechism sermon. "I shall only Answer, Whatsoever may truly serve to the Peace and Tranquility of the People comes within their reach, agreeable to the Rule of Reason, and the Word of God."[65] Reason obviously dictated that what had been said two tumultuous decades previously might have to be said differently in a quite new century. Principles did not change, but application did.

Times had changed. How could they be sure that God was for them? asked Willard in 1704, following another French and Indian massacre on the western frontier. Fear God and keep His commandments. God's people are safe when rulers are faithful to their trust, "when good and wholesome Laws, and careful execution of them, *Sobriety, Righteousness,* and *Godliness* are upheld among the People, and all manner of open wickedness is born down, and that which is secret is searched out as far as may be."[66] Massachusetts still endeavored to preserve the fabric of theocracy, and attempts were made by acts and resolves to renew the ecclesiastical laws of the former era, but the pressure of many elements made their execution increasingly difficult.[67] The Baptists were with them to stay, and social attitudes worked in favor of accepting them with less asperity. In England public opinion had been long in their favor, and in New England liberty of worship had been guaranteed to them by the provisions of the new charter.

Baptist growth was still slow in the seventeenth century, however. This may be explained in part by the barrage of sermons against them which may have kept down the number of conversions. It is impossible to accurately measure the effectiveness of preaching, and statistics cannot tell the whole story, but while by 1700 Baptists abounded in all the border towns of Rhode Island, on the islands near Cape Cod, in some of the villages of Plymouth community, and in the Piscataqua

64. *Prognosticks of Impending Calamities,* p. 17.
65. *Compleat Body,* p. 624.
66. *Israel's True Safety,* pp. 20, 32, 11.
67. Susan Martha Reed, *Church and State in Massachusetts, 1691-1740,* p. 190.

region, it has been estimated that there were only ten organized Baptist churches in Massachusetts with a comprehensive membership of approximately three hundred persons.[68]

Willard did not live to see the culmination of this trend, but eleven years after his death Cotton Mather preached the ordination sermon of a Baptist minister, Elisha Callendar, and spoke on "Brethren Dwelling Together in Unity."[69] Some still took exception to this gesture toward toleration and acceptance, but Increase Mather also extended the right hand of fellowship.

---

68. Henry C. Vedder, *A Short History of the Baptists,* p. 302; Samuel Bownas, *An account of the life, travels, and Christian experiences in the work of the ministry of Samuel Bownas,* p. 120; George Keith, *A Journal of Travels,* pp. 22-23.

69. Cotton Mather, *Brethren Dwelling Together in Unity.* Cf. Cotton Mather, *Diary,* II, 535-536.

CHAPTER NINE

THE QUAKERS

The most dramatic threat to the orthodoxy of New England came from the camp of the Quakers. Just how radical they could be Willard experienced at first hand within his first year as assistant to Thacher at South Church. At the time of the morning sermon on Sunday, July 8, 1677, a "female" Quaker strode into church, clothed in a canvas frock, her hair disheveled, her face black as ink, followed by two others like her, says Samuel Sewall. "It occasioned the greatest and most amazing uproar that I ever saw."[1] Magistrate Simon Bradstreet, a member of South Church, immediately had them arrested and clapped into jail until they should be legally discharged, for they had so frightened the people of the church by their horrible disturbance, he said, that several women were "in great danger of miscarrying."[2] As the trial began before a tense court on August 4, Governor Leverett asked Mrs. Brewster: "Are you the Woman that came into Mr. Thatcher's Meeting-House with your Hair fruzled, and dressed in the Shape of a Devil?" "I am the Woman that came into Priest Thatcher's House of Worship with my Hair about my Shoulders, Ashes upon my Head, my Face coloured black, and Sackcloth upon my upper Garments," she calmly replied. She had come to the "bloody Town of Boston" in obedience to divine inner compulsion, she continued, to entreat the city like a modern Jonah to repent and to put an end to the "cruel Laws" which perse-cuted "Friends" for worshiping the true and living God. Spurning her lengthy testimony, the Court sentenced her to be "stript . . . to the Middle, and to be tide to a Cart's Tail at the South Meeting-House, and to be drawn through the Town, and to receive twenty Stripes," her

1. Sewall, *Diary, 5 M.H.S. Colls.,* V, 30.
2. Quoted in Hill, *History of Old South Church,* I, 219.

companions being tied to the cart with her.[3] The episode turned out to be the last flare-up of overt persecution of Quakers in New England, ending more than two decades of stern repressive measures, but there was no abatement of hostility to Quakers and the preaching of Quaker doctrine.

The leaders of Massachusetts were vitally concerned as the Quakers embarked on an extensive missionary program. The ministers took nothing for granted, for in addition to a long tradition of sermons preached in New England against the Quaker peril, numerous monitory treatises had come from New Englanders who had returned to England and had seen the Quaker menace there.[4] Thacher particularly was especially diligent in searching out and confiscating the Quaker literature left in South Church homes, with the result that the "*wolves barked more at him*" than against any others.[5] Willard early took a similar strong stand. At a conference at the Sewall home in December, 1676, he and several colleagues reached the consensus that the Quakers might easily be suppressed if ministers and magistrates agreed, and that "as to what it might injure the country, in respect of England, trust God with it."[6] Three years later the Reforming Synod, voicing a communal concern, declared:

> humane Inventions, and Will-worship have been set up even in Jerusalem. Men have set up their Thresholds by Gods Threshold, and their Posts by his Post. Quakers are false Worshippers. . . . Wherefore it must needs be provoking to God, if these things be not duly and fully testified against.[7]

Just what were the Quaker ideas that so alarmed the ministers? George Fox, emphasizing the divine light, had rejected the ideas of total depravity and the authority of the Bible; stressing the inward, he had rejected external ordinances, the sacraments, the established church, and paid ministries. Similarly, Robert Barclay, systematizing Quaker

3. Joseph Besse, ed., *A Collection of the Sufferings of the People Called Quakers*, II, 261-265.

4. Cf. John Norton, *The Heart of New-England Rent at the Blasphemies of the Present Generation*, p. 81; John Wilson, *A Seasonable Watch-Word*, p. 6. From England had come the treatises of: Francis Higginson, *A Brief Relation of the Northern Quakers* (1653); Thomas Welde, *The Perfect Pharisee under Monkish Holiness* (1653). Cf. also Cotton Mather's account, *Magnalia Christi Americana* (Hartford, 1853), I, 364-365.

5. Cotton Mather, *op. cit.*, I, 492.

6. Sewall, *op. cit.*, 30.

7. "The Necessity of Reformation," 3; Walker, *Creeds and Platforms*, p. 428.

theology in fifteen elaborated propositions, directly challenged West-minster doctrine in his highly reputed *An Apology for the true Chris-tian Divinity,* reissued in English in 1678, two years after the original Latin edition. Quakerism, it has been observed, was a radical and logical culmination of the dynamic principle in the Puritan movement. The first Puritans subtracted the pope, the mass, images and five of the seven sacraments; Presbyterians subtracted the rule of bishops and substituted the authority of elders; Independents and Congregational-ists subtracted centralized government and emphasized the autonomy of the local congregation; Baptists subtracted infant baptism and com-posed church membership with professed regenerates; but Quakers went all the way and subtracted all ritual, ordered worship, and profes-sional ministries in their emphasis on the inwardness of religion.[8] Such radical subjectivity abolished everything objective in the Christian tradi-tion, and to a man the clergy of New England rose up to withstand it as a vicious threat to the faith.

The Challenge of George Keith

The spirit of agitation was kept alive in the 1680s by Quakers who from time to time delivered special messages to the governor and disturbed public worship at the time of the sacraments. The champion of them all, however, was George Keith, an unflinching Quaker apostle who arrived in Boston in 1688. Born in Scotland and educated as a Presbyterian, with a Master of Arts degree from the University of Aberdeen, he was one of the most learned of the Quakers, and a close associate of Fox, Barclay, and William Penn. Coming to Boston, he immediately posted a public challenge to the ministers to meet him in debate, a device that had worked to the advantage of Quakers among the common folk in outlying villages. Willard and his colleagues had no intention of granting him a similar opportunity in Boston, and tersely snubbed him with a public answer of their own.

> Having received a Blasphemous and Heretical Paper subscribed by one George Keith, our answer to it and him is, If he desires Conference to instruct us, let him give us his Arguments in writing, as well as his assertions: If to inform himself, let him write his Doubt: If to cavil and disturb the Peace of the Churches (which we have cause to suspect) we have neither the list nor leisure to attend his Motions: If he would have a Publick Audi-ence, let him Print: If a Private discourse though he may know

8. Howard Brinton, *Friends for 300 Years,* p. 11. On Fox see William C. Braithwaite, *The Beginnings of Quakerism,* Chapters 1-3.

where we dwell, yet we forget not what the Apostle John [sic] saith, Ephes. 2.10.

July the 12th   John [sic] Allen, Joshua Moody,
1688   Samuel Willard, Cotton Mather.[9]

Foiled and angered, by the rebuff as much as by the charge, Keith took them up and published a ten-page criticism with a taunt against the "Night-birds and Beasts of Prey" who feared to meet him in debate.[10] The next year he published all the correspondence with an attack on the New England doctrines of the ministry, worship, constitution, government, sacraments, and sabbath in *The Presbyterian and Independent Visible Churches Brought to the Test.*[11] No longer able to ignore him, the Boston ministers issued *The Principles of the Protestant Religion Maintained,*[12] a spirited counterwork, which, though written in the polemical style of Cotton Mather, evidences Willard's incisiveness and controversial acumen.

Taking up the cudgels against Keith, they warned that heretics "with Fraud would persuade . . . the Saints of the Most High to unchurch themselves by parting with all the meanes of Communion between them and their God." Baffled in former days, the "Hydra of Error" now had new sprouts, Quakerism being the worst, they thought. In it they found

the Vomit cast forth in the by-past ages by whole kennels of those creatures, for whom the Apostle to the Philippians has found a name, licked up again for a new-Digestion, and once more expos'd for the poisoning of mankind; and it is especially the more ignorant & unwary, & envious part of mankind which it is adapted unto; few swallow it but the more silly & feeble sort of souls, & those in whom the Light (which they so much adore) affords little better Directions, than those of an Ignis fatuus.

Indeed, Quakerism was, they thought, the peculiar plague of their age, and it was the particular disgrace of the English to have these people "who tho' they tremble, yet beleeve not, but oppose and muddy the

9. Ethyn W. Kirby, *George Keith (1638-1716),* p. 52. On Keith see also Rufus M. Jones, *The Quakers in the American Colonies,* pp. 445-446; William B. Sprague, *Annals of the American Pulpit,* V, 25-29.

10. Kirby, *op. cit.,* p. 53.

11. Philadelphia, 1689.

12. The full title continues: And Churches of New England, in the Profession and Exercise thereof Defended, Against all the Calumnies of one George Keith, A Quaker, in a Book lately Published at Pensilvania, to undermine them both. By the Ministers of the Gospel in Boston.

whole of that Religion, by which we draw near to God." But while they were out to reclaim their lapsed and to furnish the colonies with an antidote for this contagion, they thanked God that, though this "Choak-weed" of Protestantism had taken root within the borders of New England, it was only in the more "obscure nooks and skirts of the Country which These do make any figure in."[13]

They wrote cuttingly, they felt constrained to explain even in that age, for only in this way were some properly rebuked. The work had not the least effect in silencing Keith, however; he promptly replied with *The Pretended Antidote Proved Poyson.*[14] Cotton Mather responded with still another work, but Willard concentrated his efforts in preaching, employing arguments similar to those in their composite work against Keith.

The Word and the Spirit

Divine truth is mediated by the Scriptures, Willard declared from the pulpit of South Church, denouncing those who "pretend themselves born possessed of Truth enough to serve their turn, and so greatly enriched with a treasure of a Light within, that they make it one supreme principle article of their Religion."[15] Quaker disjunction of Word and Spirit was clear from Fox's affirmation concerning the inner light of the Spirit in every man, heathen and sinners included, a fact which he claimed to have learned directly from the Lord Jesus Christ "by his immediate Spirit and power" like the writers of the Scriptures, and only afterward from the Scriptures themselves.[16] Explicitly denouncing Calvinists, Barclay declared such inward revelations to be absolutely necessary and clear in themselves; since this saving light was wrought in all, heathen Chinese and Indians, Greek philosophers, Socrates and others were Christians. God had now raised up faithful evangelists to preach this everlasting gospel that all might come to mind the light and know the Christ within.[17]

13. *Principles of the Protestant Religion,* "The Preface."

14. Or, the True Principles of the Christian & Protestant Religion Defended, And the Four Counterfit Defenders thereof Detected and Discovered. . . . Cf. Cotton Mather, *Little Flocks Guarded against Grievous Wolves* (Boston, 1691).

15. Willard, *Heavenly Merchandize,* p. 35.

16. Fox, *Journal* (ed., T. Ellwood, 1901), I, 34f., 36; *ibid.* (ed., H. Penny, 1911), II, 63; *The Heathens Divinity, Set upon the Heads of all called Christians, That say they had not known that there had been a God or a Christ, unless the Scriptures had declared it unto them; Gospel-Truth Demonstrated* (1706), p. 322; *The Great Mystery of the Great Whore* (1659), p. 185; cited by Geoffrey F. Nuttall, *The Holy Spirit in Puritan Faith and Experience,* viii, 14.

17. Robert Barclay, *An Apology for the true Christian Divinity,* pp. 13-14, 30, 70-71, 163, 168-169, 171, 176, 178, 180, 184-185, 188.

God had indeed imparted revelation immediately to men of His choice in ancient times, Willard explained in 1688, but "since the Canon is perfected, such Revelation is ceased."[18] Keith's contention that God still revealed many things extra-scripturally—the inward call to the ministry, to prayer, to the performance of religious duties, and answers to prayer—presupposed prior Scriptural precepts and revelations, Willard and his colleagues explained. To speak of new promises and new duties, they said, was to make a new Gospel, in spite of warnings against it (Galatians 1). And Keith's pretension to expound the Scriptures by Christlike or apostolic inspiration overlooked the fact that it was still Scripture exposition, not new revelation.[19]

The Spirit and the Word always went together, Willard affirmed in sermon after sermon, echoing his Puritan mentors. In sincere covenant renewal with God, for instance, believers gave themselves to be "led by his Spirit" and "directed by his Word."[20] In preaching, but also in profitable Scripture reading, one had to pray for the illumination of the Spirit, for none knows the mind of God in Scripture but the Spirit-author.[21] Meditating on the Scriptures, one would attain more intimate communion with God, and the conviction that they were the Word of God would be authenticated inwardly by the testimony of the Spirit. Though the Scriptures were sufficient and perspicacious, to understand them aright (literally and spiritually) one needed the illumination of the Spirit; nonetheless one had to diligently search out the mind of the Spirit by reading, meditation, hearing, praying, and inquiring. "These are put together, as the Agent and the Instrument," explained Willard, and the Word thus conjoined with the Spirit was the only guide for salvation.[22]

In every aspect of spiritual life the Word and the Spirit were conjoined, Willard continued. The Spirit brought sinners to conviction through the ministry of the Word, using not only the law devaluated by the Quakers, but also the gospel in the New Testament.[23] He gave the quickening efficacy to the converting Word.[24] In bringing men to faith He illuminated their minds, giving them an infallible assurance of the

18. *Compleat Body of Divinity*, p. 28. Sermon delivered in September, 1688.
19. *Principles of the Protestant Religion*, p. 18. Cf. Keith, *Presbyterian and Independent Visible Churches Brought to the Test*, Chapter I, Section 6, and Chapter III.
20. *Necessity of Sincerity* (bound with *Covenant-Keeping*), p. 147.
21. *Heavenly Merchandize*, pp. 110, 2.
22. *Compleat Body*, pp. 20, 24, 32, 37, 22.
23. *Mercy Magnified*, p. 98; *Law Established by the Gospel*, pp. 12, 35. Cf. Barclay, *op. cit.*, pp. 77-78.
24. *Barren Fig Trees Doom*, p. 133.

truth.[25] Against the Quaker claim that assurance of faith and salvation
were gained by the Spirit's inward testimony, never from the Scripture
(it would be building upon the human principle of observation to
compare one's faith with Scriptural marks), Willard asserted that both
the directing Word and the efficient Spirit gave assurance of one's
"good estate"—the Word affording ground for self-reflection, and the
Spirit enabling one to understand Scriptural promises and evidences,
and to receive His testimony as one compared himself with them.[26]
Similarly, the guide for Christian living was given in the gospel, not by
immediate inspiration.[27] The Word was God's testimony: not to trust
it cast reflection on God Himself.[28] In sum, man's salvation was
advanced through many steps—conviction, conversion, sanctification,
glorification—and "as the whole of this is the Spirit's work, so he makes
use of the Word of God in every part of it."[29]

Truly, concluded Willard, they were an "unhappy Generation," who,
believing that the Spirit within led them into all truth, arrived at such a
height of "spiritual frenzy" that they contemptously called the written
Word of God a "dead Letter," a "paper Divinity," and accused all who
bound themselves to this "directory" of being despisers of the Spirit
and His teachings.[30]

The Institutions of Worship

Fox, explaining his mission in life, affirmed that he felt a command
to turn people to that "inward light" by which they might be turned
from the worship of "prayings and sings, which stood in forms without
power," and from "mens inventions and windy doctrines."[31] Their
manner of worship, explained Isaac Pennington, was "to wait on the
Lord, to meet in the silence of the flesh, and to watch for the stirrings
of his life" before praying, speaking, or singing.[32] "All other worship,"
summed up Barclay, "both praises, prayers, or preachings, which man
sets about in his own will, and at his own appointment, which he can

25. *Compleat Body*, p. 326.

26. *Ibid.*, p. 506. Cf. Barclay, *op. cit.*, pp. 81-82.

27. *Compleat Body*, p. 571. Cf. Barclay, *op. cit.*, pp. 78-79.

28. *Compleat Body*, p. 643.

29. *Ibid.*, p. 817.

30. *Peril of the Times Displayed*, pp. 139-140. Cf. Barclay, *op. cit.*, p. 78: the
Scripture is "outward" and "of itself a dead thing."

31. Fox, *op. cit.* (bi-centenary edition, London, 1891), I, 35ff.

32. Isaac Pennington, *The Works of the Long-Mournful and Sorely Distressed
Isaac Pennington*, IV, 57f.

both begin and end at his pleasure . . . are all superstition, will-worship, and abominable idolatry in the sight of God, which are now to be denied and rejected, and separated from in this day of his spiritual arising."[33]

To the clergy of New England this was reprehensible error, and taking their stand on the Westminster Confession and the Savoy Declaration they affirmed that reading of the Scriptures, preaching and hearing the Word of God, singing Psalms, and administration of the sacraments were all parts of the worship commanded by God. The Reforming Synod accordingly branded the Quakers "false worshippers" who had set up their own "Will-worship" within the Puritan Jerusalem.[34]

George Keith challenged the ministers of Boston to name one instance where praying without the Spirit was commanded in Scripture, but they avoided being speared on the horns of this dilemma by making a distinction. If it were taken to mean *"in sensu Composito,"* to pray in a graceless and Spiritless state, or to rest on one's natural abilities, they said, there was no such command in the Word of God; but if the phrase was taken *"in sensu Diviso,"* that men without the Spirit as well as those who had the Spirit were commanded to pray, the case was quite different, for prayer was a moral duty, and lack of grace did not discharge anyone from moral obligations. Simon Magus surely had neither the Spirit nor saving grace, yet he was commanded by Peter to pray for grace and conversion. As for praying by inspiration only, they pointed out that Abraham prayed for Ishmael by a natural sanctified affection, and Paul prayed three times about his thorn out of a sense of affliction, persuaded (without inspiration) that God could help him.

Keith's denunciation of singing with artificial music—with notes and tunes—and singing from a book, they thought hardly worth reply. How did one make melody without notes and tones? Was singing only a confused noise? Or did the Spirit tune men's voices by immediate inspiration? And singing from a book, they countered, reflecting the polemic of John Owen, made no case for praying from a book. In prayer one spoke while others joined with amens, but singing required joint expression by all, and what was to be sung as well as the proper meter had to be known by all. Surely Keith would not say that this came to all alike by immediate inspiration! So, until better materials came along they intended to use the Psalms of David, which they found suited to all conditions of the people of God. Christ and His disciples

---

33. *Op. cit.,* pp. 321-322.
34. "The Necessity of Reformation," p. 3; in Walker, *op. cit.,* p. 428.

had used them (Matthew 26:30), and Paul had advised their use (Colossians 3:16). And they were inspired—something that could not be said for contemporary compositions.[35]

In deriding externals of stated worship, such as the ringing of church bells to call people together, and the using of an hour-glass to time the services, Keith had become quite trivial, they thought. Since neglect of public worship was sin (Hebrews 10:25), reliance on Keith's expedients was absurd. His inward spiritual bell (the gospel bell ringing in the heart) was a "fancy" more fabulous than anything in Aesop, and his light within they considered a rather unreliable time clock.[36]

Pure formality truly was an enemy of godliness, Willard declared from the pulpit of South Church, but the other extreme was no less so. Those who under "pretext of Scriptural service" and imagined perfection rejected external worship, deemed preachers unnecessary, despised sacraments, and epithetized aids as "superstitious," were to be avoided as "filthy dreamers."[37] The duties of instituted worship, he explained in catechism sermons the next year, depend upon God's revealed will. The second commandment obligated men to receive, observe and preserve purely and entirely all the Scripturally prescribed forms of worship. These "media" were prescribed to help men worship and promote holiness. Man as creature needed this help, but as fallen and bereft of natural light he was in even greater need of it.[38] Among these divinely ordained New Testament institutions, Willard explained at length, reflecting Congregationalist and Reformed traditions, were "Gospel Churches" for the public worship of God and the "stated ordinances which are to be administered in these Churches": public prayer (1 Timothy 2:8), preaching of the Word (1 Corinthians 1:21; II Timothy 4:1, 2), the sacraments of baptism and the Lord's Supper (Matthew 28:19; Luke 22:18; I Corinthians 11:26), and church discipline (II Corinthians 10:13; Matthew 18:18; John 20:23). Once more scoring those who cast off these ordinances under the pretense of spiritual worship, Willard concluded: "those who are gotten above Ordinances, are fallen beneath Christians."[39]

35. *Principles of the Protestant Religion*, pp. 55-57. Cf. Keith, *op. cit.*, Chapter 4, Section 8.

36. *Principles of the Protestant Religion*, pp. 132-133; Cf. Keith, *op. cit.*, Chapter 9, Section 3.

37. *Peril of the Times Displayed*, pp. 29, 138, 140.

38. *Compleat Body*, pp. 609-610, 612. Sermons preached September 25 and October 21, 1701.

39. *Compleat Body*, pp. 617-620. Sermon preached December 16, 1701. On the traditional three marks of the church, cf. Heppe, *Reformed Dogmatics*, pp. 669f.

The Sacraments

Precedents within English Puritanism earlier than Quakerism had progressively weakened the importance of sacraments, but whereas William Dell, John Saltmarsh, and William Erbury had deprecated their use, Quakers deliberately, systematically, and pronouncedly rejected them. Fox, anxious to justify his spiritual interpretation, declared: "they tell People of a Sacrament, for which there is no Scripture"; "but the Baptism by the Spirit into one Body, this we own; . . . the Bread that we break is the Communion of the Body of Christ, the Cup we drink is the Communion of the Blood of Christ, all made to drink into one Spirit."[40] Similarly Barclay argued that baptism and communion were properly inward and spiritual (Calvin, he claimed, really did not know what to say about the body of Christ), that the word "sacrament" was not to be found in Scripture, that the Gospel put an end to "carnal" ordinances.[41]

All this was dangerously wrong, Willard warned in preaching up covenant keeping in 1682. These ordinances actually were "the very means of holiness," he emphasized, and these "contemptuous" folk who rejected visible ordinances as carnal and unsuited to the dispensation of grace were "subverters" of covenant duties, "enemies" of God's people who had gained "too much charity" in the world, offering great temptation "to lose much ground."[42]

The term "sacrament," Willard and his colleagues rebutted Keith, though not used in the New Testament, had been used in the church for ages to express that which was evidently Scriptural. The words "sign" and "seal," implying as much, were used of circumcision (Romans 4:11), and by parity of reasoning they were applicable to baptism and the Lord's Supper (I Peter 3:21; I Corinthians 11:26). Infant baptism they defended in the manner of Willard's polemic against the Baptists. They attacked Keith's faulty exegesis of a number of New Testament passages. Colossians 2:11, 12 could not be cited as an instance showing that circumcision and baptism were not outward, for the apostle was arguing from the sign to the thing signified. And as for Matthew 28:19 referring to baptism without mentioning water, they said, the very word implied it, and the gospel often enough did indicate that water was the element used. Furthermore, Paul thanked God that he had baptized so few, not with a slur upon the authenticity or honor of the ordinance, but because there was no reason for him to baptize person-

---

40. Fox, *Gospel-Truth Demonstrated* (ed., G. Whitehead, et al.), p. 24; *Epistles*, p. 57; and *Journal*, II, 129; quoted in Nuttall, *op. cit.*, p. 100.
    41. *Op. cit.*, pp. 21, 394, 383.
    42. *Covenant-Keeping the Way to Blessedness*, p. 98.

ally; on Keith's reasoning, they retorted, he would have done wrong in baptizing *any*. Nonetheless, New England Puritans never muted the necessity of inward baptism, they continued, for though Quakers held to it alone, they emphasized baptism both with water and the Holy Spirit. In much the same way they scorned Keith's allegation that the Lord's Supper had no inward spiritual signification for New England Congregationalists. They emphasized both the outward institution of Christ and the spiritual feeding upon Him, they explained, the outward being but a sign of the inward, and as a sign enjoined by Christ Himself they did not dare to omit it.[43]

Willard's catechism sermons affirmed essentially the same points. While it was obviously wrong to observe the sacrament merely as a form, he declared, it was equally wrong to call it valueless because in and of itself it was without efficacy to produce what it signified, for God had appointed it as a means for obtaining grace. "They therefore that slight and contemn it, pretend to be wiser than Christ; and by despising one of God's appointments, do expose themselves to his righteous displeasure."[44] Shortly before his death Willard prepared a number of sermons on the sacraments which elaborated once again the traditional Reformed viewpoint. The heavenly-mindedness of Quakers was an illusion, he said, for the spiritual vision of the New Testament era was still divinely limited, since God had chosen, while time endured, to reveal Himself mediately also through the sacraments.

> Nor need we to spend time in shewing the Vanity of this Allega-
> tion of Men against this: for tho' the Gospel be a more spiritual
> Dispensation than that of the law in several respects, yet this is a
> great Truth, that there is this difference between God's dis-
> covering of himself to his People in this Life, and that which is to
> come; that here it is Mediate, and there it will be Immediate:
> Here we must see through a glass darkly, but then Face to Face, I
> Cor. 13:11.[45]

The Professional Ministry

In the ideal church, according to Quaker teachers, every man and woman was enabled through the guidance of the Spirit to become his own teacher. Capitalizing upon a development that had become vigor-

---

43. *Principles of the Protestant Religion,* pp. 136-139, 141-145. Cf. Keith, *op. cit.,* Chapter 10, Sections 1-4.

44. *Compleat Body,* p. 366.

45. *Ibid.,* p. 843. Cf. Nuttall, *op. cit.,* pp. 90-91, and Heppe, *op. cit.,* pp. 627, 629ff., 636ff., for the traditional Puritan and Reformed position.

ous in England, Fox encouraged all to express themselves, moved by the indwelling Spirit.

> Lett it be your Joy to heare or see ye Springs of life breake forth in any . . .such as are Tender, if they should be moved to bubble forth a few words & speake in ye seed & lambs power suffer & beare y^t that is ye Tender, & if they should goe beyond their measure beare it in ye meeting for peace sake & order.[46]

Quakers therefore abandoned not only a separated ministry but also a purely male ministry. "What, are all true Christians Priests?" asked Fox. "Yes: What are Women Priests? Yes, Women Priests."[47] Quaker women thereupon preached in England, and they came to the American colonies to preach.

Quakers did not despise education in itself, but emphasis upon a ministry depending upon the Spirit rather than learning eventually led them to bear testimony both against the learned and "hireling" ministry maintained by Anglicans, Presbyterians, and Independents. Barclay argued that since all true spiritual knowledge was revealed and received by the light or gift of God (and only in this way was a true minister ordained and equipped), those so qualified were to preach without human commission or literature, and having received it freely they were to give it without hire or bargaining. Covetousness and excess would be curtailed if at most they (like Paul) would receive only voluntary gifts of food and clothing. If such voluntary support was not forthcoming, perhaps the preaching had been powerless and deserved nothing.[48]

This Quaker witness, dictated by the English practice of forced tithes in support of established ministers, was turned on the similar situation in New England where all were compelled to contribute to the support of the Congregational ministry. This doctrine, broadcast by numerous itinerant self-appointed Quaker preachers, not only challenged orthodox faith, it was a direct threat to the ecclesiastical system of Massachusetts. Materialism and worldliness were already crowding in upon the religious interests of New England, causing many to begrudge payments for the church's ministry, and it is understandable that New England leaders did not look on with indifference as Quaker missionaries crisscrossed the land, aggravating the situation by their preaching. One of the provoking evils calling for reform, declared the assembled ministers at the Synod of 1679, was the withholding of wages from the

46. Fox, *Journal* (ed., H. Penny), I, 222; cf. also his *Works* (Philadelphia, 1831), pp. 365-367; quoted in Nuttall, *op. cit.,* p. 86.

47. Fox, *Epistles*, p. 244; quoted in Nuttall, *op. cit.,* p. 87.

48. *Op. cit.,* p. 257. Cf. Braithwaite, *Second Period of Quakerism*, xix, 524-553; and Frederick B. Tolles, *Quakers and the Atlantic Culture*, pp. 3, 25.

faithful laborers who toiled for the welfare of men's souls. The Scriptures expressly taught, they stated, that all who were taught of the Word of God, not only church members, were to support those who ministered; if people were unwilling to do what justice and reason dictated, the magistrate was to see to it that they did their duty.[49] But as the century wore on, with the imposition of taxes to meet mounting defense costs, and the introduction of a new form of money, inflated currency left clerical salaries often quite inadequate. An abstract from an account book kept by the deacons of South Church reveals that in the face of rising costs of living Willard's salary was not increased during the period. A large gift of appreciation was given to him from the treasury of the church in 1693, however, accompanied by an additional subscription by the membership of the church.[50] But while Willard seems not to have complained for himself, he did speak out often in behalf of others.

In much the same way that he had answered the deprecation of the Baptists earlier, Willard joined his colleagues in rebutting the attacks of Keith on the ministry. Quakers, unsuccessful in getting ministers to cease preaching against their errors, they said, sought to persuade people that they owed ministers no maintenance, "and if they can starve them out, the business is done." Ministerial support should be voluntary and from charity, Keith declared, citing I Corinthians 9:14f. Quite the contrary, replied the ministers: for the apostle in arguing for ministerial support from Old Testament regulations for priests and Levites, argued from the lesser to the greater. And if, as judicious scholars reasoned, the tribe of Levi comprised one fortieth of the people but was allotted the portion of three tribes, the implication was obvious! Far from being "Alms of Mercy," ministerial maintenance was a debt of justice according to ample New Testament teaching (Galatians 6:6; I Timothy 5:17, 19; I Corinthians 9). As for Christ sending forth His disciples with a prohibition against taking anything from others, this was a special precept; until He bade others to do this they were to rely on His providence, and not to do so would be to tempt God. Nor was Paul's practice normative; according to his own statement maintenance was his due, but though he chose not to take it no one was to suffer because of it. Besides, as he himself said, though he took no wages from the churches of Achaia, he did from others (II Corinthians 11:8-10). Furthermore, voluntary practice during days of persecution was not meant to be obligatory for others in times of peace. In spite of all of

---

49. "Necessity of Reformation," pp. 8, 11; in Walker, *op. cit.,* pp. 432, 434.
50. Hill, *op. cit.,* I, 228n., 294n. On the general situation see Samuel E. Morison's "Introduction," in Sibley, *Biographical Sketches,* IV, 4.

Keith's railing, however, New England ministers, they claimed, could never be charged with oppressing people.[51]

Willard's catechism sermons on the ten commandments vigorously championed the same ideas. The ministry was an ordinance established by the second commandment, he declared; hence maintenance was not left to human liberty but appointed by Christ. Support was to be proportionate to the people's blessings, though the method might be prudential. Suitable respect, enjoined by the fifth commandment, Willard explained to those who were inclined to forget New England's tradition of social stratification, required proper maintenance for the ministry. "God hath ever since He had a Church in the World, taken care of the Comfortable Supply of those who Serve Him in *Religious Orders*," he reminded them. It was reasonable that faithful ministers who spent their time in behalf of men's souls should live without fear of "outward Concerns." Support was an act of justice, therefore, not of voluntary alms or charity. If ministers, who were duty-bound to devote themselves exclusively to their calling, broke this commandment in taking additional employment, church members were no less guilty by withholding their "Comfortable & Honourable Subsistence," thereby necessitating the neglect of their "proper" work in order to support themselves. Since the ministry was a public calling serving the "publick Benefit," he declared in his exposition of the eighth commandment, the public owed a sufficient and honourable support to those who served "at the Altar." And interpreted positively, this commandment required cheerfulness in liberal distribution![52]

Aided by social forces, Quakers at length, a decade after Willard's death, were granted exemption from the law compelling support of the Congregational ministry. But it was an uphill fight all the way, and Willard, for one, to the end of his life fought to preserve the New England system.

51. *Principles of the Protestant Religion,* pp. 41-55, 58-61. Cf. Keith, *op. cit.,* Chapter 4, Section 10.
52. *Compleat Body,* pp. 618-620 (December 16, 1701); pp. 639-640, 650 (April 4, 1704); pp. 693, 710 (April and July, 1705).

CHAPTER TEN

HISTORY AND THE JUDGMENTS OF GOD

Willard had a philosophy of history, or more accurately a theology of history, and this ultimately explains his dedication to the role of defender and propagandist of the orthodox faith. He was certain about the direction of history—where it had come from and where it was going. He kept a sharp eye on what was happening in New England, but he also took note of significant developments and trends in the religious world across the sea. To him this interest was no idle avocation of a clerical hobbyist: all previous history was a prologue to, and all contemporary history determined the success or failure of New England's errand into the wilderness. All this he interpreted according to the lights of recorded revelation as he read it.

His ideas were developed not in scientific or systematic treatises—the more profound intricacies he waived aside as more "nice" than edifying—but in sermons, often on special and noteworthy occasions.

A product of the second century of the Reformation, he did not transcend the limitations and presuppositions of the seventeenth-century frame of reference. The inherited fund of ideas with which he worked was the Hebrew view of civilization, recast with Christian insights by the writers of the New Testament and the early church fathers, especially Augustine, and reaffirmed in the Protestant Reformation. This is to say, he had a providential view of history.

History as Providential

History to him was conceived in the mind of God. It was the outworking of the eternal plan of God, who contrived an "Eternal idea

170

of all things" that were to be and saw all things in one "perfect and eternal view" without any "successive intuition." As an intelligent and wise "Artificer" God had an idea of all His works before He willed them: "if therefore God works in time, we presuppose that he Purposed so to do before Time." Thus the manifold happenings of time were to be traced back to the divine decree.

> The Decree involves everything in it, and hath left nothing uncertain as to that; it extends it self to all Effects and Events, Eph. 1.11. It reacheth to *Sparrows*, Matth. 10.29. And *Hairs,* Ver. 30. To *Goards* and *Worms,* Jon. 4. And as it neglects not the Least Things, so it orders the Greatest; all Changes in *Kingdoms* and *Monarchies,* Dan. 4.32. And things most *Eventual,* Prov. 16.33. *The lot is cast into the lap: but the whole disposing thereof is of the Lord.* Yea, even the Arbitrary Contingent Actions of Reasonable Creatures, Acts 2.33.[1]

Every second cause was decreed by the divine first cause, for in pursuing eventuation "up to the top" one comes upon God. Arminians made history a kind of divine patchwork with their affirmation of human contingency, whereas in reality conditions had also been decreed. "The Conditions of things are but *Media* in his Decrees, and only intend, that he will bring about such Ends, by such Means; and having once proposed, he never varied."[2] God's great design thus precedes the observable chain of events that transpire within a decreed scheme of causation.

History had a beginning. Whatever God foreordained "he brings to pass in his Works," causing it to pass by his transient efficiency "from Not-Being to Being . . . and to such a Being." Eternity is solely the prerogative of God, all else was created and had a beginning. Everything that exists follows the principle of succession of hours, days, years, and ages, "and where there is a Succession, there is no Eternity, but a Beginning." Time is but the measure of the creature's duration, and being a measure it must have limits. The world's beginning could be discerned from the "Original" of nations, and investigation of antiquity disclosed when and where it was first peopled, for the closer one got to it the more numerous the "Monuments" of antiquity became. The number of years since man's creation, as Willard counted them up in the Scripture, was "considerably short of Six Thousand Years." To him it was unreasonable to think that the world should have stood for many thousands of ages before man was placed on it. The most ancient

1. *Compleat Body of Divinity,* pp. 101-103.
2. *Ibid.,* p. 91.

histories, he found, began with the Assyrian monarchy and the reign of "Ninus," Abraham's contemporary, the records before that being confused fragments of things "meerly Mythological" and "very Fabulous." Furthermore, the invention of the arts was relatively recent, "many of them were but of Yesterday, in comparison, and have not at this Day arrived in Perfection, but have new Experiments added to them continually."[3]

The only exception to philosophy's maxim *"Ex nihilo nihil fit"* was God, and faith alone comprehended it. The world, Willard observed pre-scientifically, was created in equinox from a created mass of formless, unindividuated, uninhabitable, chaotic matter which had been maintained in this state for literally twelve hours (John 11:9), and then orderly fashioned into the present frame of things in literally six days (Exodus 20:11; Genesis 1). Man was introduced last, after divine deliberation, and placed on the "Globe" as a special creature who, in addition to vegetative, motive, and sense life, possessed a soul. He is, accordingly, a reasonable creature who

> can both propound to himself his own End, and make choice of the Means of Way leading unto it. . . . None can either compel or hinder him in his Choice, but he can follow the Dictates of his own Understanding: From whence it follows, that all his humane Actions are Voluntary & Deliberate.

It was precisely this that gave significance to man's relationship to God in history, for man's chief purpose as "head of the Lower World," was "to direct himself, and improve the other Beings, to the Glory of his, and their Creator."[4]

History was also in God's hands. Having created the world God did not leave it to guide itself, nor did He put it into man's hands—He kept His own finger on everything. He "drives the great and whole trade of the world," said Willard, in language Boston merchants would understand. Five arguments buttressed this providential view of history. The wise and orderly management of the world of irrational things implied it. The control of the affairs of rational beings, sometimes defeating and frustrating man's most skillfully contrived designs, argued One above them. He who made it incumbent on men to care for their own was hypothetically under similar obligation, Willard observed; in fact "the whole world is a sucking Infant depending on the Breasts of Divine Providence." The preservation of the Bible and the Church throughout the ages in the face of persecution was a proof of providence. And the

3. *Ibid.*, pp. 105, 108.
4. *Ibid.*, pp. 109-111, 114-116, 119, 122-124, 128.

objections or scruples of men were easily answered: "chance" was only
what men saw, and contingent second causes though real were determined by the first cause. One, therefore, either had to believe in
providence or deny his Christianity, asserted Willard. And without faith
one "must needs despair."

> How can he Sanctify God in the Fires; Rejoice in the *Want* of all
> things; Uphold his Profession in *Integrity,* when he is *sore broken
> in the Place of Dragons;* Suffer cheerfully the *Loss* of Estate,
> Liberty, yea Life itself in the Defence of the *Truths of Christ;* if
> he doth not believe that there is the Wisdom & Power of God
> Managing of those Affairs? [5]

Puritan congregations, compared with today's, had incredible appe-
tites for lengthy expositions of doctrine, and Willard's discourses on
providence at South Church were as detailed as the standard manuals of
dogmatics. Providence, he methodically explained to the choice gather-
ings of townfolk at his catechetical lectures, was the continuation of
the divine efficiency begun in creation; it extended universally to all
times, places, and things; it was exact in its operation, and it followed
God's fixed and unalterable counsel. There could be nothing fortuitous
in such a scheme, nothing in the least accidental or circumstantial. But
certainty of futurition did not violate the contingency of second causes,
for rational agents acted voluntarily, though in subordination to the
rules of providence. God was immediately present in every effect
(Amos 3:6) as the absolute cause (Acts 17:28). In carrying out His
great design God worked mediately in second causes so that they did
nothing except what He determined and enabled them to do (II
Chronicles 24:24; Amos 5:9; I Corinthians 1:27, 28; Judges 7:2), still
second causes really acted as if there were no first cause. [6]

Ordinarily God acted according to natural law, according to the
principle imprinted on things in creation, Willard explained, but in
extraordinary instances He could alter His method by miraculously
"skipping over" or "inverting" the natural order, since the ratification
of the gospel miracles was not frequent. God did two things in all
this: He conserved and He governed. Every creature was not
only dependent on God for existence and the power to operate, he also
needed to be rightly directed to attain his own subordinate purpose and
the final purpose of glorifying God. Man's concurrence in this scheme
Willard subsumed under divine government. "Except He who Made this
great Vessel, and Upholds it, be also it's *Pilot*," Willard continued, in

5. *Ibid.,* pp. 105, 129-132.
6. *Ibid.,* pp. 133-136. Cf. Heppe, *Reformed Dogmatics,* Chapter XII.

figures those who knew the sea and New England's treacherous shore-
line would understand,

> it will never shape a true *Course,* but be Lost. He holds the *Card*
> and *Compass,* and sits at *Helm:* And though Rational Beings are
> called upon to Eye the *Pole-Star,* yet did not He direct these,
> they would also miscarry: . . . God having *Made* a World, doth
> not leave it to be managed by another, as the *Shipwright* doth his
> Ship. He only knows every Nook and Corner, every Rock, and
> Shelve, and Quick sand; and how to carry it Clear of all, into the
> *Port* it is Bound for.[7]

This divine government was both common and special, common in
the sense that all creation—rain, hail and snow, wind and tempest—acts
at His arbitrary command, in ways Willard thought defied physical
explanation by man; and special in the sense that God dealt with man
from the beginning by way of covenant. When man, abusing his free
will, fell from the covenant of life, God entered into a covenant of
grace with him, a transaction which gave meaning to all of history:
"truly, the main drift or design of the whole book of God, in the old
and new Testament, is to give us an account of this affair."[8]

To the Puritan mind, therefore, Biblical history was of immense
value. God had a practical design in preserving much of recordable
history in the Bible: by rightly using "Scripture history" they were able
to draw lessons applicatory to their own lives. Anyone properly steeped
in this knowledge had in his possession the key to unlock the mystery
and meaning of contemporary events. "No providences pass before us
but we ought to observe them," counseled Willard, "so as to use them
for our advantage."[9] Equally important, scanning "the current of
Scripture history" one could not fail to note the recurrent order of rise
and fall. "Godly and zealous Rulers in State & Church were taken from
them, and they presently fell into their Apostacies, and hereby God was
stirred up to Anger against them, and all manner of evils thereupon over
took them, and wasted them."[10] When they repented and reformed,
they rose again. Everything moved from a definite beginning to a
determined end; history not only disclosed significant periodicity in
this eternally plotted line of time, it also revealed God's moral and
spiritual purposes in dealing with men.

7. *Compleat Body,* pp. 136-144.
8. *Ibid.,* pp. 145-148, 153-157, 246.
9. *Truly Blessed Man,* p. 280.
10. *Prognosticks of Impending Calamities,* pp. 28-29.

The Significance of the Christian Era

The Christian era began with the most important event of all history—Christ's "coming in the Flesh" to accomplish atonement and void all that had been "figured" in the law—and it would continue until Christ came again in the great and general judgment.[11] The incarnation was the great dividing line of history, distinguishing between the prophetic and typical prefigurements of the time of the law and the clear universality of the gospel day.[12] The covenant dispensation under "Jewish Paedagogy" was brought to an end with the destruction of the second temple and the dispersion of the Jewish nation by the Romans, and subsequent time became that of the "Gospel Constitution of the Church." This Church, the kingdom of heaven, the mediatorial kingdom purchased by Christ's blood, He Himself ruled from the "throne" until His second coming, though outwardly it was administered by the settled and unalterable institutions of Christ.[13]

From its inception this Church, understood in the large sense of all who make an "Orthodox Profession of the faith and truth as it is in Jesus," had a checkered career. Light and darkness alternated within it, an imperfection that will continue until the last judgment ushers in a period of great light. In the apostolic age and that immediately succeeding it—during the lifetime of those who had seen and conversed with the apostles—the light of knowledge was bright, and there was a great deal of holiness. But troubles too, for "Errours and Heresies . . . sprang up even in the Apostles days."[14] For this reason Willard, like his colleagues, read the fathers critically with Scriptures in hand, and though he occasionally cited Tertullian and Augustine with approbation, the fathers in general, he felt, interpreted the Christian religion "too laxely."[15] Gnostics, Manicheans, Marcionites, tritheites and others troubled the church,[16] and by degrees the light became dimmer till at length "gross ignorance, error, and superstition" brought a "sable cloud" upon the church.[17] As the world turned Arian in denying the divinity of Christ the orthodox were diminished to the point that it "was once said, *One Athanasius against the whole world.*" But the Nicene Council gave "plump testimony against the Blasphemy" vented

11. *Checkered State of the Gospel Church*, pp. 4-5.
12. *The Fountain Opened*, pp. 33-35.
13. *Checkered State of the Gospel Church*, pp. 6-7.
14. *Ibid.*, pp. 8-10, 12-14, 16.
15. *Compleat Body*, p. 834. As examples of his citation of Tertullian and Augustine, see *Mercy Magnified*, pp. 59, 381-382, and *Compleat Body*, p. 738.
16. *Compleat Body*, p. 94.
17. *Checkered State of the Gospel Church*, p. 14.

by Arius to the dishonor of the Son of God.[18] Declension worsened as "Antichristianism" grew to its height in what is now called the Middle Ages, graphically described by this Puritan divine as the time when "the fogs of the bottomless pit grievously obscured the Sunlight of the Gospel."[19] The Roman Church so perverted and encumbered the teaching of Christ with doctrinal and ritualistic observances of her own invention that she became the very antithesis of all she claimed to be, the antichrist. No less than others, therefore, Willard denounced its "Blind Popish Errors, concerning Merits, Satisfaction, many Mediators, &c."[20]

With the Reformation came a great "clearing time," a time second in importance only to the advent of Christ and the apostolic age in its manifestations of grace.[21] Wonderful accomplishments had been made since the Reformation, but not without opposition. "Rome and Hell have carried on a plot, ever since the Reformation in England," he declared, "to blow up the Protestant interest there."[22] It was because their fathers could not fully achieve there the spiritual potentialities they envisioned that they turned their eyes to the new world.

Willard shared the conviction that the New England enterprise had been launched at the apex of the Reformation era, that it was an event without parallel except that of Abraham leaving Ur or the children of Israel fleeing Egypt. The design of the founders was to settle and secure religion for themselves and their posterity according to God's way, he reiterated,[23] and there was no place in all the world where a people had been "brought to such perfection and considerableness, in so short a time."

From the beginning, therefore, New England was under special obligation to make good because of its covenant relationship with God. No people since the time of the Jews, with the exception of the Scots, were as avowedly a covenant people. "Thus stands the cause between God and us," declared John Winthrop aboard the *Arbella*, "wee are entered into Covenant with him for this worke, . . . [and] hee . . . will expect a

18. *Ibid.*, p. 14; *Compleat Body*, p. 319; *Heavenly Merchandize*, p. 104.
19. *Checkered State of the Gospel Church*, p. 14.
20. *Covenant-Keeping The Way to Blessedness*, "Preface." On Puritan attitudes to Roman Catholicism, see Mary Augustana Ray, *American Opinion of Roman Catholicism in the Eighteenth Century*, p. 15. Cf. also Miller and Johnson, *The Puritans*, pp. 9-10.
21. *Checkered State of the Gospel Church*, p. 14; *Fountain Opened*, p. 115.
22. *All Plots*, p. 225.
23. *Ne Sutor Ultra Crepidam*, p. 4; cf. also *Covenant-Keeping the Way to Blessedness*, p. 114; "The Necessity of Reformation," p. iii, in Walker, *Creeds and Platforms*, pp. 423-424.

strikt performance of the Articles contained in it."[24] The legitimacy of this collective commitment Willard never questioned; the ways of God with New England were in many respects like His dealings with ancient Israel. "That the body of a Professing People are, as such, *in Covenant with God*" was sufficiently witnessed in Scripture.[25] God in entering into this type of relationship with a people voluntarily bound Himself to deal with them according to special terms. The heathen world He might treat as He pleased, "upon his meer Prerogative," but a professing People in visible covenant with Him He treated "according to the tenour of that Covenant, in which there are Conditionate Promises and Threatenings."[26] A chosen people were the recipients of special favors and under special obligations. The whole creation was under God's "common" government, all rational creatures experienced His "special" government, but His own people were led and guided "inwardly by his Spirit, outwardly by his Ordinances, and Providences."[27] Complete submission was implicit. "A People that are in Covenant with him, have acknowledged and submitted to his Sovereignty over them; . . . When therefore they depart from his Obedience, and *turn aside to their crooked wayes,* they therein depart from their Allegiance."[28]

This obviously meant that New Englanders had a corporate responsibility in keeping the covenant, Willard warned. "Now what concerns such a People as they are a Body, or a Company of Professors standing under the Obligations of such a Covenant, referrs unto this life and the Affairs of it, for they will not be considered or treated after this life as a people."[29] God's promises for their collective weal, such as their safety, he explained, "are *Temporary;* and both the Promises and Threatenings which are ratified to them refer to this World, and the blessings or the evils that are to be met withal here." Ultimately the power to comply with the terms of such a covenant came from God, "that so they may keep close to their duty," but this was not meant to encourage human passivity. New Englanders too often exhibited the fatal tendency of the ancient Israelites to depend on the covenant absolutely, "and accordingly to cry, *The Temple of the Lord,* as if that were their security." Like Jeremiah, therefore, Willard also warned against reliance on external things, emphasizing that the presence of the Lord was only for those who obeyed His will, and only in this way

24. Winthrop, "A Modell of Christian Charity," *Winthrop Papers, 1623-1630,* II; reprinted in Smith, Handy and Loetscher, *American Christianity,* I, 101.
25. *Israel's True Safety,* p. 9.
26. *Rules for Discerning the Present Times,* p. 24.
27. *Mercy Magnified,* pp. 53-54.
28. *Reformation the Great Duty of an Afflicted People,* p. 36.
29. *Rules for Discerning the Present Times,* pp. 24-25.

would they be preserved from disaster. God could be said to be for them only when they were for Him, and walked "in conformity to the terms of the Covenant, with which the promises are connected, & unto which they are restrained."[30] It all boiled down to this: "A people in visible Covenant stand upon their good behaviour, as they carry it so they may expect it shall go with them."[31]

The Four Horsemen

The New England experiment had hardly got under way before the declension they so much feared and warned against began in their Bible commonwealth. "A little after 1660," observed Thomas Prince from the vantage point of the next century, "there began to appear a *Decay:* and this increased to 1670, when it grew visible and threatening, and was generally complained of and bewailed bitterly by the Pious among them: and yet much more to 1680, when but few of the first Generation remained."[32] Distressed at their own waning piety, the founding saints were disturbed that the new generation, increasingly absorbed in economic success and worldly pleasures, evidenced even less of the true spirit. These native born sons and daughters, strangers to the stress that fostered their fathers' strenuous piety, and growing up in a settled community, were succumbing to the spiritual drag of human nature and responding according to the laws of social change. New England leaders were too concerned about the consequences, however, to rationalize about this perennial tendency of all creative movements. To them the formula of the communal covenant worked perfectly: they had broken their allegiance, and the divine threatenings automatically went into effect.

Within a few years it seemed that the four horsemen of the Apocalypse—conquest, war, pestilence, and death—galloped across New England. Here was the proof of God's controversy with them: such calamities were judgments. Already as a young minister at Groton Church Willard made the standard points. God invariably dealt with an externally covenanted people according to the terms of promises and threats, and though He sovereignly reserved the right to vary His method, "as to the essence of the Covenant, he thus stands positively and absolutely engaged to reward obedience, and to punish disobedience." His judgments were so many "documents" to be carefully read. The Bible itself pointed out the monitory significance of Noah's flood and Sodom's overthrow. If New Englanders made no better use of their

---

30. *Israel's True Safety,* pp. 10, 6-7.
31. *Sermon Preached upon Ezekiel,* p. 3. Cf. Jeremiah 7:4.
32. Thomas Prince, *Christian History,* I, 94.

privileges than Israel, he warned, "we may expect to be visited as well as they were, and not only may we argue *a pari*, but also *ab impari*, from the lesser to the greater; if Israel so privileged were not spared, how much less shall we be spared, who exceed them in priviledges." God's judgments came in a host of ways, sometimes immediately by unseen hands, sometimes mediately by devils, men, brute beasts, and the elements. They were often ordinary like sickness, famine, and pestilence, but sometimes extraordinary like possession by devils. They could be personal or epidemical, outward or spiritual, but they were all from God—they were "speaking Providence."[33] This was the explanation of the strange hysteria of Elizabeth Knapp, the crop failure of 1672, King Philip's War in 1675, the smallpox epidemic in 1677-78, the fires and the shipwrecks, and the hostility of the Stuart government.

But one of the blessings of their special relationship to God, Willard reminded the General Court and the people of New England in 1682, was that a way of recovery was open to a covenanted nation. "This is the priviledge of a People in visible Covenant with God, that there is no threatening denounced against them, but with a gracious reserve and room to reverse it in case of Repentance." Bad as the situation was, the limit of God's graciousness had not been reached, there could still be hope. "I cannot but be persuaded that God hath good things yet in reserve for *New-England:* but he expects your reformation, and that you acknowledge and turn from your sins." He was aghast that some churches held back from covenant renewal for fear that their judgment and condemnation would be the greater. "If these Churches are not prepared to renew their Covenant with God, they are not prepared for mercy: If the way of our Anastasie be more dangerous than our state of Apostacie, our danger is tremendous."[34]

The removal of eminent leaders by death he interpreted as an expression of the same divine displeasure. While not blind to the natural facts of life, Governor John Leverett's death at the age of sixty-three was, he thought, a "solemn stroke of displeasure," an ominous loss at a time when such "reiterated strokes" were frequent. "Indeed the voice of providence is loud," he warned. "The Plucking up of the Pillars is in order to the pulling down of the house."[35] Circumstances sometimes clearly indicated that events were "judicial and calamitous," he declared at Major Thomas Savage's funeral in 1682: when such pious and useful men were taken away on the heels of ministerial warnings about

33. *Useful Instructions,* pp. 11-12, 23, 25, 31-32. Cf. Luke 17:32 and I Peter 2:4-6.
34. *The only sure way to prevent threatned Calamity,* pp. 175, 187, 191.
35. *Sermon Preached upon Ezekiel,* pp. 1, 4, 10-12.

judgment, it indicated that God was beginning to execute His threatenings. Confidently unravelling the riddle of divine providence that permitted the removal of the godly while the wicked were left, Willard explained that everything had (as the philosopher put it) two handles, and most took providence by the wrong handle.

> They interpret many dispensations to be Judicial, and so indeed they may be; but their folly is, that they interpret them so to be in respect of the persons suffering them, when as it is indeed to themselves.[36]

"I shall not make it my work to Prophesie," declared Willard at the death of John Hull a year and a half later, but went on nonetheless to ask: "When there are but a few Saints in the world, and these die apace ... what is to be thought to be at the door."[37] The same refrain was repeated at the funeral of John Eliot, who died at the age of eighty-six in 1690.[38] When William Stoughton died at the age of seventy in 1701, he pulled his old sermons out of the file, chose a different text, rearranged the arguments, and did it all over again. Though God has testified against us in many ways awaiting our reformation, he lamented, "we have rather grown worse, & remain stupid." Return to God, he warned, "lest he be provoked to anger, *and cause the Funerals of our wise and good Leaders, to be but the harbingers to the Funeral of all that is precious & pleasant among us.*"[39]

The message was reinforced by events across the sea. News of the repression of the Huguenots moved Willard to warn that this fiery trial was no strange thing, that in the providence of God New Englanders might have to face the same trial.[40] Similarly, the persecution of the Protestants in Hungary, he explained, was God permitting world rulers to persecute His people that they might be reformed; a "vastly different effect" was created in "looking upon instruments, and no further, and looking upon them as instruments, eyeing withal the hand that manageth them." Seeing God in them, he exhorted, enabled one to "discern his holy displeasure, enkindled by sin, which will tend to humble us, and drive us to Repentance."[41]

A short time later as the colony came under royal governors, a rigid censorship was imposed upon the press, and the jeremiad of judgment was suddenly muted.

36. *Righteous Man's Death,* pp. 150, 154-155.
37. *High Esteem Which God hath of the Death of his Saints,* p. 18.
38. *Barren Fig Trees Doom,* pp. 215-216.
39. *Prognosticks of Impending Calamities,* pp. 15, 32.
40. *Fiery Trial,* pp. 13, 18.
41. *All Plots,* pp. 207-210, 219-220.

Satan and His Instruments

For three agonizing years Massachusetts lay under the royal thumb. Then followed the bitter partisan struggle over the new charter. For more than a decade, therefore, the spirit of New England was torn on the rack of political, social, and religious vicissitudes. Willard had warned about impending new calamities, but though they had battled the elements, fought the Indians, and struggled with the Crown, none were prepared for the mysterious onslaught from the invisible world. The witchcraft hysteria of 1692 caught them unawares.

They had handled cases of alleged witchcraft before, but what happened at Salem village that February was without parallel in her history. Its ultimate resolution was due to the key role played by Willard behind the scenes.

More than a hundred persons had been accused by the two neurotic daughters of the Reverend Samuel Parris by the time the special Court of Oyer and Terminer was appointed on May 14.[42] The Court included three of Willard's parishioners—Samuel Sewall, Wait Still Winthrop, and Peter Sergeant.[43] When Bridget Bishop, the first to be condemned, was hanged on June 10, the governor and the Council, following an older charter practice, sought the advice of the ministers, who, carefully thumbing through the manuals of William Perkins and Richard Bernard, advised against admission of spectral evidence and urged calmness and caution.[44] Willard and others began to have serious doubts about the proceedings and the guilt of the accused when five more lives were taken on June 19. Sometime between June 30 and July 19 one of the accusers "cried out publicly of Mr. Willard Minister in Boston, as afflicting her," but she was informed that she was "mistaken in the person," and sent out of Court.[45] When the highly respected John

---

42. There is a vast literature on the witchcraft episode. A short bibliography of important primary and secondary sources is given in Miller and Johnson, *op. cit.*, pp. 826-827. George L. Burr has edited a number of the documents in *Narratives of the Witchcraft Cases, 1648-1706.* William E. Woodward has performed similar service in *Records of Salem Witchcraft, Copied from the Original Documents.*

43. For biographical detail see Hill and Bigelow, *Historical Catalogue*, pp. 259, 290, 288.

44. Cf. William Perkins, *A Discourse of the Damned Art of Witchcraft* (Cambridge, England, 1606); and Richard Bernard, *A Guide to Grand-Jury Men* (1627, 1629).

45. Robert Calef, *More Wonders of the Invisible World* (1700), in Burr, *op. cit.*, p. 360.

Alden was also accused and kept prisoner at his own home, a fast was held there on July 20, and Willard offered prayer.[46]

Willard conferred with the ministers again on August 1, because the Court, assuming that God would not permit an innocent person to be accused, still accepted all evidence offered, so that accusation meant conviction, unless the accused confessed and gave evidence by accusing others. The ministers felt at the time that though the devil might have permission to instigate those possessed to accuse innocent persons as their tormentors, such instances were rare, especially when brought before civil judicatories. Since the whole question turned upon the nature of the evidence, the ministers, after consulting certain French and Dutch ministers in New York (who without shedding further light urged circumspection), commissioned Increase Mather to codify citations from available authorities. On October 3 they endorsed his manuscript on the invalidity of spectral evidence, entitled "Cases of Conscience Concerning evil Spirits Personating Men," and hurried it off to the governor. Governor Phips thereupon resolved that the Court, which under the vigorous prosecution of Chief Justice William Stoughton had already executed twenty of the twenty-five condemned, should sit no longer, and that prosecutions on the basis of this procedure should cease.[47] Willard's preface to the treatise, reflecting sentiments expressed two decades before at Groton, stated his strong reservations about the proceedings.

> So odious and Abominable is the name of a Witch, to the Civilized, much more the Religious part of Mankind, that it is apt to grow up into a Scandal for any, so much as to enter some sober cautions against the over hasty suspecting, or too precipitant Judging of Persons on this Account. But certainly, the more execrable the Crime is, the more Critical care is to be used in exposing of the Names, Liberties, and Lives of men (especially of a Godly Conversation) to the imputation of it.[48]

After reading "Mr. Willard's Epistle to Mr. Mather's book," Judge Sewall discussed the matter with former deputy governor Thomas Danforth, who expressed the opinion, said Sewall, that "there cañot be

---

46. Sewall, *Diary, 5 M.H.S. Colls.,* V, 361-362.

47. Letter of Governor William Phips, October 12, 1692, to the home government, in Burr, *op. cit.,* p. 197.

48. Increase Mather, *Cases of Conscience Concerning Evil Spirits Personating Men,* "Christian Reader." Though postdated 1693, an earlier copy is inscribed by a contemporary, "Novr 24th. 1692." Cf. Holmes, *Increase Mather: A Bibliography,* p. 106.

a procedure in Court except there be some better consent of the Ministers and People."[49]

In trying to halt the uncritical proceedings Willard came in for his share of criticism, but also praise. One of his parishioners, the wealthy and broadminded Thomas Brattle, applauding the courageous leadership of the ministers, wrote to a clerical correspondent in England on October 8, 1692:

> in particular, I cannot but think very honourably of the endeavors of a Rev'd person in Boston, whose good affection to his countrey in general, and spiritual relation to three judges in particular, has made him very solicitous and industrous in this matter; . . . He has as yett mett with little but unkindness, abuse, and reproach from many men; but I trust that, in after times, his wisdome and service will find a more universal acknowledgment; and if not, his reward is with the Lord.[50]

There is good reason to believe that Willard influenced the popular mind in still another way. Sometime during the excitement, while the troubles were at their height, a pseudonymous and witty dialogue between S (Salem) and B (Boston) was published as *Some Miscellany Observations on our Present Debates respecting Witchcrafts.* Ostensibly written by "P.E." (Philip English) and "J.A." (John Alden) for Hezekiah Usher, and purportedly printed by William Bradford in Philadelphia, its origins seem shrouded in mystery. The type is not Bradford's; and Usher, English, and Alden—all safely hiding in New York as fugitives from reckless accusations at Salem, after being assisted in their escape by Willard—had nothing to do with the work.[51] Robert Calef in 1695 suggested Willard as "the suppos'd Author."[52] The *Observations* openly admits that there was great dissatisfaction with the proceedings against those accused of witchcraft at Salem, and that some attempts to obstruct them had been made. In answer to *S*'s anxiety that this will prove pernicious to the land in view of the already existing divisions among them, *B* replies that while the peace of the place was always to be sought, an earnest contending for the truth was also requisite. In brief, the argument is as follows. *B* assumes the existence of witches and the legitimacy of punishing them, but emphasizes the need for

49. Sewall, *op. cit.,* 367.

50. Letter of Thomas Brattle, F.R.S., October 8, 1692, in Burr, *op. cit.,* pp. 186-187.

51. Burr, *op. cit.,* p. 187n. Cf. S. G. Drake, *The Witchcraft Delusion in New England,* III, 177-178.

52. Letter of Robert Calef to Samuel Willard, September 20, 1695, in Calef, *op. cit.,* p. 38; reprinted in Drake, *op. cit.,* II, 102-103.

using caution and following the right rules in their detection. They must be indubitably proved to be witches before they are convicted: the matter of fact must be evidently done and proved, the evidence of guilt must be certain, and there must be clear proof that the accused party has done the crime. Two things were necessary to establish conclusions: a voluntary confession by the accused, and the testimony of two witnesses to one and the same fact. Many whom *S* and his fellow townmen believe "bewitched" may be "possessed" of the devil, suggests *B*. Most of their information is from afflicting spectres, *B* charges, and while it is true that the devils are under the government of God's providence, he is not ready to believe that God would use devils so extraordinarily in this case. Spectral evidence, therefore, is insufficient. *S*, thinking he has discovered the Achilles' heel of *B*, asks: "Where then is the Rectoral Holiness of God in Governing the World?" But *B* counters: "It is not for such silly Mortals as you and I to prescribe to him who sits King forever." Where was it when God allowed Naboth's life to be taken by false witnesses? When God pleases to allow such things to happen "in a way of Judgment" it is consistent with His holiness, *B* explains. It is also "doctrinal." "He can make a scourge of it to punish a Backsliding People by: he can humble his own Children by it, and make it turn to their good in the end."[53]

Much in the little treatise is akin to Willard's customary mode of thought. He was never a reckless polemicist, yet he never sacrificed truth to preserve the peace. The careful logic of the *Observations* resembles that of Willard's reasoned discourses. As his earliest report on alleged witchcraft reveals, he was capable of calm evaluation of exciting emergencies. The observation "that the more horrid the Crime is, the more Cautious we ought to be making any guilty of it," is an almost exact parallel to Willard's preface to the *Cases of Conscience.* The *Observations* does not deny the existence of witches, nor the magistrate's duty to punish the convicted. Similarly Willard's sermons nowhere contradict this belief, and always extol the office of the magistrate. His sermons and the *Observations* alike emphasize reason and right understanding of the Scriptures. Like Willard's report on Elizabeth Knapp, the *Observations* concludes that there is greater evidence to support preternatural influences than witchcraft. The admission that God may use the devil as a scourge upon apostatizing people finds parallels in Willard's Groton fast day sermon and in his frequent use of the judgment theme. In one respect the *Observations* resembles the letter of Thomas Brattle extolling Willard's early stand against the

53. *Some Miscellany Observations On our present Debates respecting Witchcrafts,* pp. 1-14.

proceedings, where Brattle refers to Philip English and John Alden as "P.E." and "J.A."[54] But it is likely that Willard and Brattle often discussed the proceedings together and that they influenced each other. It ought not to be forgotten, remarked Ebenezer Pemberton some years later, "how singularly instrumental he was in discovering the cheats and delusions of Satan, which did threaten to stain our Land with Blood and to deluge it with all manner of Woes . . . *in that Dark and Mysterious Season* when we were assaulted from the Invisible World."[55]

Ministerial influence doubtlessly accounts for the passing of a bill in the Council on October 26 calling for a fast and a convocation of ministers that they might be "led in the right way as to Witchcrafts." The "season and mañer of it," said Sewall, "is such, that the Court of Oyer and Terminer count themselves thereby dismissed." Three days later Governor Phips confirmed the Court's dismissal, and there is no record of the fast being held.[56] The new Court which convened on January 3 acquitted or reprieved those accused, and proceeded to a more critical use of evidence.

Three years later, irritated that all attempts to arrange a day of humiliation for the witchcraft butchery had been rebuffed, Willard preached at a prayer day on September 16 called by the Court in behalf of the expeditionary force sent against the French marauders on the Maine outposts, and "spake smartly at last about the Salem Witchcrafts, and that no order had been suffer'd to come forth by Authority to ask God's pardon."[57] With the defeat of the expedition, another crop failure, more sea losses, sickness, and Indian raids, the leaders concluded that God was continuing His controversy with New England, and on December 11 and 17 the Council and the House agreed on a bill for a fast day. The draft, written by Sewall, cited numerous particulars of judgment, and called upon the people to supplicate God to show them what they had done amiss.

> And, especially, that whatever Mistakes, on either hand, have been fallen into either by the body of this People, or any Orders of them, referring to the late Tragedie raised amongst us by Satan and his Instruments, through the awfull Judgment of God; He would humble us therefore, and pardon all the Errors of his Servants and People that desire to Love his Name; and be attoned to His Land.[58]

54. Letter of Brattle, in Burr, *op. cit.,* p. 178.
55. Pemberton, *Funeral Sermon,* p. 74.
56. Sewall, *op. cit.,* 367; cf. Love, *Fast and Thanksgiving Days,* pp. 263-264.
57. Sewall, *op. cit.,* 433.
58. Sewall, *op. cit.,* 440-441n.; cf. also *Massachusetts Archives,* XI, 120-121.

At the public fast on January 4, 1697, as Willard was passing up one of the aisles to the pulpit, Sewall handed him a "bill" of confession which Willard read in the service as Sewall stood in penitence.

> Samuel Sewall, sensible of the reiterated strokes of God upon himself and family; and being sensible that as to the Guilt contracted upon the opening of the late Comission of Oyer and Terminer at Salem (to which the order of the Day relates) he is, upon many accounts, more concerned than any that he knows of, Desires to take the Blame and shame of it, Asking pardon of men, And especially desiring prayers that God, who has an Unlimited Authority, would pardon that sin and all other sins; Personal and Relative: And according to his infinite Benignity, and Sovereignty, Not Visit the sin of him, or of any other, upon himself or any of his, nor upon the Land: But that he would powerfully defend him against all Temptations to Sin, for the future; and vouchsafe him the efficacious, saving Conduct of his Word and Spirit.[59]

As Willard finished the reading, the judge bowed and resumed his seat. It was a worthy exemplification of all that Willard's preaching urged.

The Signs of the Times

As the seventeenth century drew to its close Willard became even more sensitive to the signs of the times. There is an "Important Duty lying upon the People of God," he declared in 1692, "to labour after a skill in discerning the Signs of the Times in which they live." The signs were either "natural," "positive and instituted," or "mixt and moral." To natural phenomena such as comets and earthquakes he attached little significance, unlike some of his predecessors and Increase Mather. "I meddle not with them," declared Willard, "nor is there any credit to be given to those that do; and it is to be lamented that so many Christians are seduced into a good Opinion of them." But though he moved scientifically beyond some of his contemporaries in shedding superstitious interpretations of such phenomena, he firmly held to the theory that providences had moral signification. "There is a voice in every turn of providence which passeth over men, and it speaks to them, signifying what it is that God requires of them at such a time, and it highly concerns them to hear it, that so they may practice accordingly."[60]

59. Sewall, *op. cit.,* V, 445.
60. *Rules for Discerning the Present Times,* pp. 5-6, 8. Cf. Samuel Danforth, *An Astronomical Description of the late Comet or Blazing Star with a brief Theological Application thereof* (Cambridge, 1665), pp. 166f.; Increase Mather, *Kometographia* (Boston, 1683).

How could that little company of professing people in their corner of the world profitably discern the times? Intensifying the jeremiad one step further, Willard drew the distinction between signs that were indicative, monitory, and ratifying. Public calamities sometimes might be the punishments of sins that had been committed long before, he explained, "but afflictions that are Penal do usually come upon a Generation that is so afflicted." Three things were a sure indication that calamities were not merely trials but confirmations of divine anger: if, when they were obviously guilty of apostasy, reformation did not follow ministerial rebukes, and lighter afflictions did not reclaim them, they could be certain that God was intensifying His controversy with them. Once he set out to prove that their calamities were judicial, Willard had no other choice but that of making his denunciations ever more emphatic. It would have seemed blasphemous to him to suggest that God was a kind of grand inquisitor, torturing victims on the rack of suffering; but, said Willard, God in dealing with a people as a whole in judgment did proceed "gradually." If, in spite of judgments, iniquity continued, and the people became worse, they might expect worse things to come.[61]

Thus when Groton in 1694 was once again ravished by the Indians, Willard declared at a fast day at South Church that the language of providence was indeed plain. "If we had hearkened to the voice of the Rod, it would have been removed, and not continued, and harder strokes inflicted." Obstinate refusal was being visited by sevenfold punishment. Extirpation, however, was the final remedy reserved only for incorrigible impenitence; the great design of divine judgments on covenant people was reformation. They were impotent apart from the Spirit, but it was certain that a great deal more could have been done; the blame, therefore, rested not upon their impotence but upon their wilfulness. Had they been willing, but God unwilling? For shame! "Let us see and confess the naughtiness of our own hearts, and take the blame home to ourselves." Punishment, they were learning, "riseth by Sevens" as God progressively and with "leisurely steps" disciplined first with more tolerable, then with harder strokes.[62]

What would have happened to Willard's interpretation of history if the calamities suddenly ceased? Apparently anticipating the objection, Willard explained that God customarily granted merciful "intermissions"; they themselves had experienced such "notable respites" and "breathing times." God waited, like a physician, to see whether the administered "Potion" worked. Mercies that should have melted the

---

61. *Rules for Discerning the Present Times,* pp. 16-26.
62. *Reformation the Great Duty of an Afflicted People,* "To the Reader," pp. 11, 16, 28, 34-35, 48, 50-57.

hearts of the adamant had been unimproved, however, and for such incorrigibleness there was but one relevant message: *"prepare to meet thy God, Oh Israel."* Greater troubles were certain, for either God's name suffered or covenant delinquents had to be cut off.[63]

As the eighteenth century dawned Willard preached a series of sermons on the peril of the times. One had to hope for the best, he charitably observed, but the "symptoms" prompted conjectures about what was likely to come. Something new had to be added to his familiar catalogue of sins: delinquent saints were now considered socially respectable!

> But when such sins grow frequent, and those that have taken on themselves a name of being Religious, begin to indulge themselves herein; and men that allow themselves in such things are not *Reproached* for it, but are in as good Credit as the best, it then becomes a bad symptom, and saith that the times are declining and perilous.[64]

Conversions were becoming scarce, growth in grace was hardly discernible, wearying of strictness people yearned for "liberty," spiritual things were neglected with small excuse, licentious talk and obscene conduct were frequent, and to top it all the rising generation, ignorant of fundamentals, was in search of new things—the very things their progenitors had fled from in England. Yielding to the social and religious pressures toward conformity, professing Christians were increasingly becoming afraid of that "bug bear harangue of Singularity!" In the face of this, did the fact that New England was enjoying a period of prosperity mean that God was giving them up? he asked. Then surely it was a "sad prognostick."[65]

The Imminent Consummation of History

History was nearing its end, Willard believed; the last and worst period of the church's history, the "Laodicean," had dawned.[66] Christ's coming was not far off.[67]

But before the end, he assured those mystified by the "dark providences" of the time, there would be a period of glory for the church. Concomitant with the fulness of the Gentiles there would be a national

63. *Ibid.*, pp. 60, 62, 64, 67, 70-71.
64. *Peril of the Times Displayed,* pp. 64-67, 78-80, 91-92.
65. *Ibid.*, pp. 94, 97, 99, 102, 104, 108, 110, 112, 116.
66. *Fiery Trial,* p. 15.
67. *Child's Portion,* p. 96.

calling of the Jews. This special season, Congregationalists in both Englands believed, would witness a glorious exhibition of the power of the gospel, eclipsing even the apostolic and reformation ages. Christians generally agreed, Willard declared, that this prophecy referred to that nation which was Abraham's seed "according to the Flesh"; though scholars like Richard Baxter and John Lightfoot "strenuously oppugned" the idea, others such as John Owen, William Twisse, and Thomas Goodwin vigorously confuted their "pretended pleadings" against it.[68]

The subject had been dealt with rather fancifully by some—John Eliot, for instance, thought the Indians were of Jewish origin, that Ezekiel 37 referred "to the Indians as such Jews," and that the New England churches were the "preface of the New Heavens."[69] Willard's view, by contrast, was sober and balanced, following closely the lines drawn by the Westminster and Savoy divines. It was not a "fundamental" article of salvation, yet "speculation" on it offered consolation. Many Biblical texts referred to the spiritual Israel or to the Jewish return from Babylon, Willard conceded; but others predicted glorious things for the Jews in the "gospel-day," some in apostolic times, some in times not yet fulfilled. There was "a *Mystical* sense in some Prophecies about Israel," he continued, "yet they go too far, who would restrain altogether to this, as those do who deny this Doctrine: yea, there is a *Compound* sense in many of these things, and they aim both at the one and the other."[70]

Willard advanced six considerations to buttress this belief. The national calling of the Jews was mentioned distributively in the Bible with the calling of the Gentiles. Isaiah 11:11, 12 foretold a calling after Christ's appearance. Romans 11:15-16, 24 and Luke 21:24 referred to a calling following their rejection of Christ and their dispersion. According to Isaiah 26:18f., Hosea 3:3-4, and Zechariah 12:6-8 there were things not yet accomplished. And finally there was that which filled Willard with wonder—the Jews to that day, notwithstanding calamitous sufferings, had remained a people distinct.[71]

This event would be a great day for the church, Willard taught. Peace would reign, Satan would be bound, the enemies of God would lick the dust, grace would flourish and holiness abound. He would not venture a prediction on the precise time of its eventuation, but many preparatory things have been fulfilled, he said, and "we may expect that God will

68. *Fountain Opened,* "To the Reader," pp. 2-4, 23, 26, 33-36, 106-107, 115.
69. Quoted in Joseph B. Felt, *Ecclesiastical History of New England,* II, 10, 12, 22.
70. *Fountain Opened,* pp. 107-110.
71. *Ibid.,* pp. 110-113.

make short work of it when it draws nigh its accomplishment." At the moment they were passing through an evil time; yet those "going off the stage" who were solicitous about their posterity could comfort themselves with the thought that the day was not far off, "and though we may not live to see the dawnings of it, yet our Posterity may see the breaking of it."[72] Since those happy times were to be ushered in by prayer, exhorted Willard (citing Psalm 122:6 and Isaiah 62:6-7), they were to pray for the conversion of the Jews—though how actively the church folk of Massachusetts proselyted the handful of Jews already living among them,[73] is not known. "When therefore God shall pour such a spirit of Prayer on his people in this regard, it will be a blessed Prognostick of that glorious time, hastening."[74]

As to the millennium, while Increase and Cotton Mather bubbled over with chiliastic hopes and predictions of its imminent establishment on earth, Willard had more reserve. Citing an old error, attributed to Cerinthus by Eusebius, which put such a carnal interpretation on many passages referring to Christ's return (a kingdom set up for a thousand years with saints possessing the earth and reigning over the ungodly with great pomp), Willard judged: "it smells so much of the flesh." He also rejected the literal interpretation some advanced of the resurrection of the just on the earth, a thousand years before the general resurrection of the wicked and the final determination of all things, after which Christ would return to heaven with His saints. "Whether it shall be thus or otherwise," declared Willard, "the day shall determine." There was insufficient Biblical evidence to make it a necessary point of faith, and it was attended with so many intricacies that it was irresolvable. Everything alleged in its support could be reduced either to Christ's first coming, the New Testament era in general, or the time of the triumphant church in the eternal kingdom.[75] The resurrection and the judgment were to occur together, he explained, and as for those who alleged a resurrection antecedent to the thousand years, he left them "to abound in their own sense, craving liberty to differ from them, as in a Point extra-fundamental."[76]

The eventuality of the judgment, however, was certain. It would be presumptuous to specify its locale, he thought, though he believed it would be in "this lower world," so that the place of sinning would be

72. *Ibid.*, pp. 116-123.

73. Sewall, *op. cit.*, VI, 9. Cf. also Leon Huhner, *Jews in America in Colonial and Revolutionary Times*, pp. 74-79.

74. *Fountain Opened*, pp. 124-126.

75. *Child's Portion*, pp. 93-95.

76. *Compleat Body*, p. 541.

the place of judgment.[77] Of greater concern was the fact that all had to reckon with it personally, a point he drove home in an unusual instance. South Church was deeply shocked in 1698 on learning that one of its members, a nineteen-year-old girl who had fallen into prostitution, had murdered her second illegitimate child. She was sentenced to die, and in the hope that this "unhappy mother" would show some sign of repentance Willard preached two public sermons in her presence on "Impenitent Sinners Warned of their Misery and Summoned to Judgment." "It is every whit as certain that men shall come into Judgment, as that they shall Dye," Willard warned, and for sinful men to break the covenant of grace there is the menace of "double damnation"—personal judgment immediately following death, and the general judgment reserved for the great and last day. "Abominations" as great as those of the condemned girl existed and had not been brought to light in New England, he feared; he preached the doctrine therefore as a deterrent. "Now, what a check would such reflections as these are, thoroughly believed, and fixedly entertained, give to the mad youngster, in the midst of all his frolicks, and mar all the mirth of his greedy lusts, turning it into bitterness?"[78]

God was the governor of the world He had created, therefore there had to be a day of account. And it wouldn't be long, Willard predicted. Some prophecies still had to be fulfilled, but he was certain that they were in the last days, "the winding up of the time that we live in." Before long the sign of the Son of Man (its meaning was conjectural) would appear in the heavens, and Christ would return with the voice of the archangel and the sound of the last trumpet "to wind up the great work of special government which had been managed from the Creation, and to settle the determinations of it for Eternity."[79] Then God, who in the beginning put man under the law with sanctions, who opened a new covenant for sinners by which life was secured for believers in Christ, will reveal His righteousness and mercy in the great trial, revealing what they did with this rule. Those who never had the revelation of grace would be judged by the moral law of relative justice, which, since all men naturally are sinners, will mean their condemnation. But some in the same condemnation will be acquitted, for

77. *Ibid.*, p. 422.

78. *Impenitent Sinners Warned of their Misery and Summoned to Judgement,* "To the Reader," pp. 31, 34, 36, 41. Willard's suspicions had some foundation. For studies of this phase of social conduct in New England, see Thomas J. Wertenbaker, *The First Americans,* p. 199; C. F. Adams, "Some Phases of Sexual Morality and Church Discipline in Colonial New England," *M.H.S. Procs.,* June, 1891; Edmund S. Morgan, "The Puritans and Sex," *N.E.Q.,* XV (1942), 591-607; Emil Oberholzer, *Delinquent Saints,* pp. 127-129.

79. *Compleat Body,* pp. 420-423.

the law of the covenant has been answered by a surety, and the trial will determine whether they have title to this satisfaction. "This therefore must be the Rule of Chancery in that Court," declared Willard, "viz. Whether they are in Christ by Faith?"[80]

The watchword to all, therefore, was: get ready for that day. For the faithful the issue of the great judgment would be consummate bliss; for sinners woeful condemnation. And it is certain, Willard proclaimed in a culminant jeremiad, that

> when damned Sinners are Everlastingly Roaring and Howling under the Extremity of Infernal Plagues and Torments, these shall be Eternally Singing of Hallelujah's, Rejoycing and making Melody in the Presence of God and the Lamb, causing Heaven to ring, from one end to another with Acclamations of Joy, tuned to an Heavenly Consort, in prospect of those things which they see and possess; and in Acknowledgments of the unspeakable Grace by which they had been saved: Which if Hell can be acquainted withal, and might but have a peep-hole to discover, how would it fill them with unspeakable Bitterness, Tortures, and Blasphemies?

But for believers Willard had an encouraging word. Whatever the trials of this life,

> think in the severest of them, though it seems thus now, yet ere long my Saviour will come and fetch me home to his own Place; the Joyful Marriage Day is drawing on apace; the Bridegroom is but making ready for it, suiting all things for so stately a Solemnity: A little while, and I shall see him come with Glory, I shall meet him, and go with him, and enjoy him Eternally.[81]

*   *   *   *   *

As the fall term opened at Harvard in 1707, Willard went up to Cambridge on August 11 to expound the Scriptures to the students, but becoming ill he returned home before prayer time. Samuel Sewall called the next day and he spoke of "great pain in's head, and sickness at his stomack." He "believ'd he was near his end," said Sewall, and asked him to submit his oral resignation to the governor and the Council. Soon after Sewall left he "fell very sick, and had three sore Convulsion Fits to our great sorrow and amazement."[82]

By September 7 he had recovered sufficiently to baptize a child and administer the Lord's Supper at South Church. Five days later he cut his finger eating oysters, "went up to his study, called his wife, thanked

80. *Ibid.*, pp. 547-551.
81. *Ibid.*, pp. 556, 558-559.
82. Sewall, *op. cit.*, VI, 193.

her for her kindness, prayed God to bless them all; then fell into a convulsion." Sewall hurried to his pastor's home as soon as he heard he was seriously ill, and entered the crowded chamber just as Pemberton was concluding his prayer. As the other left, Sewall stayed and recounts, "In a few minutes saw my dear Pastor expire." It took everyone by surprise, for the doctors were in another room consulting what to do. "There was a dolefull cry in the house."[83]

At the funeral the next day the fellows and students of the college led the procession to the old burial ground beside King's Chapel, and Ebenezer Pemberton escorted Mrs. Willard. The two Mathers, James Allen, Thomas Bridge, Benjamin Wadsworth, and Benjamin Colman carried the body. Until such a time as South Church could build a new tomb, Willard was laid in Sewall's tomb next to his old college tutor, Joshua Moody.

Pemberton's text for the sermon fittingly summarized the life that epitomized the New England mind as a champion of orthodoxy in an era of change.

> Who then is a faithful and wise Servant, whom his Lord hath made Ruler over his Household, to give them meat in due Season? Blessed is that Servant whom his Lord when he cometh shall find so doing (Matthew 24:45, 46).

83. *Ibid.*, 194.

Bibliography

I. *Primary Sources*

A. **Manuscripts**

"Boston Sermons 1671-1679," manuscript in the library of the Massachusetts Historical Society. The particular sermons, copied by John Hull, a member of South Church, are designated by date.

Willard, Samuel, "Common-place book," Folio. In the library of Harvard University.

B. **The Works of Samuel Willard**

All Plots against God and his People Detected and Defeated, as it was delivered in a Sermon At a Fast kept by the first gathered Church in Boston, Jan. 25, 1682 (bound with *The Child's Portion.* Boston, 1684).

The Barren Fig Trees Doom. Or, a Brief Discourse wherein is set forth the woful Danger of all who abide Unfruitful under Gospel-Priviledges, and Gods Husbandry. Being the Substance of Sixteen Sermons Preached on Christ's Parable of the Fig-Tree (Boston, 1691).

The Best Priviledge. Or, a Sermon wherein the Great Advantage of enjoying the Oracles of God is displayed, and the Duty of such as have them is urged. Preached on the Lecture in Boston, on June 19th. 1701 (Boston, 1701).

"A briefe account of a strange and unusuall Providence of God, befallen to Elizabeth Knap of Groton in 1671-1672," in *Collections of the Massachusetts Historical Society,* XXXVIII, 555-570.

Brief Directions to a Young Scholar Designing the Ministry, for the Study of Divinity (Boston, 1735).

A Brief Discourse Concerning that Ceremony of Laying the Hand on the Bible in Swearing (London, 1689).

A Brief Discourse of Justification. Wherein This Doctrine is plainly laid down ¬according to the Scriptures. As it was Delivered in Several Sermons on this Subject (Boston, 1686).

A Brief Reply to Mr. George Keith, in Answer To a Script of his, Entituled, A Refutation of a Dangerous and Hurtful Opinion, Maintained by Mr. Samuel Willard, &c. (Boston, 1703).

Brotherly Love Described and Directed. As it was Casuistically handled in Two Sermons, Preached on the Lecture in Boston, in the year 1701 (bound with *The Christians Exercise by Satans Temptations.* Boston, 1701).

The Character Of a good Ruler. As it was Recommended in a Sermon Preached before his Excellency the Governour, and the Honourable Counsellors, and Assembly of the Representatives of the Province of Massachusetts-Bay in New-England. On May 30, 1694. Which was the Day for Election of Counsellors for that Province (Boston, 1694).

The Checkered State of the Gospel Church. Being the Substance of a Sermon prepared for, and in part Preached on September 18th. 1701. Being a Day of Publick Fasting and Prayer (Boston, 1701).

The Child's Portion: Or the unseen Glory of the Children of God, Asserted, and proved: Together with several other Sermons Occasionally Preached, and now published (Boston, 1684).

The Christians Exercise by Satans Temptations: Or, An Essay to discover the methods which this Adversary useth to Tempt the Children of God; and to direct them how to escape the mischief thereof. Being the Substance of several Sermons Preached on that Subject (Boston, 1701).

A Compleat Body of Divinity in Two Hundred and Fifty Expository Lectures on the Assembly's Shorter Catechism. Wherein the Doctrines of the Christian Religion are unfolded, their Truth confirm'd, their Excellence display'd, their Usefulness improv'd; contrary Errors & Vices refuted & expos'd, Objections answer'd, Controversies settled, Cases of Conscience resolv'd; and a great Light thereby reflected on the present Age (Boston, 1726).

Covenant-Keeping The Way to Blessedness, Or, A Brief discourse wherein is shown the Connexion which there is between the Promise, on God's Part, and Duty, on Our Part, in the Covenant of Grace; As it was Delivered in several Sermons Preached in Order to Solemn Renewing of Covenant (Boston, 1682).

The Danger of Taking God's Name in Vain. As it was Delivered in a Sermon (Boston, 1691).

The Doctrine of the Covenant of Redemption. Wherein is laid the Foundation of all our Hopes and Happiness. Briefly Opened and Improved (Boston, 1693).

The Duty of a People that have Renewed their Covenant with God. Opened and Urged in A Sermon Preached to the second Church in Boston in New-England, March 17, 1679-80; after that Church had explicitly and most solemnly renewed the Ingagement of themselves to God, and one to another (Boston, 1680).

Evangelical Perfection, or How far the Gospel requires Believers to Aspire after being compleatly Perfect. As it was Delivered on a Lecture at Boston, on June 10th. 1694 (bound with *The Fountain Opened.* Boston, 1700).

The Fear of an Oath. Or, Some Cautions to be used about Swearing, If we would approve ourselves Truly Godly. As it was Discoursed in a Sermon, Preached at Boston, on the Lecture; January 30, 1700-1 (Boston, 1701).

The Fiery Tryal no strange thing; Delivered in a Sermon Preached at Charlestown, February 15, 1681. Being a Day of Humiliation (Boston, 1682).

The Fountain Opened: Or, The Great Gospel Priviledge of having Christ exhibited to Sinfull Men. Wherein Also is proved that there shall be a National Calling of the Jews. From Zech. xiii. 1 (Boston, 1700).

The Heart Garrisoned. Or, The Wisdome, and Care of the Spiritual Souldier above all things to safeguard his Heart. Delivered in a Sermon which was Preached to the Honoured Gentlemen of the Artillery Company, on the Day of their Election, at Boston in New-England June 5, 1676 (Cambridge, 1676).

Heavenly Merchandize: Or the Purchasing of Truth Recommended, and the Selling of it Disswaded; As it was Delivered in Several Sermons; Upon Prov. 23.23 (Boston, 1686).

The High Esteem Which God hath of the Death of his Saints. As it was Delivered in a Sermon Preached October 7. 1683. Occasioned by the Death of the Worshipful John Hull Esq: Who Deceased October 1, 1683 (Boston, 1683).

Impenitent Sinners Warned of their Misery and Summoned to Judgement. Two Sermons at Boston, Nov. 6 and 10, 1698. Occasioned by the Amazing Instance of a Miserable Creature, condemned for Murdering her Infant, begotten in Whoredom. To which are subjoined the Solemn Words spoken to her, on those opportunities. Published for the Warning of others (Boston, 1698).

Israel's True Safety: Offered in a Sermon, Before His Excellency, the Honourable Council, and Representatives, of the Province of the Massachusetts-Bay in New-England, on March 15th. 1704. Being a Day Set a part for Solemn Fasting and Prayer (Boston, 1704).

The Just Man's Prerogative. A Sermon Preached Privately, Sept. 27. 1706. On a Solemn Occasion; For the Consolation of a Sorrowful Family, Mourning over the Immature Death, of a Pious Son, viz. Mr. Simeon Stoddard, who was found Barbarously Murdered, in Chelsea-Fields near London, May 14. 1706 (Boston, 1706).

The Law Established by the Gospel. Or, A Brief Discourse, wherein is Asserted and Declared, the Great Honour which is put upon the Law of God, in the Gospel way of Justification by Faith alone. Being the Substance of A Sermon Preached on the Lecture in Boston, September 20. 1694 (Boston, 1694).

Love's Pedigree. Or A Discourse shewing the Grace of Love in a Believer to be of a Divine Original. Delivered in a Sermon Preached at the Lecture in Boston. Febr. 29. 1699-1700 (Boston, 1700).

The Man of War. A Sermon Preached to the Artillery Company at Boston, on June 5, 1699. Being the Anniversary day for their Election of Officers (Boston, 1699).

Mercy Magnified on a Penitent Prodigal, Or a Brief Discourse, wherein Christs Parable of the Lost Son found, is Opened and Applied, As it was Delivered in Sundry Sermons (Boston, 1684).

Morality Not to be Relied on for Life. Or, A Brief Discourse, discovering the One Thing Wanting, which leaves the legalist Short of Life Eternal. Delivered in a Sermon on the Lecture in Boston, May 23d. 1700 (Boston, 1700).

The Mourners Cordial Against Excessive Sorrow. Discovering what Grounds of Hope Gods People have concerning their Dead Friends (Boston, 1691).

Ne Sutor Ultra Crepidam. Or Brief Animadversions Upon the New-England Anabaptists late Fallacious Narrative; Wherein the Notorious Mistakes and Falsehoods by them Published, are Detected (Boston, 1681).

The Necessity of Sincerity in renewing Covenant: Opened and urged in a Sermon Preached to the Third Gathered Church in Boston, New England; June 29, 1680 (bound with *Covenant-Keeping the Way to Blessedness.* Boston, 1682).

The only sure way to prevent threatned Calamity: As it was delivered in a Sermon, Preached at the Court of Election, May 24, 1682 (bound with *The Child's Portion.* Boston, 1684).

The Peril of the Times Displayed. Or the Danger of Mens taking up with a Form of Godliness, But Denying the Power of it. Being the Substance of several Sermons Preached (Boston, 1700).

The Principles of the Protestant Religion Maintained, And Churches of New-England, in the Profession and Exercise thereof Defended, Against all the Calumnies of one George Keith, A Quaker, in a Book lately Published at Pensilvania, to undermine them both. By the Ministers of the Gospel in

Boston [James Allen, Joshuah Moodey, Samuel Willard, Cotton Mather]
(Boston, 1690).

Prognosticks of Impending Calamities. Delivered in a Sermon Preached on the
Lecture at Boston, July 17. 1701. Occasioned by the Death of the Truly
Honourable, William Stoughton, Esq. Lieutenant Governour, &c. of the
Province of the Massachusetts-Bay, in New-England (Boston, 1701).

Promise-Keeping. A Great Duty. As it was Delivered in a Sermon (Boston, 1691).

Reformation The Great Duty of an Afflicted People. Setting forth The Sin and
Danger there is in Neglecting of it, under the Continued and Repeated
Judgements of God. Being the Substance of what was Preached on a Solemn
Day of Humiliation kept by the Third Gathered Church in Boston, on
August. 23d. 1694 (Boston, 1694).

A Remedy Against Despair. Or a Brief Discourse wherein Great Sinners are
Encouraged, and Directed how to improve the consideration of the Great-
ness of their Sins in Praying to God for Pardon. Being the Substance of Two
Sermons Preached at the Lecture in Boston, 1699 (Boston, 1700).

The Righteous Man's Death a Presage of evil approaching: A Sermon Occasioned
by the Death of Major Thomas Savage Esq; Preached, Febr. 19. 1681 (bound
with *The Child's Portion.* Boston, 1684).

Rules for the Discerning of the Present Times. Recommended To the People of
God, in New-England. In a Sermon Preached on the Lecture in Boston;
November 27th. 1692 (Boston, 1693).

A Sermon Preached upon Ezekiel 22.30, 31. Occasioned by the Death of the
much honoured John Leveret Esq; Governour of the Colony of the Massachusetts. N-E. (Boston, 1679).

The Sinfulness of Worshipping God With Men's Institutions. As it was Delivered in
a Sermon (Boston, 1691).

Some Brief Sacramental Meditations, Preparatory for Communion at the Great
Ordinance of the Supper (Boston, 1711).

Some Miscellany Observations On our present Debates respecting Witchcrafts, in a
Dialogue Between S. & B. By P.E. and J.A. (Philadelphia, 1692).

Spiritual Desertions Discovered and Remedied. Being the Substance of divers
Sermons Preached for the help of dark Souls, labouring under Divine
withdrawings (Boston, 1699).

A Thanksgiving Sermon Preach'd at Boston in New England, December, 1705. On
the Return of a Gentleman from his Travels (London, 1709).

The Truly Blessed Man: Or, the Way to be Happy here, and For Ever: Being the
Substance of Divers Sermons Preached on, Psalm xxxii (Boston, 1700).

*Useful Instructions for a professing People in Times of great Security and
Degeneracy:* Delivered in several Sermons on Solemn Occasions (Cambridge,
1673).

Walking with God, The Great Duty and Priviledge of true Christians. In Two
Sermons, Preached on the Lecture, in the year, 1700 (Boston, 1701).

C. The Polemical Works of George Keith

The Presbyterian and Independent Visible Churches Brought to the Test, and
examined according to the Doctrin of the holy Scriptures, in their Doctrin,
Ministry, Worship, Constitution, Government, Sacraments, and Sabbath
Day. . . . With a Call and Warning from the Lord to the People of Boston
and New-England to Repent, &c (Philadelphia, 1689).

The Pretended Antidote Proved Poyson. Or, The True Principles of the Christian
& Protestant Religion Defended, And the Four Counterfeit Defenders there-

of Detected and Discovered; the names of which are James Allen, Joshua Moodey, Samuell Willard and Cotton Mather, who call themselves Ministers of the Gospel in Boston, in their pretended Answer to My Book. . . .(Philadelphia, 1690).

A Refutation of a dangerous and hurtful Opinion maintained by Mr. Samuel Willard, an Independent Minister at Boston, & President at the Commencement in Cambridge in New England, July 1, 1703 (New York, 1703).

An Answer to Mr. Samuel Willard (One of the Ministers at Boston in New England), His Reply to My Printed Sheet, called, A Dangerous and hurtful Opinion maintained by him, viz. That the Fall of Adam, and all the sins of Men necessarily come to pass by virtue of God's Decree, and his Determining both of the Will of Adam, and of all other Men to sin (New York, 1704).

II. *Secondary Sources*

Adams, Brooks, *The Emancipation of Massachusetts* (Boston and New York, 1887).

Adams, Charles Francis, ed., *Antinomianism in the Colony of Massachusetts Bay, 1636-1638.* Including The Short Story and other Documents (Boston, 1894).

— — — — — —, "Some Phases of Sexual Morality and Church Discipline in Colonial New England," *Proceedings of the Massachusetts Historical Society,* Second Series, VI (Cambridge, 1891), 477-516.

— — — — — —, *Three Episodes in Massachusetts History* (2 vols., Boston, 1893).

Adams, James Truslow, *The Founding of New England* (Boston, 1921).

— — — — — —, *Provincial Society,* 1690-1763 (New York, 1927).

Albertson, Dean, "Puritan Liquor in the Planting of New England," *New England Quarterly,* XXIII, 477-490.

Amesii, Gvilielmi [William Ames], *Anti-Synodalia Scripta,* vel Animadversiones in Dogmatica illa, quae Remonstrantes in Synodo Dordracena, exhibuerunt & postea divulgarunt (Amstelodami, A. MDCXXXIII).

Ames, William, *The Marrow of Theology,* translated with an introduction by John Dykstra Eusden (Boston and Philadelphia, 1968).

Andrewes, Charles M., *The Colonial Period of American History: The Settlements* (Vol. I, New Haven, 1934).

Atkins, Gaius Glenn, and Fagley, Frederick L., *History of American Congregationalism* (Boston and Chicago, 1942).

Backus, Isaac, *A History of New England.* With Particular Reference to the Denomination of Christians called Baptists (2 vols., Newton, Massachusetts, 1871).

Bailyn, Bernard, *The New England Merchants in the Seventeenth Century* (Cambridge, 1955).

Bainton, Roland H., *Christian Attitudes Toward War and Peace.* A Historical Survey and Critical Re-evaluation (New York, 1960).

Bangs, Carl C., "Arminius and Reformed Theology" (typed Ph. D. dissertation, University of Chicago, 1958).

— — — — — —, "Arminius and the Reformation," *Church History,* XXX (1961), 155-170.

Barclay, Robert, *An Apology for the true Christian Divinity* (Philadelphia, n.d.).

Barclay, Robert, *The Inner Life of the Religious Societies of the Commonwealth:* Considered Principally with Reference to the Influence of Church Organization and the Spread of Christianity (London, 1876).

Benedict, David, *A General History of the Baptist Denomination in America and other Parts of the World* (New York, 1848).
Berkhof, Louis, *Reformed Dogmatics. Historical* (History of Dogma) (Grand Rapids, Michigan, 1937).
——————, *Systematic Theology* (Grand Rapids, 1941).
Berkouwer, G. C., *Divine Election* (Grand Rapids, 1960).
——————, *Faith and Justification* (Grand Rapids, 1954).
——————, *Faith and Perseverance* (Grand Rapids, 1958).
——————, *Faith and Sanctification* (Grand Rapids, 1952).
——————, *Man: The Image of God* (Grand Rapids, 1962).
——————, *The Person of Christ* (Grand Rapids, 1955).
——————, *The Providence of God* (Grand Rapids, 1952).
Besse, Joseph, ed., *A Collection of the Sufferings of the People Called Quakers* (London, 1753).
Boas, Ralph and Louse, *Cotton Mather. Keeper of the Puritan Conscience* (New York, 1928).
Boleman, B. A., "Success: The Puritan Highroad to Hell; Preaching in New England in the Seventeenth Century," *Journal of Religion,* XXIII (1943), 206-213.
Boorstin, Daniel J., *The Americans. The Colonial Experience* (New York, 1958).
Bownas, Samuel, *An account of the life, travels, and Christian experiences in the work of the ministry of Samuel Bownas* (London, 1759).
Bradford, Alden, *New England Chronology: From the Discovery of the Country by Cabot in 1497 to 1800* (Boston, 1843).
Braithwaite, William C., *The Beginnings of Quakerism* (rev. ed., Cambridge, England, 1955).
——————, *The Second Period of Quakerism* (Cambridge, England, 1921).
Brauer, Jerald C., "Puritan Mysticism and the Development of Liberalism," *Church History,* XIX (1950), 151-170.
——————, "Reflections on the Nature of English Puritanism," *Church History,* XXIII (1954), 99-108.
——————, "The Rule of the Saints in American Politics," *Church History,* XXVII (1958), 240-255.
Braziller, George, *Witchcraft at Salem* (New York, 1969)
Breen, Quirinus, "John Calvin and the Rhetorical Tradition," *Church History,* XXVI (1957), 3-21.
Brinton, Howard, *Friends For 300 Years:* The History and Beliefs of the Society of Friends Since George Fox Started the Quaker Movement (New York, 1952).
Bronkema, Ralph, *The Essence of Puritanism* (Goes, Holland, 1929).
Brown, R. Katherine, "Freemanship in Puritan Massachusetts," *American Historical Review,* LIX (1953-1954), 865-883.
Brown, W. Adams, "Covenant Theology," *Encyclopedia of Religion and Ethics* (Edinburgh, 1908-22), Vol. 4, pp. 216-224.
Brown, John, *Puritan Preaching in England.* A Study of Past and Present (New York, 1900).
Bruce, F. F., *The English Bible; a History of Translations* (New York, 1961).
Buffington, Arthur Howland, "The Isolationist Policy of Colonial Massachusetts," *New England Quarterly,* I (1927), 158-179.
——————, "The Puritan View of War," *Publications of the Colonial Society of Massachusetts,* XXVIII (Boston, 1935), 67-86.
Bulkeley, Peter, *The Gospel Covenant: Or the Covenant of Grace Opened* (London, 1646).

Burr, George L., ed., *Narratives of the Witchcraft Cases. 1648-1706* (New York, 1914).
Burr, Nelson R., et al., *A Critical Bibliography of Religion in America* (2 vols.), (Vol. IV, *Religion in American Life*), (Princeton, 1961).
Burrage, Champlin, *The Early English Dissenters In the Light of Recent Research (1550-1641)*, (2 vols., Cambridge, 1912).
Burrage, Henry S., "The Contest for Religious Liberty in Massachusetts," *Papers of the American Society of Church History,* VI (1893), 149-168.
————, *A History of the Baptists in New England* (Philadelphia, 1894).
Butler, Caleb, *History of the Town of Groton* (Boston, 1848).
Byington, Ezra Hoy, "John Eliot, The Puritan Missionary to the Indians," *Papers of the American Society of Church History,* VIII (1896), 111-145.

Calamandrei, Mauro, "Neglected Aspects of Roger Williams' Thought," *Church History,* XXI (1952), 239-258.
Calef, Robert, *More Wonders of the Invisible World,* reprinted in S. G. Drake, *The Witchcraft Delusion in New England* (Roxbury, 1866).
Calvin, John, *The Institutes of the Christian Religion* (7th American ed., 2 vols., Philadelphia, 1936).
Campbell, Douglas, *The Puritan in Holland, England, and America* (2 vols., New York, 1892).
Case, Shirley Jackson, *The Christian Philosophy of History* (Chicago, 1943).
Chamberlain, N. H., *Samuel Sewall and the World He Lived In* (Boston, 1898).
Chapman, Clayton H., "The Life and Influence of Reverend Benjamin Colman, D.D." (typed Ph. D. dissertation, Boston University, 1948).
Chauncy, Charles, *Gods Mercy,* shewed to His People in giving them a Faithful Ministry and Schooles of Learning for the continual supplyes thereof (Cambridge, 1655), 14f.
Christie, Francis A., "The Beginnings of Arminianism in New England," *Papers of the American Society of Church History,* Second Series, III (1912), 151-172.
Clark, Herman F., "John Hull. Colonial Merchant, 1624-1683," *Proceedings of the American Antiquarian Society,* XLVI, 197-218.
————, "John Hull, Mintmaster," *New England Quarterly,* X (1937), 668-684.
Clarke, John, *Ill Newes from New England* (London, 1652).
Cogswell, William, ed., *The New England Historical and Genealogical Register* (50 vols., Boston, 1847-1896).
Colie, Rosalie L., *Light and Enlightenment.* A Study of the Cambridge Platonists and the Dutch Arminians (Cambridge, 1957).
Cragg, G. R., *From Puritanism to the Age of Reason.* A Study of Changes in Religious Thought Within the Church of England 1660-1700 (Cambridge, 1950).
————, *Puritanism In the Period of the Great Persecution. 1660-1688* (Cambridge, 1957).
Crisp, Tobias, *Christ Alone Exalted,* in the Perfection and Encouragement of the Saints, Notwithstanding Sins and Trials, Being the Complete Works of Tobias Crisp, D.D. . . .containing Fifty Two Sermons (7th ed., 2 vols., London, 1832).
Cross, Arthur Lyon, *The Anglican Episcopate and the American Colonies* (New York, 1902).
Crouse, H. M., "Causes of the Great Migration," *New England Quarterly,* V (1932), 3-36.
Curti, Merle, *The Growth of American Thought* (New York, 1943).

Danckaerts, Jasper, *The Journal of Jasper Danckaerts,* 1679-1680, ed. by Bartlett B. James and J. Franklin Jameson (New York, 1913).

Danforth, Samuel, *A Brief Recognition of New England's Errand into the Wilderness* (Cambridge, 1671).

Dargan, Edwin Charles, *A History of Preaching* (Grand Rapids, 1954).

Davies, Godfrey, *The Restoration of Charles II, 1658-1660* (San Marino, 1955).

DeJong, Peter Y., *The Covenant Idea in New England Theology* (Grand Rapids, 1945).

Dexter, Henry Martin, *The Congregationalism of the Last Three Hundred Years, As Seen in its Literature:* With Special Reference to certain Recondite, Neglected, or Disputed Passages (New York, 1880).

The Dictionary of American Biography (20 vols., 1928-1936).

The Dictionary of National Biography (22 vols., London, 1908-1909).

Dorfman, Joseph, *The Economic Mind in American Civilization, 1606-1865,* I (New York, 1946).

Dow, George F., *Everyday Life in the Massachusetts Bay Colony* (Boston, 1935).

Doyle, J. A., *The Puritan Colonies* (vols. II and III in his *The English in America,* London, 1882).

Drake, S. G., *The Witchcraft Delusion in New England* (Roxbury, 1866).

Dunton, John, *Letters Written From New England* (ed. by W. H. Whitmore, *Publications of the Prince Society,* IV, London, 1867).

Earle, Alice M., *Child Life in Colonial Days* (2nd ed., New York, 1927).

– – – – – –, *Customs and Fashions in Old New England* (New York, 1893).

– – – – – –, *Home Life in Colonial Days* (New York, 1898).

– – – – – –, *The Sabbath in Puritan New England* (7th ed., New York, 1893).

East, Robert A., "Puritanism and New Settlement," *New England Quarterly,* XVII (1944), 255-264.

Ellis, Arthur B., *History of the First Church in Boston, 1630-1880* (Boston, 1881).

Emerson, Everett H., "Calvin and Covenant Theology," *Church History,* XXV (1956), 136-144.

Evans, Charles, *American Bibliography* (vol. I, *1639-1729,* Chicago, 1903).

Ewell, John Lewis, "Judge Samuel Sewall (1652-1730). A Typical Massachusetts Puritan," *Papers of the American Society of Church History,* VII (1895), 25-54.

Faust, Clarence H., and Johnson, Thomas H., *Jonathan Edwards.* Representative Selections with Introduction, Bibliography, and Notes (New York, 1935).

Felt, Joseph B., *The Ecclesiastical History of New England* (2 vols., Boston, 1855-1862).

Fleming, Sandford, *Children and Puritanism.* The Place of Children in the Life and Thought of the New England Churches 1620-1847 (New Haven, 1933).

Foote, Henry W., *Annals of King's Chapel,* I (Boston, 1882).

Forbes, Allan, *Towns of New England and Old England, Ireland and Scotland* (New York, 1936).

Foster, Frank H., "The Eschatology of the New England Divines," *Bibliotheca Sacra,* XLIII (1886), 6-19.

Gaustad, Edwin Scott, *A Religious History of America* (New York, 1966).

George, Charles H. and Katherine, *The Protestant Mind of the English Reformation, 1570-1640* (Princeton, 1961).

Gerstner, John H., *Steps to Salvation.* The Evangelistic Message of Jonathan Edwards (Philadelphia, 1960).

Gray, Stanley, "The Political Thought of John Winthrop," *New England Quarterly,* III (1930), 681-705.

Green, Samuel Abott, *The Early Records of Groton, Massachusetts, 1662-1707* (Groton, 1880).
— — — — — —, "The Geography of Groton," *Groton Historical Series,* I (Groton, 1886), No. XV.
— — — — — —, *Groton During the Indian Wars* (Groton, 1883).
— — — — — — —, *Groton in Witchcraft Times* (Groton, 1883).
— — — — — —, *An Historical Sketch of Groton, Massachusetts, 1655-1890* (Groton, 1894).
— — — — — —, "List of Ministers, with Their Dates of Settlement, and of Death or Dismissal," *Groton Historical Series,* II (Groton, 1890), Article IV.
— — — — — —, *The Population of Groton at Different Times* (Cambridge, 1888).
— — — — — —, "The Population of Groton at Different Times," *Groton Historical Series,* II (Groton, 1890), Article V.
— — — — — —, "A Register of Births, Deaths, and Marriages in Groton, 1664-1693," *Groton Historical Series,* I, No. XIII.
— — — — — —, "Simon Willard and the Nonacoicus Farm," *Groton Historical Series,* I, No. XII.
Greenwood, Francis W. P., *History of King's Chapel* (Boston, 1833).
Griffiths, Olive M., *Religion and Learning* (Cambridge, England, 1935).
Grislis, Egil, "Calvin's Doctrine of Baptism," *Church History,* XXXI (1962), 46-65.
Hall, Thomas, *Vindicae Literarum* (London, 1655).
Hall, Thomas C., *The Religious Background of American Culture* (Boston, 1930).
Haller, William, *Liberty and Reformation in the Puritan Revolution* (New York, 1955).
— — — — — —, *The Rise of Puritanism* (New York, 1938).
Haller, William, Jr., *The Puritan Frontier Town Planting in New England Colonial Development 1630-1660* (New York, 1951).
Harbison, E. Harris, "The 'Meaning of History' and the Writing of History," *Church History,* XXI (1952), 97-107.
Harkness, R. E. E., "Principles of the Early Baptists of England and America," *Crozer Quarterly,* V (1928), 440-460.
Haroutunian, Joseph, *Piety Versus Moralism* (New York, 1932).
Harrison, A. W., *Arminianism* (London, 1937).
— — — — — —, *The Beginnings of Arminianism to the Synod of Dort* (London, 1926).
Heppe, Heinrich, *Reformed Dogmatics.* Set Out and Illustrated From the Sources (rev. and ed. by Ernst Bizer, London, 1950).
Hill, Hamilton A., and Bigelow, George F., *An Historical Catalogue of the Old South Church (Third Church) Boston. 1669 1882* (Boston, 1883).
Hill, Hamilton A., *History of the Old South Church (Third Church) Boston. 1669-1884* (2 vols., Boston and New York, 1890).
Hodge, A. A., and Hodge, J. A., *The System of Theology contained in the Westminster Shorter Catechism* (New York, 1888).
Hodge, Charles, *Systematic Theology* (3 vols., Grand Rapids, n.d. A reprint of the work first issued 1871-1873).
Holmes, Thomas James, *Cotton Mather. A Bibliography of His Works* (Cambridge, 1940).
— — — — — —, *Increase Mather. A Bibliography of His Works* (Cleveland, 1931).
Hornberger, Theodore, "Benjamin Colman and the Enlightenment," *New England Quarterly,* XII (1939), 227-240.
— — — — — —, "Puritanism and Science," *New England Quarterly,* X (1937), 593-615.

204

How, Samuel, *The Sufficiency of the Spirits Teaching without human Learning:* or a Treatise tending to prove humane Learning to be no help to the spiritual understanding of the Word of God (London, 1639).

Howe, Mark De Wolfe, and Eaton, Louis F., Jr., "The Supreme Judicial Power in the Colony of Massachusetts Bay," *New England Quarterly,* XX (1947), 291-316.

Hubbard, William, *A Narrative of the Indian Wars in New England 1607-1677* (1677).

Hudson, Winthrop S., "Baptists Were Not Anabaptists," *The Chronicle,* XVI (1953).

──────, "The Morison Myth Concerning the Founding of Harvard College," *Church History,* VIII (1939), 148-159.

──────, "Who Were the Baptists?," *Baptist Quarterly,* XVI (1955-56).

Huehns, Gertrude, *Antinomianism in English History.* With Special Reference to the period 1640-1660 (London, 1951).

Huhner, Leon, *Jews in America in Colonial Times and Revolutionary Times* (New York, 1959).

Hull, John, *The Diaries of John Hull,* Mint-Master and Treasurer of the Colony of Massachusetts Bay, *Transactions and Collections of the American Antiquarian Society,* III (Boston, 1857).

Huntsinger, Laura M., *Harvard Portraits:* A Catalogue of Portrait Paintings (Cambridge, 1936).

Hutchinson, Thomas, *A Collection of Original Papers,* reprinted as *Hutchinson Papers* (Albany, 1865).

Hutchinson, Thomas, *The History of the Colony and Province of Massachusetts-Bay* (ed. by Lawrence Shaw Mayo, 2 vols., Cambridge, 1936).

Jackson, Samuel M., ed., *The New Schaff-Herzog Encyclopedia of Religious Knowledge* (12 vols., New York, 1908-1912).

Jernigan, M. W., *The American Colonies, 1492-1750* (New York, 1929).

Johnson, Edward, *A History of New England* (London, 1654), reprinted as *Johnson's Wonder-Working Providence,* ed. by J. Franklin Jameson (New York, 1910).

Jones, Richard F., "Science and English Prose Style in the Third Quarter of the Seventeenth Century," *Publications of the Modern Language Association,* XLV (1930), 977-1009.

──────, "The Attack on Pulpit Eloquence in the Restoration: An Episode in the Development of the Neo-Classical Standards for Prose." *Journal of English and Germanic Philology,* XXX (1931), 188-217.

──────, "Science and Language in England in the Midseventeenth Century," *Journal of English and Germanic Philology,* XXXI (1932), 315-331.

Jones, Rufus M., *The Quakers in the American Colonies* (New York, 1910).

Jordan, W. K., *The Development of Religious Toleration in England.* From the Accession of James I to the Convention of the Long Parliament (Cambridge, 1936).

──────, *The Development of Religious Toleration in England.* From the Convention of the Long Parliament to the Restoration, 1640-1660: The Revolutionary Experiments and Dominant Religious Thought (Cambridge, 1938).

──────, *The Development of Religious Toleration in England.* Attainment of the Theory and Accomodations in Thought and Institutions (1640-1660), (Cambridge, 1940).

Josselyn, John, *An Account of Two Voyages to New England* (London, 1674).

Keith, George, *A Journal of Travels from New Hampshire to Caratuck, on the continent of North America* (London, 1706).

Kevan, Ernest F., *The Grace of Law, A Study of Puritan Theology* (Grand Rapids, 1965).

Kimball, E., *The Public Life of Joseph Dudley* (New York, 1911).

King, Henry M., *Rev. John Myles and the Founding of the First Baptist Church in Massachusetts* (Providence, 1905).

Kirby, Ethyn Williams, *George Keith (1638-1716)* (New York, 1942).

Kittredge, G. L., *Witchcraft in Old and New England* (Cambridge, 1929).

Knappen, M. M., *Tudor Puritanism. A Chapter in the History of Idealism* (Chicago, 1939).

Kromminga, D. H., *The Millennium in the Church. Studies in the History of Christian Chiliasm* (Grand Rapids, 1945).

Lancour, H. Harold, "Passenger Lists of Ships Coming to North America, 1607-1825," *Bulletin of the New York Public Library*, XLI (1937), 389-410.

Latourette, Kenneth Scott, *Three Centuries of Advance, A. D. 1500-A. D. 1800 (A History of the Expansion of Christianity*, III) (New York, 1939).

Lea, Henry Charles, *Materials Toward a History of Witchcraft* (New York, 1957).

Leach, Douglas Edward, "The Military System of Plymouth Colony," *New England Quarterly*, XXIV (1948), 342-364.

Levy, Babette Mae, *Preaching in the First Half Century of New England History* (Hartford, 1945).

Littell, Franklin H., *The Anabaptist View of the Church* (Boston, 1958).

–––––––, "The Claims of the Free Churches," *The Christian Century*, LXXVIII (1961).

Love, W. DeLoss, Jr., *The Fast and Thanksgiving Days of New England* (Boston and New York, 1895).

Löwith, Karl, *Meaning in History. The Theological Implications of the Philosophy of History* (Chicago, 1949).

Lyttle, C., "A Sketch of Theological Development at Harvard University, 1636-1805," *Church History*, V (1936), 301-329.

McCulloh, Gerald O., ed., *Man's Faith and Freedom. The Theological Influence of Jacobus Arminius* (New York and Nashville, 1962).

McGiffert, Arthur Cushman, *Protestant Thought Before Kant* (New York, 1911).

McNeill, John T., "The Doctrine of the Ministry in Reformed Theology," *Church History*, XII (1943), 77-97.

–––––––, *The History and Character of Calvinism* (New York, 1954).

Marvin, A. P., *The Life and Times of Cotton Mather* (Boston, 1892).

Mather, Cotton, *Brethren Dwelling Together in Unity* (Boston, 1718).

–––––––, *Diary*, 2 vols., *Collections of the Massachusetts Historical Society*, Seventh Series, VII, VIII.

–––––––, *Magnalia Christi Americana: or, The Ecclesiastical History of New England* (London, 1702).

–––––––, *Parentator*. Memoirs of Remarkables in the Life and Death of the Ever-Memorable Dr. Increase Mather (Boston, 1724).

–––––––, *A Pillar of Gratitude* (Boston, 1700).

–––––––, *Wonders of the Invisible World* (Boston, 1693; reprinted London, 1862).

Mather, Increase, *A Briefe History of the Warr with the Indians in New-England* (Boston, 1675).

–––––––, *Cases of Conscience Concerning Evil Spirits Personating Men* (Boston, 1693).

––––––, *Diary*, *Proceedings of the Massachusetts Historical Society*, Second Series, XIII.

––––––, *The Divine Right of Infant-Baptisme*. Asserted and Proved from Scripture and Antiquity (Boston, 1680).

Miller, Perry, ed., *The American Puritans*. Their Prose and Poetry (Garden City, 1956).

––––––, "Declension in a Bible Commonwealth," *Proceedings of the American Antiquarian Society*, LI (1941), 37-94.

––––––, *Errand Into the Wilderness* (Cambridge, 1956).

––––––, "The Half-Way Covenant," *New England Quarterly*, VI (1933), 676-715.

––––––, *"Jonathan Edwards"* (n. p., 1949).

––––––, "The Marrow of Puritan Divinity," *Publications of the Colonial Society of Massachusetts*, XXXII (1938), 247-300.

––––––, *The New England Mind. The Seventeenth Century* (Cambridge, 1954).

––––––, *The New England Mind. From Colony to Province* (Cambridge, 1953).

––––––, *Orthodoxy in Massachusetts* (Cambridge, 1933).

––––––, " 'Preparation for Salvation' in Seventeenth Century New England," *Journal of the History of Ideas*, 4 (1943), 253-286.

––––––, "The Puritan Theory of the Sacraments in Seventeenth Century New England," *Catholic Historical Review*, XXII (1937), 409-425.

Miller, Perry, and Johnson, Thomas H., *The Puritans* (New York, 1938).

Mitchell, W. Fraser, *English Pulpit Oratory from Andrewes to Tillotson*. A Study of its Literary Aspects (London, 1932).

Moehlman, Conrad Henry, "The Baptist View of the State," *Church History*, VI (1937), 24-49.

Moller, Jens G., "The Beginnings of Puritan Covenant Theology," *The Journal of Ecclesiastical History*, XIV (1963), 46-67.

More, Paul E., and Cross, Frank L., *Anglicanism*. The Thought and Practice of the Church of England, Illustrated from the Religious Literature of the Seventeenth Century (Milwaukee, 1935).

Morgan, Edmund S., "The Case Against Anne Hutchinson," *New England Quarterly*, X (1937), 635-649.

––––––, "The Puritans and Sex," *New England Quarterly*, XV (1942), 591-607.

––––––, *The Puritan Dilemma*. The Story of John Winthrop (Boston, 1958).

––––––, *The Puritan Family* (Boston, 1944).

Morison, Samuel Eliot, *Builders of the Bay Colony* (Boston and New York, 1930).

––––––, *Harvard College in the Seventeenth Century* (2 vols., Cambridge, 1936).

––––––, *The Founding of Harvard College* (Cambridge, 1935).

––––––, "The Harvard School of Astronomy in the Seventeenth Century," *New England Quarterly*, VII (1934), 3-24.

––––––, *The Intellectual Life of Colonial New England* (New York, 1956).

––––––, "Virginians and Marylanders at Harvard College," *William and Mary Quarterly*, XII (1933), 1-9.

Morris, Edward D., *The Theology of the Westminster Symbols* (Columbus, 1900).

Mosteller, James D., "Baptists and Anabaptists," *The Chronicle*, XX (1957).

Mullett, Charles F., "Toleration and Persecution in England, 1660-1689," *Church History*, XVIII (1949), 18-43.

Murdock, Kenneth B., *Increase Mather*. The Foremost American Puritan (Cambridge, 1925).

––––––––, *Literature and Theology in Colonial New England* (Cambridge, 1949).

Neal, Daniel, *The History of the Puritans* (3 vols., London, 1837).

Newman, A. H., "Antinomianism," *The New Schaff-Herzog Encyclopedia of Religious Knowledge*, I (New York, 1908).

Niebuhr, H. Richard, and Williams, Daniel D., *The Ministry in Historical Perspectives* (New York, 1956).

Nobbs, Douglas, *Theocracy and Toleration*. A Study of the Disputes in Dutch Calvinism From 1600-1650 (Cambridge and New York, 1938).

Norton, Arthur O., "Harvard Text Books and Reference Books of the Seventeenth Century," *Publications of the Colonial Society of Massachusetts*, XXVIII (1935), 400-449.

Norton, John, *The Heart of New-England Rent at the Blasphemies of the Present Generation* (London, 1660).

Nuttall, Geoffrey F., *The Holy Spirit in Puritan Faith and Experience* (Oxford, England, 1947).

––––––––, *Visible Saints*. The Congregational Way. 1640-1660 (Oxford, England, 1957).

Notestein, Wallace, *A History of Witchcraft in England 1558-1718* (Washington, 1911).

Oberholzer, Emil, Jr., *Delinquent Saints:* Disciplinary Action in the Congregational Churches of Massachusetts (New York, 1956).

Osgood, Herbert L., *The American Colonies in the Seventeenth Century* (2 vols., New York, 1904 and 1907).

––––––––, *The American Colonies in the Eighteenth Century* (2 vols., Glouchester, Massachusetts, 1958).

Palfrey, John G., *The History of New England* (5 vols., Boston, 1858-1890).

Parkes, Henry F., "Morals and Law Enforcement in Colonial New England," *New England Quarterly*, V (1932), 431-452.

Payne, Ernest A., "Who Were the Baptists?," *Baptist Quarterly*, XVI (1955-56).

Parrington, Vernon L., *Main Currents in American Thought* (New York, 1927 and 1930).

Pearson, A. F. Scott, *Church and State*. Political Aspects of Sixteenth Century Puritanism (Cambridge, England, 1928).

Pemberton, Ebenezer, *A Funeral Sermon on the Death of that Learned & Excellent Divine, The Reverend Mr. Samuel Willard*. Pastor of the Church of Christ in Boston, and Vice-President of Harvard College (Boston, 1707).

Pennington, Isaac, *The Works of the Long-Mournful and Sorely Distressed Isaac Pennington* (London, 1681).

Perkins, William, *A Christian and Plain Treatise on the Mode and Order of Predestination and on the Amplitude of Divine Grace* (London, 1598), in *Works* (London, 1626-1631).

Persons, Stow, *American Minds*. A History of Ideas (New York, 1958).

Peterson, Harold L., "The Military Equipment of the Plymouth and Bay Colonies: 1620-1690," *New England Quarterly*, XX (1947), 197-208.

Pettit, Norman, *The Heart Prepared: Grace and Conversion in Puritan Spiritual Life* (New Haven, 1966).

Pope, Charles Henry, ed., *Willard Genealogy*. Materials gathered chiefly by Joseph Willard and Charles Wilkes Walker (Boston, 1915).

Pope, Robert G., *The Half-Way Covenant* (Princeton, 1969).

Potter, A. C., *Catalogue of John Harvard's Library* (Cambridge, 1919); also reprinted in *Publications of the Colonial Society of Massachusetts*, XXI (1920), 190-230.

Powell, Chilton L., "Marriage in Early New England," *New England Quarterly*, I (1928), 323-334.

Pratt, Antoinette Marie, *The Attitude of the Roman Catholic Church Towards Witchcraft and the Allied Practices of Sorcery and Magic* (Washington, D.C., 1915).

Prince, Thomas, *Christian History* (Boston, 1743).

Quincy, J., *The History of Harvard University* (2 vols., Cambridge, 1840).

Ray, Mary Augustina, *American Opinion of Roman Catholicism in the Eighteenth Century* (New York, 1936).

Reed, Susan Martha, *Church and State in Massachusetts. 1691-1740* (Urbana, 1914).

Richardson, Caroline Francis, *English Preachers and Preaching. 1640-1670* (New York, 1928).

Robinson, Charles F., and Robinson, Robin, "Three Early Massachusetts Libraries," *Publications of the Colonial Society of Massachusetts*, XXVIII (1935), 107-175.

Robbins, Chandler, *A History of the Second Church, or Old North, in Boston* (Boston, 1852).

Rugg, Winnifred King, *Unafraid. A Life of Anne Hutchinson* (Boston, 1930).

Sainsbury, W. N., and Fortescue, J. W., *Calendar and State Papers, Colonial Series, America and West Indies* (London, 1856—).

Sabine, G. H., *History of Political Theory* (New York, 1937).

Schaff, Philip, *The Creeds of Christendom*, with a History and Critical Notes (6th ed., 3 vols., New York, 1931).

Schneider, Herbert Wallace, *The Puritan Mind* (New York, 1930).

Schrenk, Gottlob, *Gottesreich und Bund im älteren Protestantismus, vornehmlich bei Johannes Coccejus* (Gutersloh, 1923).

Scudder, Townsend, *Concord: American Town* (Boston, 1947).

Sewall, Samuel, *Diary of Samuel Sewall, 1674-1729, Collections of the Massachusetts Historical Society*, Fifth Series, V and VI (Boston, 1878, 1879).

Seidman, Aaron B., "Church and State in the Early Years of the Massachusetts Bay Colony," *New England Quarterly*, XVIII (1945), 211-233.

Shewmaker, William O., "The Training of the Protestant Ministry in the United States of America, Before the Establishment of Theological Seminaries," *Papers of the American Society of Church History*, Second Series, VI, 75-202.

Shipton, Clifford K., "Immigration to New England, 1680-1740," *Journal of Political Economy*, XLIV (1936), 225-256.

——————, "Literary Leaven in Provincial New England," *New England Quarterly*, IX (1939), 203-217.

——————, "New England Clergy in the Glacial Age," *Publications of the Colonial Society of Massachusetts*, XXXII (1933), 24-54.

——————, "The New England Frontier," *New England Quarterly*, X (1937), 25-36.

——————, "A Plea for Puritanism," *The American Historical Review*, XL (1935), 460-467.

——————, "Secondary Education in the Puritan Colonies," *New England Quarterly*, VII (1937), 646-661.

Sibley, John L., *Biographical Sketches of Graduates of Harvard University* (3 vols., Cambridge, 1873-1885).

Shurtleff, Nathaniel B., ed., *Records of the Governor and Company of the Massachusetts Bay in New England* (5 vols. in 6 parts) (Boston, 1853-1854).

Simpson, Alan, *Puritanism in Old and New England* (Chicago, 1956).

Simpson, Samuel, "Early Ministerial Training in America," *Papers of the American Society of Church History*, Second Series, II, 117-129.

Smith, H. Shelton, Handy, Robert T., and Loetscher, Lefferts A., *American Christianity*. An Interpretation with Representative Documents, I (New York, 1960).

Solt, Leo F., "Anti-Intellectualism in the Puritan Revolution," *Church History*, XXIV (1956), 306-316.

———————, "The Fifth Monarchy Men: Politics and the Millennium," *Church History*, XXX (1961), 314-324.

Spiller, Robert E., Thorp, Willard, Johnson, Thomas H., and Canby, Henry Seidel, *Literary History of the United States* (4 vols., New York, 1948-1959).

Sprague, William B., *Annals of the American Pulpit*, I (Boston, 1857).

Starkey, Marion L., *The Devil in Massachusetts* (New York, 1949).

Stearns, Raymond P., "Assessing the New England Mind," *Church History*, X (1941), 246-262.

———————, *Congregationalism in the Dutch Netherlands*. The Rise and Fall of the English Congregational Classes. 1621-1635 (Chicago, 1940).

———————, "New England Way in Holland," *New England Quarterly*, VI (1933), 747-792.

———————, *The Strenuous Puritan:* Hugh Peter, 1598-1660 (Urbana, 1954).

Swift, Lindsay, "The Massachusetts Election Sermons," *Publications of the Colonial Society of Massachusetts*, I (1895), 388-451.

Thorning, Joseph F., *Religious Liberty in Transition* (Washington, D. C., 1931).

Toppan, R. N., *Edward Randolph. 1676-1703* (5 vols., *Publications of the Prince Society*, Boston, 1898-1909).

Torbet, Robert G., *A History of the Baptists* (Philadelphia, 1950).

Trent, W. P., et al., *The Cambridge History of American Literature*, I (New York, 1917).

Trinterud, L. J., "The Origins of Puritanism," *Church History*, XX (1951), 37-57.

Trueblood, D. Elton, *Robert Barclay* (New York, 1968).

Tyler, Moses C., *A History of American Literature*, II (New York, 1878).

Upham, C. W., *Salem Witchcraft*, with an Account of Salem Village and a History of Opinions on Witchcraft and Kindred Subjects (Boston, 1867).

Vaughan, Alden T., *New England Frontier, Puritans and Indians, 1620-1675* (Boston, 1965).

Vedder, Henry C., *A Short History of the Baptists* (Philadelphia, 1907).

Walcott, Robert R., "Husbandry in Colonial New England," *New England Quarterly*, IX (1936), 218-252.

Walker, George L., *Some Aspects of the Religious Life in New England*, With Special Reference to Congregationalists (Boston, 1897).

Walker, Williston, *The Creeds and Platforms of Congregationalism* (Boston, 1960; first published in New York, 1893).

———————, *History of the Congregational Churches in the United States* (The American Church History Series, III. *The Congregationalists*, New York, 1904).

———————, *Ten New England Leaders* (Boston, 1901).

Ward, Nathaniel (pseudonym, Theodore de la Guard), *The Simple Cobler of Aggawam* (London, 1647).

Warfield, Benjamin B., "The Polemics of Infant Baptism," *The Presbyterian Quarterly*, XIII (1899), 313-334; reprinted in *Studies in Theology* (New York, 1932), 389-408.

––––––––, "Predestination in the Reformed Confessions," *The Presbyterian and Reformed Review,* XII (1901), 49-128; reprinted in *Studies in Theology* (New York, 1932), 117-231.

––––––––, *The Westminster Assembly and Its Work* (New York, 1931).

Warren, Austin, *The New England Conscience* (Ann Arbor, 1966).

Watson, Thomas, *A Body of Divinity* (London, 1890).

Weeden, W. B., *Economic and Social History of New England* (2 vols., Boston, 1890).

Wendell, Barrett, *Cotton Mather. The Puritan Priest* (New York, 1891).

––––––––, *The Temper of the Seventeenth Century in English Literature* (New York, 1904).

Wertenbaker, Thomas J., *The First Americans (History of American Life Series,* III, New York, 1927).

––––––––, *The Puritan Oligarchy* (New York, 1947).

Whitehill, Walter M., *Boston. A Topographical History* (Cambridge, 1959).

Whitlock, Glen E., "The Call to the Ministry in the Reformed Tradition," *Theology Today,* XVII (1960), 311-322.

Whitmore, W. H., ed., *The Andros Tracts* (Boston, 1868-1874).

Willard, Joseph, "Memoir of Rev. Samuel Willard, M.A.," *The American Quarterly Register,* XII (Boston, 1839), No. 2.

––––––––, *Willard Memoir: or, Life and Times of Major Simon Willard:* With Notices of Three Generations of His Descendents, and Two Collateral Branches in the United States; also Some Account of the Name and Family in Europe, from an Early Day (Boston, 1858).

Willard, Widney, *Memoirs of Youth and Manhood* (2 vols., Cambridge, 1855).

Williams, Roger, *The Bloudy Tenent of Persecution, for Cause of Conscience* (London, 1644).

––––––––, *The Bloody Tenent yet more Bloody* (London, 1652).

Wilson, John, *A Seasonable Watch-Word* (Cambridge, 1677).

Winslow, Ola Elizabeth, *John Eliot, "Apostle to the Indians"* (Boston, 1968).

––––––––, *Meetinghouse Hill* (New York, 1952).

––––––––, *Samuel Sewall of Boston* (New York, 1964).

Winthrop, John, *The History of New England from 1630 to 1649* (ed. by James Savage, Boston, 1853).

––––––––, "A Short Story of the Rise, Reign, and Ruine of the Antinomians, Familists & Libertines, That infected the Churches of New England," *Publications of the Prince Society,* XXI (Boston, 1894).

Wisner, Benjamin, *The History of the Old South Church in Boston* (Boston, 1830).

Wolcott, Robert R., "Husbandry in Colonial New England," *New England Quarterly,* IX (1936), 235.

Wollebius, Johannes, *Christianae Theologiae Compendium* (Basel, 1626); transl. by Alexander Ross, *The Abridgment of Christian Divinity* (London, 1650).

Wood, Nathan E., *The History of the First Baptist Church of Boston (1665-1899)* (Philadelphia, 1899).

Woodward, William E., *Records of Salem Witchcraft, Copied from the Original Documents* (2 vols., Roxbury, Massachusetts, 1864).

Wright, Conrad, *The Beginnings of Unitarianism in America* (Boston, 1955).

Wright, L. B., *Middle Class Culture in Elizabethan England* (Chapel Hill, 1935).

Wright, Luella M., *The Literary Life of the Early Friends. 1650-1725* (New York, 1932).

Wright, Thomas G., *Literary Culture in Early New England. 1620-1730* (New
  Haven, 1920).
Ziff, Larzer, *The Career of John Cotton.* Puritanism and the American Experience
  (Princeton, 1962).

Index

Adams, Charles F., 123n, 125n, 126n, 127n, 129n, 130n, 133n, 191n
Adams, James T., 70n, 71n
affliction. *See* providence
Agricola, Johannes, 122
Alden, John, 37, 181-182
Allen, James, 54, 64, 68, 71, 83, 84, 104, 159, 193
Alsted, Johan H., 22, 42
Ames, William, 21, 22, 42, 94, 114, 125; *de Conscientia,* 21; *Medulla SS. Theologiae,* 22, 42, 125n
Anabaptists, 81; Münster, 138, 147, 165, 179. *See also* Baptists
Andover, First (North) Church, 49
Andros, Sir Edmund, 63, 64-72, 73, 91, 93, 153; Lady Andros, 66
Anglican Church, 12, 54, 66, 72, 95, 98, 107, 119, 121
Anglicans, 41, 48, 49, 54, 55, 61, 62, 64, 65, 66, 70, 72, 73, 121, 167
Anne, Queen, 87
anti-Christ, Roman Catholicism as, 176
anti-clerical spirit, 150
anti-intellectualism, in New England, 19
Antinomianism, 14, 44, 122-134; its long history, 122; and immediate revelation, 123-126; and justification, 126-130; and sanctification, 130-134
Aquinas, Thomas, 22
Arians, 175
Aristotle, 21
Arminianism, 12, 44, 98-121, 122, 126, 171; Keith's Quaker Armin-
ianism, 104-107; five points of opposition to Calvinism, 107-118; and moralism, 118; Keith's Anglican Arminianism, 119-121
Arminius, Jacobus, 98
Artillery election sermons, 32, 34, 46, 81
astronomy, 21, 186
Athanasius, 175
Augustine, 41, 90, 109, 111, 112, 116, 170, 175

Backus, Isaac, 135n, 136n, 137n
Bahama Islands, 17
Bailey, John, 83
Bailyn, Bernard, 35n, 37n, 99n, 119n
Ball, John, 100
baptism, 24, 36, 139, 165; infant baptism, 19, 136, 138, 142ff., 165; of Benjamin Franklin, 40n; an ordinance, 164
Baptists, 44, 55, 135-155, 158; first Baptist congregation in Massachusetts, 136; church organized in Boston, 136; church reestablished on Noodles Island, 136; disputation at First Church, Boston, 137; sentenced to banishment, 137; build meetinghouse in Boston, 137; Russell's *Brief Narrative,* 138; and infant baptism, 138, 141, 142ff.; and liberty of conscience, 139, 140; and the ministry, 141, 146ff.; and church-state relations, 141, 151ff.; growth of, 154
Barclay, Robert, 157, 158, 160, 161n,

213